A BIGGER FIELD
AWAITS US

A BIGGER FIELD AWAITS US

THE SCOTTISH FOOTBALL TEAM THAT FOUGHT THE GREAT WAR

ANDREW BEAUJON

CHICAGO
REVIEW
PRESS

Published by Chicago Review Press Incorporated
814 North Franklin Street
Chicago, Illinois 60610
ISBN 978-0-89733-736-6

Extract from *The Little Field Marshal: A Life of Sir John French* by
Richard Holmes © Richard Holmes 1998. Reproduced by permission
of Sheil Land Associates Ltd.

Extracts from *Tyneside Irish: 24th, 25th, 26th and 27th (Service) Battalions
of Northumberland Fusiliers* by John Sheen and published by Pen and
Sword Books; *Tyneside Scottish: 21st, 22nd and 23rd (Service) Battalions
of the Northumberland Fusiliers* by Graham Stewart and John Sheen and
published by Pen and Sword Books; and *The German Army of the Somme*
by Jack Sheldon and published by Pen and Sword Books. All reproduced
by permission of Pen and Sword Books.

Extracts from *McCrae's Battalion* by Jack Alexander. Published by
Mainstream Publishing. Reprinted by permission of the Random House
Group Limited. © 2003.

Library of Congress Cataloging-in-Publication Data
Is available from the Library of Congress.

Typesetting: Nord Compo

Printed in the United States of America
5 4 3 2 1

CONTENTS

PEOPLE TO REMEMBER

Heart of Midlothian Players and Organization

James "Jimmy" Boyd: A member of the famous Mossend Swifts, later known as the West Calder Swifts, also known as the "cow-punchers," Boyd was brother to Hearts goalkeeper Archie Boyd and had signed with Hearts a few months before enlistment and hadn't yet made the first team.

Alfred "Alfie" Briggs: Alfie Briggs grew up in Glasgow and played half-back, one of the toughest positions in turn-of-the-century football. He and his fellow midfielders were charged with blunting opponents' attacks and returning the ball to Hearts' forwards. Briggs built machines at the Singer Sewing Works in Clydebank before signing to Hearts in 1912.

Patrick "Paddy" Crossan: Hearts' right back and by many accounts the most popular member of the 1914–1915 team. Paddy had a highly developed sense of humor, and his teammates only slightly sarcastically called him "the Handsomest Man in the World," because his dark good looks helped bring women into the traditionally male preserve of football.

Duncan Currie: Played fullback on the other side of the goal from Paddy. Currie was a hairdresser from Kilwinning, south of Glasgow. A leader on and off the field, he became a sergeant in McCrae's battalion.

Ernest "Ernie" Ellis: Ellis was an Englishman who joined Hearts from Barnsley Football Club in Yorkshire. He signed with Hearts in May 1914 and hadn't had much time with the team when they enlisted. Ellis was married and had a daughter, Kitty, who was born while he was in France.

Elias Fürst: The president of the club and the son of Jewish immigrants from Eastern Europe, Fürst became a rabid football fan as a child and helped the club avoid financial ruin by reorganizing its finances at the turn of the century.

Tom Gracie: Hearts' manager John McCartney spotted Gracie when he played for Liverpool, but he was a Scottish lad and leaped at the chance to return home to play for Hearts. He was Hearts' top goal scorer in their 1914–1915 season.

Harry Graham: Harry joined Hearts from Raith Rovers and became one of the team's top scorers, despite working as an inside forward charged with creating chances for the other players. Graham had asthma, which kept him from joining the Sixteenth Royal Scots. He eventually joined the Royal Army Medical Corps, instead.

James "Jimmy" Low: Low was a student at Edinburgh University when he joined Hearts and wasn't featured in the famous photo of Hearts just after they enlisted—he had to skip the photoshoot to make it to class. Low scored eighteen goals for Hearts. He enlisted in the Sixteenth Royal Scots but was moved to the Sixth Battalion, Seaforth Highlanders, where he took a commission.

John McCartney: Hearts' manager and a famous player in his own right as a youth, McCartney was a pioneer of the "scientific game" that helped Hearts dominate Scottish football. During the war he began a charity that sent footballs to soldiers. He managed Hearts until 1919, when the team fired him and hired his son in his place.

Annan Ness: Ness played for Hearts' reserve team, but once they had enlisted his previous military experience with the Royal Army Medical Corps proved invaluable, and he was quickly made a sergeant in the Sixteenth Royal Scots. Ness was the only member of the initial group of Hearts players who enlisted to stay with McCrae's battalion until it was disbanded in 1918.

George Sinclair: A winger for Hearts who was already a reservist at the beginning of the war and was called up quickly to work as a driver for the Royal Field Artillery.

James Speedie: An insurance clerk from Edinburgh, Speedie signed with Hearts in 1913 and joined the army before the rest of his teammates. He served with the Queens Own Cameron Highlanders and fought at the Battle of Loos.

Henry "Harry" Wattie: A forward for Hearts and the heir to Bobby Walker, Harry was an artist on the field. He was also Paddy's best friend and brother to Mary Alice, Paddy's girlfriend. Quiet and unassuming, he became a star player for Hearts anyway, preferring to let his talent on the pitch do his talking.

William "Willie" Wilson: Paddy's teammate at the junior team Arniston Rangers and later at Hearts, Willie became one of Hearts' top scorers. A recurrent shoulder injury kept him out of fighting with the rest of his team in France.

Edinburgh Politicians

Sir George McCrae: A successful businessman and enthusiastic Territorial Army reservist in Edinburgh, McCrae helped straighten out Edinburgh's tortured finances and organized some big building projects around the city, including installing electric lights and rebuilding the North Bridge. A career in national politics followed and foundered a little when McCrae was appointed to the Local Government Board, where he fought for improved housing. A patriot and natural salesman, McCrae answered Lord Kitchener's call with a plan to fill an Edinburgh battalion quickly.

Sir Robert Cranston: A former lord provost (mayor) of Edinburgh, Cranston led the Fifteenth Royal Scots, a battalion that was already recruiting when Sir George began his campaign, and which fought alongside McCrae's battalion at the Somme.

Sir James Leishman: A member of Edinburgh's city council, Leishman was also on Hearts' board and helped Sir George with recruiting.

Sixteenth Royal Scots

Lieutenant Colonel Arthur Stephenson: Replaced McCrae as commander of the Sixteenth Royal Scots in November 1916.

Captain Peter Ross: Leader of A Company at the Somme.

Captain Napier "Nap" Armit: Leader of B Company at the Somme.

Captain Lionel Coles: Leader of C Company, which included the Hearts men, at the Somme.

Captain Andrew Whyte: Leader of D Company at the Somme.

British Military Leaders

Sir John French: The first leader of the British Expeditionary Force, French clashed with Kitchener and his subordinate, Douglas Haig, over the direction of the war. French was a hero of the Boer War, in which the British barely prevailed over a rag-tag group of farmers. A womanizer and perpetual debtor, French tried to blame Haig for the military disaster at Loos in 1915, an act that contributed to French being fired and Haig assuming command.

Sir Douglas Haig: Haig carried the British to their eventual victory in 1918, but not before amassing one of the largest butcher's bills of all time. Obsessed with the idea of breaking through the German trench lines, he tried offensive after offensive in which thousands of men died. Long thought of as a bungler and the "accidental victor" of the war, some historians believe Haig was in fact a successful general whose attitudes toward his men can only be viewed fairly within the confines of his time.

William Robertson: The first, and to date only, man to rise from enlisted private to field marshal, "Wullie" Robertson was chief of the Imperial General Staff from 1916 to 1918 and was Haig's main point of contact in the British government.

Edward Ingouville-Williams: The commander of the Thirty-Fourth Division, which included the Sixteenth Royal Scots, "Inky Bill" was popular with his men and chafed at restrictions that kept generals behind the lines.

Sir William Pulteney: The commander of III Corps, which included the Thirty-Fourth Division.

British Civilian Leaders

Herbert H. Asquith: Prime minister of Britain at the outbreak of the war, H. H. Asquith had to reconstruct his government after the journalist Charles Repington, acting in part on information furnished by Sir John French, wrote of the crippling lack of munitions, particularly shells, on the Western Front. Asquith's coalition government lasted until December 1916.

David Lloyd George: A media-savvy Welshman, Lloyd George was secretary of state for war when he succeeded Asquith as prime minister, and held the job throughout the remainder of the war.

King George V: The son of Edward VII and a friend of Haig's, the king was also cousin to Kaiser Wilhelm of Germany and Tsar Nicholas II of Russia.

Other Military Leaders

Erich von Falkenhayn: Chief of the German general staff until August 1916.

Paul von Hindenburg: Replaced Falkenhayn in 1916, Hindenburg and Erich Ludendorff became the de facto heads of Germany for the remainder of the war, sidelining Kaiser Wilhelm.

Kaiser Wilhelm II: Germany's last emperor and the grandson of Queen Victoria.

General Joseph Joffre: Commander of the French forces until the end of 1916, when he was replaced by Robert Nivelle, who was soon replaced by Gen. Philippe Pétain after prosecuting a disastrous offensive.

INTRODUCTION
The Handsomest Man in the World

The earth shuddered and convulsed all around the Handsomest Man in the World. Large objects fell and exploded nearby. He felt the overpressure from their blasts. He felt dirt spray him again and again, each wave stinging like midges.

Paddy Crossan was prone. His knees were bent, his fingers splayed, twitching in the chalky dust. He tried to gather his thoughts. He could remember pulling himself out of that chalk, could still feel the white powder in his nose. The debris covering him made him look like a poorly buried corpse. He had been in a shell hole; he remembered dragging his body over the lip.

He couldn't see or hear properly. He couldn't stand—he'd get hit. He couldn't run.

Running was something Paddy remembered. Running was something Paddy loved. They had been running toward the village.

It was a Saturday. Saturdays used to be the best days. That's when he and his best friend, Harry, used to take to the pitch at Tynecastle in Edinburgh and run for an hour and a half.

This dirt. Paddy used to play football on dirt and mud before he made it to Tynecastle. Where was Harry? Harry was one of the people who called Paddy the Handsomest Man in the World. Harry often suggested that Paddy had given the title to himself. Paddy wasn't exactly a beauty, but he had . . . something. His dark hair and stare, always fixed at a point off in the distance, drew more than a few admirers to Tynecastle. Women didn't spend much time at football grounds. That was where men wrapped themselves in team scarves and pissed against the walls and yelled at Crossan to keep his eyes on the forwards.

Harry had been running toward Contalmaison, too. So had Duncan, Annan, Ernie, and Jimmy. They'd all played for Hearts, though Jimmy had joined after he left, and Annan was on the reserve team. They'd worn long-sleeved maroon jerseys and white shorts, tall black socks with maroon-and-white stripes at the top. They all wore khaki now.

They'd been with Coles. Lionel Coles had led them out of the jumping-off trench earlier that morning. He smoked a pipe as C Company moved down into Sausage Valley. They went toward the right side of Sausage Redoubt, toward the Kipper Trench, just like they'd practiced. They weren't running. They'd been ordered to walk, approaching the German lines in waves.

The sun had been in their eyes when they went over, some men shouting. Up top there must have been a dozen machine guns raking the air with deadly enfilade fire. When some shells hit the ground, the chalky dust they kicked up made it look like it was snowing. The Grimsby lads who were supposed to be to their left were just gone. Shrapnel from German artillery took out some of the lads from his company before they'd had a chance to run.

And yet somehow much of C Company had managed to make it across the brown pockmarked ground, past the German trench they called Kipper, to the second line. There, at the entrance to a communication trench called Wood Alley, his teammate Alfie Briggs was shot. Jimmy Scott from Raith Rovers went down. How had they kept going?

They made it to Peake Wood, on the side of the little copse that faced the village of Albert. Through all the dust and smoke you couldn't see the town. A golden statue of the Virgin Mary hung precariously from the town's basilica; the Tommies believed that when she fell the war would end. But you could see Contalmaison.

At least that's what the map called it. The village was now little more than piles of rubble and chunks of chalk, with trees in neat rows broken and burned by shellfire. They were resting in the sunken road that approached the village, the mounds of earth on either side of them higher than their helmets, the little valleys between them filled with pieces of wood and iron and men.

There were men from other units with them—the Grimsby Chums, the Eleventh Suffolks. They said everyone else was gone. Paddy ran, they all ran. Where the road opened up, they found three machine guns waiting for them. Ernie fell in front of the barbed wire. Friendly shells were supposed to have cut that barbed wire. Jimmy went down.

Paddy was still running. Two men from the Suffolks were next to him. Duncan was hit in the shoulder. Where was Harry? Paddy saw the earth heave and crumble in front of him. The dust hit his eyes and coated his face. The last thing he remembered seeing was Contalmaison behind a cloud of dust.

How long had he been under the earth? It was night when he started to come to. He could see very little. The Suffolks were next to him, but they weren't moving. His head felt so strange. The loud noises made him feel sleepy, almost bored. He started to crawl. There were bodies everywhere. Some of them still had their canteens. He had never been so thirsty. He scavenged.

Not long ago, the Handsomest Man in the World had made extra money each summer competing in sprinting contests, often under a false name so reporters who covered Hearts wouldn't find out. Now he moved slowly, close to the ground, hoping no one would see him. He wondered if he'd ever again know what it feels like to run.

1

A COMPANY
OF SPORTSMEN

In November 1914 the war came to Edinburgh in the form of a very
long line around a squat beaux arts concert hall that had opened just
months before with a grand dome up top and cheap wooden seats in
the upper circle for working people. The seats were designed to bring
sweet music into tough lives and to amplify the sounds from the stage.
The massive pipe organ in the gallery shook everyone's bum when
the maestro played a low note, and you might even get a little bit of
that buzz if a speaker had a low voice. On this Friday night the buzz
was outside, as four thousand people waited for two thousand seats in
weather the meteorological office had somewhat unhelpfully predicted
as "variable, fair or fine to showery."

You came to the Usher Hall through wet streets crowded by tall
sandstone edifices that are now pinkish gray and glow gold at sunset.
But in 1914 they were a somber gray, slathered with greasy dust from
the coal that barely warmed the tenement flats and storefronts on the
way. As you approached the Usher, heading down Lothian Road from
Fountainbridge, maybe, or cutting through Bread Street Lane if you were
canny, you entered the square where the city's famous castle, at once
visible by a gap in the skyline, watched over the street artists working.

Men wore long coats over their jackets and ties, their hats beacons of class: flat caps for the working classes; derbies, bowlers, and even sometimes top hats for those up the ladder. Women wore wide-brimmed hats that were simple and dark, sometimes with bows for effect, and their long coats covered simple dresses—shirtwaists over long, narrow skirts whose hemlines, inspired by daring Parisians, were just starting to creep up above the ankle. Such fashionable lasses might have kept their hands warm with muffs, another item that had lately come into style.

There was no admission price for the most desirable ticket in town, just your time, which you burned up happily waiting with everyone else desperate to cheer Sir George McCrae and the lads from Hearts.

Hearts is a nickname for the Heart of Midlothian Football Club. It was founded in 1874 in Gorgie, an area west of the city center whose forty thousand or so residents lived in tenements, in small flats off dark stairs in Georgian buildings, or, if they were from the artisan or skilled working classes, in terraced or colony houses where they didn't have to share space with dozens of other families. The team took its name from the seventh of Sir Walter Scott's *Waverley* novels, telling the story of an eighteenth century riot against an officious captain of the city guard. By 1914 it was a professional operation whose official rival was, and remains to this day, Hibernian Football Club. "Hibs" play in Leith, north of the city center.

Gorgie was a thriving commercial district in 1914. Like the nearby areas of Dalry and Shandon, it hosted a multitude of businesses and light industry—tanners, brewers, rubber works, printers, bakers, furniture makers, dairies, and even farms. Suburban railroads and tramways shuttled people around town; the Union Canal just to the south ran thirty-two miles to Falkirk, where it connected with the Forth and Clyde Canal into Glasgow.

The 1911 census counted just over half a million people in Edinburgh, then and now a breathtakingly beautiful city. Its castle sits on a four-hundred-foot-high volcanic plug that overlooks the Old and New Towns of the city center; a road runs eastward down the hill from the fortress about a mile to the Palace of Holyroodhouse, near the cliffs of the Salisbury Crags and the eight-hundred-foot-high hill Arthur's Seat. From the top of Arthur's Seat you can peer down on Leith and its docks on the Firth of Forth, a large estuary where the river Forth empties into the North Sea.

While Glasgow was a center of shipbuilding and heavy industry, Edinburgh's character was influenced heavily by the businesses of finance and law. Edinburghers are famously distant and taciturn to outsiders. Edinburgh is one of those cities in which interlocking personal connections and a Calvinistic suspicion of ambition and success practically turn it into a small town; the phrase "A kent yer faither"—I know your father—is a supremely Edinburgh way of putting down anyone who might otherwise feel entitled to feel good about their accomplishments.

And yet it was in Edinburgh that George McCrae flourished without a father. He was the rarest of men in class-bound turn-of-the-century British society: a genuinely self-made man. McCrae was born up north in Aberdeen in 1860,[1] the illegitimate son of a housemaid named Jane Buchan, who may have invented a last name and a father for the boy's birth certificate. They moved to Edinburgh, where she raised George in her brother's house. He was apprenticed to a hatter named Robert Nicol, "having been left at the age of ten to fight his own battles," as he put it four decades later.[2]

George was hardworking and ambitious; six years after he entered his employ in Dunfermline, Nicol put the boy in charge of the family's business, which he ran from its Edinburgh shop. At eighteen, McCrae added to his obligations by joining the British Army's volunteer force as a reservist. Two years later he left the Nicol family and established a hats-and-hosiery business on Cockburn Street in Edinburgh's Old Town, later expanding it into a company with headquarters on Princes Street, Edinburgh's showiest address. Even at the start of his career, McCrae showed a talent for getting attention: he made a huge pair of gloves and drove them around town with a banner that read "Made to Measure by McCrae!" and a giant bowler cap that walked around town.[3]

At twenty-nine McCrae entered city government and immediately set to work straightening out Edinburgh's tortured finances; he became the city's treasurer two years later and in 1894 implemented the Corporation Stock Act that brought in £120,000, simplified the city's accounts, and saved it significant money on legal fees and interest. He changed Edinburgh's physical landscape as well, providing crucial support for the city to install electric lighting, acquire tramways, and rebuild the North Bridge that joins the Royal Mile to Princes Street.

In 1897 he became a candidate for lord provost, then the equivalent of mayor in a Scottish city, but lost to Sir Mitchell Mitchell-Thomson. Undeterred, McCrae set his sights on national politics, winning a seat in Parliament in 1899. There his nuts-and-bolts experience with local finances proved invaluable, and he contributed to projects including London's water bill, providing physical training and school meals to poor Scottish children, and construction of housing projects in Dunfermline and Rosyth near the naval yards on the other side of the Firth of Forth from Edinburgh.

Throughout he remained a loyal member of the Fourth Royal Scots, who wore red tunics and were known as the "Water Rats" because its men were reputed as teetotalers. McCrae supported the 1907 act that created the Territorial Army, charged with defense of the homeland as well as serving as a reserve to the main British Army. In 1881 he was a sergeant and marched in a huge downpour past Queen Victoria. He received a commission in 1883 as a lieutenant and by 1905 took command of the regiment as a colonel. The Territorial Army turned the Fourth Royal Scots into the Sixth Royal Scots, and when George McCrae turned over command the unit was one of the best-run in the country. He was knighted in 1908 by King Edward at Buckingham Palace: "A draper who was three times treasurer of the city of Edinburgh, and is regarded in the House of Commons as an expert on financial subjects," the King's Birthday Honours list read.[4]

Sir George McCrae, photographed in 1901 by Sir (John) Benjamin Stone.
Collection of the National Portrait Gallery, London

McCrae married Eliza Cameron Russell in 1880 and had three sons and five daughters. McCrae never acknowledged his own illegitimacy. Jane Buchan lived with him by 1901 under the name Jane McCrae, their secret safe until she died the next year, when he listed himself simply as her employer on her death certificate. As the genealogist Alex Wood has written, Sir George's rags-to-riches tale was acceptable in turn-of-the-century Britain; his unclear paternity was not.

"Lizzie" died of cancer in late 1913. War came soon after her death and all three of her sons served their country: George was a captain in the Fourth battalion of the Royal Scots, the Queen's Edinburgh Rifles. William was in the Royal Artillery's First Lowland City of Edinburgh Heavy Battery. Kenneth was somewhere in Buenos Aires at the war's outbreak; Sir George had no idea where he was until six weeks later, when a telegram arrived from Liverpool: "I have come home for service," it said, to Sir George's pride.

Britain needed the McCrae boys. It needed all the men it could get. Although a formidable naval power, its professional army was minuscule compared to those on the continent. Germany had four and a half million men in its army. Austria-Hungary had three million. France and Russia, Britain's partners in the Triple Entente that linked the countries' interests, had four million and six million men at the ready, respectively. Unlike those countries, Britain had an all-volunteer army—the army, and most British people, found conscription repugnant.

But in June 1914 a nineteen-year-old Bosnian nationalist Gavrilo Princip set in motion forces that would eventually challenge many British self-conceptions. Archduke Franz Ferdinand was heir to the Austro-Hungarian throne, a decaying empire that barely held on to a collection of Baltic states, including Bosnia and Herzegovina. He was visiting Sarajevo on June 28, when Princip succeeded where one of his coconspirators had failed earlier in the day with an ineffective bomb: Franz Ferdinand's driver got them out of that situation but later took a wrong turn that dumped them into an alley right where Princip happened to be standing. Princip took advantage of the mix-up and placed bullets in the archduke and his wife, Sophie, before the driver could reverse out.

Europe's leaders were bound together at the time by a series of complex alliances and blood ties that defy easy taxonomy. Kaiser Wilhelm II of Germany was a cousin to both King George V of Britain, who had taken the throne in 1910, and Empress Alexandra of Russia. Germany had a close alliance with Austria-Hungary. Anti-Serb riots followed in Vienna and Brno. Led by Franz Ferdinand's uncle Emperor Franz Joseph I and encouraged by Kaiser Wilhelm, the Austro-Hungarian government issued to Serbia a set of demands on July 23, among them to help Austria-Hungary suppress the "subversive movement directed against the integrity of the Monarchy," arrest officers it suspected of colluding with the rebels, and to censor publications that "shall incite to hatred and contempt."

Serbia felt it had little choice but to comply. It agreed to all conditions but asked that a judicial inquiry Austria-Hungary demanded be conducted by the Permanent Court of Arbitration at the Hague instead of in Serbia. The capitulation wasn't enough. Austria-Hungary declared war on Serbia on July 28.

Russia had close relations with its fellow Slavic state Serbia and began mobilizing its military. Austria-Hungary moved its forces against Russia in turn. Germany was bound by an alliance to Austria-Hungary and declared war on Russia on August 1. It also declared war on France, which was allied to Russia.

Britain and Germany had signed a treaty in 1839 guaranteeing Belgian neutrality, but Germany's long-established plan for a war with France required a swift route to Paris, and poor little Belgium was simply in the way. Britain and Germany had been circling each other like the biggest, most belligerent kids on the playground for years. For the most part, the competition was limited to the seas, where each tried to keep the bigger navy afloat. That contest came ashore when Britain issued its own ultimatum to Germany: stay out of Belgium. German troops crossed the border that night. At 11:00 PM on August 4 Britain declared war.

The British people greeted war with unprecedented patriotism and optimism. Following a report in the *Daily Mail* of Irish soldiers singing it, a music-hall song called "It's a Long Way to Tipperary" became an anthem for the nation as it headed to a war most thought would be over quickly, probably by Christmas. Mass-market newspapers had been a part of daily life for only about twenty years; just as many people caught up on current affairs at the cinema, from newsreels that played before features.

It was through newspapers and posters that Lord Herbert Kitchener, a military hero and Britain's newly appointed secretary of state for war, called for one hundred thousand volunteers to join the country's armed forces. His request inspired a famous propaganda poster featuring an illustration of Kitchener pointing at the reader, his eyes regarding them sternly between his field marshal's cap and squirrel-sized mustache. "Join Your Country's Army!" it read, "God Save the King."

The new forces were to be neither part of the regular army, which embarked for France on August 9, nor the territorials, whom many in the army looked down upon as weekend warriors trained in the least sporting deeds of all—homeland defense.

This new army would be made up of "pals," a term Gen. Henry Rawlinson suggested as a way to win recruits. Pals' battalions would let a man serve with others from his town or profession. The first was a stockbrokers' battalion from London. Others followed in Liverpool, Bristol, and Glasgow, which formed a "tramways battalion" in the Highland Light Infantry. A month after Rawlinson's suggestion, there were more than fifty pals' battalions. Edinburgh formed the Fifteenth Royal Scots in September 1914. The battalion was to be filled by Col. Sir Robert Cranston, one of the city's former lord provosts, and recruited around town as well as ethnic Scots whose families had moved to the English city of Manchester. "Scotland for Ever!" read a recruiting poster there. It reassured potential soldiers that "by joining this battalion you are with all your Manchester companions."

Recruiting fever swept Britain concurrent with a grassroots effort to shame those who didn't sign up. Patriotic Britons began harassing young men on the street, pressing white feathers, a symbol of cowardice, into the hands of any seemingly healthy person who appeared to be "hanging back."

The pressure began to fall quite heavily on professional football players and their fans as autumn advanced and the hopes of a quick war crumbled. Able-bodied men who played football or attended matches either "did not understand the situation or they were cowards and traitors," Labour MP J. H. Thomas said in a speech in London.[5] A cartoon in the magazine *Punch* showed the magazine's titular character hectoring a football player: "No doubt you can make money in this field, my friend, but there's only one field today where you can get honour."[6] And the wealthy social reformer Frederick Charrington led a crusade against football that was taken up by many in the press. Charrington was physically ejected from a match in London that September after haranguing the crowd at halftime.

Football had its roots in the posh playing fields of Oxford University, where students accustomed to appending *-ers* to abbreviated words (*champers* for Champagne, *brekker* for breakfast) wrested the term *soccer* out of the term *association football*. In Scotland most people just called it *football*, and by the mid-1870s, it was the country's most popular diversion, particularly among the working classes. There was more than a hint of condescension in Charrington's effort: there were no similarly loud campaigns to send fox hunters to the Western Front. It's not a coincidence that Charrington campaigned against drinking and music halls before football got under his skin—he and other elites were consistently eager to deny the working classes any small pleasures they could eke out of life.

More to the point, the criticism was predicated in part on the misapprehension that football teams had stashed away terrific numbers of men. "I think that the public have forgotten that there is, after all, a very small number of professional football players in the kingdom," Sir James Leishman, a local politician and a shareholder in Hearts, told a reporter for the *Edinburgh Evening News* in November. "If every man enlisted probably they would not be able to fill three regiments. In Scotland I question if there are any more than 300 or 400 men who are making their living playing football. In Edinburgh I suppose there would be probably 50 or 60."[7] William Wilton, who managed the Glasgow Rangers Football Club, said the team's gate receipts were down 50 percent in October, which indicated that "a big proportion of the new recruits had been taken from the ranks of football spectators"—many of whom were already committing their labors to the war effort through Glasgow's heavy industry sectors like shipbuilding.[8]

Still, football's governing bodies in Britain could not ignore the escalating drumbeat of criticism. In September the English Football Association mandated that member clubs' fields, or "pitches," be made available for drilling exercises, and took further steps to help with recruitment efforts, including speakers at halftime and patriotic posters throughout their grounds.

Hearts manager John McCartney got his club on board even earlier. McCartney was a large man with an enormous mustache and had been an accomplished football player before the turn of the century. One of his first acts as Hearts' manager was to nail a sign above the club's boardroom that read "YOU MUST ALWAYS GIVE THE PUBLIC WHAT THE PUBLIC WANTS!"[9]

Two members of Hearts, Neil Moreland and George Sinclair, were reservists and got called up quickly when war was declared. In the middle of August, McCartney arranged for Hearts players to take part in weekly drill sessions on grounds behind Usher Hall on Grindlay Street. Annan Ness, a member of the club's reserve team who'd had some military experience before he joined, ran the drills, which members of Hibernian joined.

Football clubs had legitimate worries about losing their men to the military. The professional game was still quite young, and the clubs operated on thin margins. Hearts had just installed a new grandstand in their stadium, Tynecastle, that eventually cost £12,000—a fortune at the time. "The contractors," Leishman said, "must be paid." Competition with other teams had pushed player salaries up, and the law was unclear about whether the clubs would still have to pay players if they enlisted.

Hearts faced another situation that many would consider a good problem to have: their team in 1914 was really, really good.

This success had a lot to do with McCartney's aggressive recruitment of promising players around Scotland and Northern England as well as the style of play he encouraged, which some called "scientific"—the team passed the ball frequently, bewildering opponents who were used to converging on the ball in a scrum.

They were becoming an excellent team. Hearts had finished third in the Scottish League in the 1913–1914 season, but as the new season opened that August it was clear McCartney had found the pieces he needed. On August 15, 1914, Hearts opened their season against Glasgow's Celtic at home. It was the first league game for goalkeeper Archie Boyd, for defender James Frew, and for forward Tom Gracie, who McCartney had plucked from Liverpool. Winger James Speedie was making his second appearance on the first team in a league match. He had played at Tranent Juniors with another first-team man, Harry Wattie, an Edinburgh boy who'd grown up supporting Hearts.

The game was only twenty minutes in before Hearts' Alfie Briggs brought down Celtic striker John Browning in the penalty area. Referee Tom Dougray called for a penalty kick, taken by Celtic center forward Jimmy "the Sniper" McColl. McColl kicked a hot ball at the Hearts goal, but Boyd stopped it, sending a loud cheer ringing out over Gorgie from the eighteen thousand in attendance. The noise urged Hearts forward. Five minutes later, Hearts midfielder Peter Nellies, who worked part-time as a coal miner, threaded the Celtic defenders and passed the ball to Wattie, who scored after a feint.

But just before halftime team captain Bob Mercer tore a ligament in his knee. There were no substitutions in those days; if a player was injured, his team simply did without him. After the half Speedie was hurt, too, and had to hobble off the field for five minutes. Forward Willie Wilson was also seen limping. At this point, with nine men on the field, Hearts began what a sportswriter at the game called a "rare exhibition of grim resolution and unflinching pluck." Celtic began a pitiless assault on Hearts' half of the field, but Frew, who was filling in for Duncan Currie, ably guarded the goal alongside Wattie's best friend, Paddy Crossan.

Crossan was having the game of his life, clearing one attack after another and wearing down the Glaswegians. In the eighty-first minute,

Celtic's Patsy Gallacher, an Irish forward who played on the inside right, was also injured and had to retire. Gracie spotted an opening between Celtic defender Alec McNair and goalkeeper Charlie Shaw, who had moved out of position; he calmly put the ball into the untended net. Suddenly, a writer who used the byline "Linx" wrote, "there was no more popular individual in the capital."[10]

After they downed Celtic, Hearts rolled across Scotland crushing the dreams of other teams: Raith Rovers fell 3–1 the next week, followed by a 6–0 spanking of Hibs, and blanking three consecutive teams before conceding a single goal to Glasgow's Rangers on September 19. (Hearts still won.) By the night of the Usher Hall meeting, they'd lost only one game, to Dumbarton, and tied one other, against Queen's Park on October 24. It was hard to see how any other team might take that season's title from them.

Not everyone in Edinburgh was cheering. On Monday, November 16, the *Evening News* carried a letter written by someone identifying herself as "a Soldier's Daughter." It was two days after Hearts had soundly beaten Falkirk at Tynecastle, a game during which winger James Speedie had surprised McCartney and his teammates by volunteering to join the Queen's Own Cameron Highlanders during a halftime appeal. "A Soldier's Daughter" was in no mood to congratulate him, nor Wilson and Wattie for their thrilling goals:

> Might I suggest that while the "Heart of Mid-Lothian" continue to play football, enabled thus to pursue their peaceful play by the sacrifice of the lives of thousands of their countrymen, they might adopt, temporarily, a nom de plume, say, the "White Feathers of Midlothian."
>
> By this simple device the taint of rottenness imputed to the "Heart of Mid-Lothian" by their use of this classic title would be removed, and at the same time they would secure a peculiarly appropriate badge for an ornamental body of athletes and their followers.

The letter hurt. On Thursday, November 19, the *Evening News* informed the public that Sir George McCrae had volunteered his services to the crown, "and has offered to raise a Territorial battalion for active service in the field." Lord Kitchener, it noted, had agreed to be an honorary colonel.

On Saturday, the same day Hearts pounded Partick Thistle 2–0 at their home ground of Firhill, the *Evening News* ran an editorial called "Sir G. M'Crae Raises the Flag." It tipped Sir George's hand: "Under the auspices of the Heart of Mid-Lothian Club half a battalion of excellent soldiers could be raised with ease."

McCrae knew that securing the recruitment of some of Hearts' players would not only dampen criticism of footballers for shirking but would command tremendous press coverage, and encourage many of their fans to join up as well. He wanted to raise the battalion in a week, a feat that would perhaps not coincidentally show up Cranston's Fifteenth Battalion. Lord provost was a post McCrae had never been able to obtain.

Three days later Sir George addressed a meeting of the Edinburgh and District Trades Council at Melbourne Hall, where he told the representatives of various trades that he'd already had 250 applications for 31 vacancies of officers. Men could join as long as they were 5'3" or taller, he said, and in answer to a question from the audience said he was personally of the opinion that no one should be turned away for having false teeth. He identified himself as a working man, then made a three-part argument for why members of the skilled trades should use their influence to convince other working men to fight.

The first was that if Germany won the war, it would be disastrous. The second was that he was appalled by the thought that anyone would say the working classes weren't doing their duty. Finally, he did not believe in conscription. Anyone who came forward now would not only defend Britain against the horrible prospect of a triumphant Germany but also against it acting like a continental power where all the country was engaged in the mechanics of war. British people who saved the voluntary force were the "freest of men in the freest of countries."

The next morning was November 25, a Wednesday. The *Scotsman* carried a message from McCrae:

TO THE YOUNG MEN OF EDINBURGH

The present crisis is one of supreme gravity. World-wide issues are trembling in the balance.

I appeal with confidence to the patriotism and generous enthusiasm of my fellow-citizens.

The noblest and highest duty finds expression in personal service.

I say to the Young Men in this ancient capital of a free country—

"You are strong; be willing."

On you rests the awful responsibility of unnecessarily prolonging this devastating war. If you will only come forward in sufficient numbers you can stop the War.

All cannot go, but if your home ties permit, and you shirk your obvious duty, you may escape a hero's death, but you will go through life feeling mean.

In the presence of the God of Battles; ask of your conscience this question—

DARE I STAND ASIDE?

George McCrae

That same day Leishman asked John McCartney to come to a meeting at his shop on George Street in Edinburgh's New Town. Leishman told McCartney that Britain faced a dire situation with regard to man power to fight the war. Sir George made a surprise appearance—some might call it an ambush—at the meeting. He asked McCartney whether any of his team would join the battalion he was planning. McCartney demurred, saying he'd have to speak to the team's board first. He returned to Tynecastle and called an emergency meeting.

The directors also punted. McCartney would have to ask the players themselves, they said, but they decided that anyone who joined would get half wages when on active duty, and full pay as long as they could play while they served. So the coach called an all-team meeting, and addressed his players in a subdued voice. Any players who wanted to enlist should stand, he said.

The room was silent for a while, McCartney later wrote, and then one by one they began to stand: Ernie Ellis, Tom Gracie, Duncan Currie, Willie Wilson, Norman Findlay, Bob Preston, Harry Wattie, Alfie Briggs, Jimmy Frew, Annan Ness, Bob Mercer, George Bryden, Harry Graham, Willie Aitken, and Walter Scott.

Sir George had arranged a medical examination for volunteers.

Mercer, Bryden, Graham, Aitken, and Scott couldn't pass the medical exam and were rejected. Mercer's knee kept him out; Bryden was found to have a weak heart; and the others had various respiratory conditions, not uncommon in Edinburgh at the time. The city was aptly nicknamed "Auld Reekie" on account of the smoke and soot that rose and fell from its chimneys.

Three players surprised their mates by remaining seated: brothers Jimmy and Archie Boyd, and Paddy Crossan. The Boyds were keen to join but wanted to consult with their mother first. She refused to let them both go—someone had to support her, she argued. Since Archie had a fiancée, Jimmy decided to take his spot. Crossan, on the other hand, just needed some time to think, apparently. He had an "edge" about him, a team historian wrote, and made decisions on his own time.

Paddy joined later the next day, but not before the *Evening News* sent a photographer to Tynecastle. Ellis, Gracie, and Currie stood flanked by McCartney and team trainer Jimmy Duckworth. Wilson, Findlay, and Preston sat with their arms crossed in the second row, next to Watttie, who had Duckworth's hand on his shoulder and his own hands on his thighs. Briggs, Frew, and Ness lounged on the ground in front of their teammates, with Jamie Low shown in an inset; he'd had to leave to make a class at Edinburgh University, where he was studying agriculture. All wore their maroon jerseys and white shorts. In a version of the photo the *Evening News* didn't use, Ness held Blackie, the Tynecastle cat.

HEARTS' PLAYERS WHO HAVE JOINED THE ARMY.

The *Evening News* photo of Hearts players after they enlisted on November 25.
Standing, from left: John McCartney, Ernie Ellis, Tom Gracie, Duncan Currie.
Seated: Willie Wilson, Norman Findlay, Bob Preston, Harry Wattie. On the
ground: Alfie Briggs, Jimmy Frew, Annan Ness. Inset: Jamie Low.
Edinburgh Evening News, November 26, 1914

News of Hearts' enlistment quickly passed from newspaper to newspaper around Britain. A year before, a group called the Young Scots had
successfully pushed Britain's Parliament to consider a bill that would
give Scotland—united with England since 1707—its own legislature and
many powers of home rule. The bill was scheduled for another read
in Westminster in May 1914, but war ended any such moves toward
independence for nearly a century. Scotland would fight for Britain
without reservation.

McCrae's gamble had the desired effect on football's critics. On
November 26 the Irish Unionist MP Sir John Lonsdale proposed that
Britain should, through legislation, immediately "commandeer all the
football grounds for military purposes." Lonsdale noted before the House
of Commons that a recruiting drive the Saturday previous, before thousands of people at a number of grounds in England, obtained "only *one*
recruit to the colors."

"I saw that in the newspapers," Prime Minister H. H. Asquith answered. "But I am very glad to say that in Scotland a very different response was made." The cheers that greeted Asquith muffled any further noise of legislation from the group Scottish League president William Ward called the "stop-the-game croakers."

———————

At the Usher Hall on November 27, most of the people outside had managed to pack into the theater, overwhelming its seats and aisles. McCrae and the Hearts players entered to a cheer so loud that people reported hearing it several streets away. McCrae brought a cardboard soldier onstage with him, a question mark in a blank space where his face should have gone.

Anyone hoping to hear them had to wait first for the politicians who eagerly basked in the Hearts' volunteers' patriotic glow. Charles Price, an MP for Edinburgh, spoke first, reading a letter to McCrae from Thomas McKinnon Wood, the secretary for Scotland. "I am very much pleased to hear that your patriotic effort to raise a new Edinburgh battalion is meeting with such success," McKinnon Wood had written, "and hope that the meeting on Friday will bring you hundreds of recruits. Scotland has proved that she can be trusted to give a noble response to the national appeal, and I am confident that Edinburgh will give you what you are asking."[11]

Alexander Ure, who'd become Lord Strathclyde on retiring from Parliament the year before, followed Price, enjoying what a reporter for the Dundee *Courier* called "a very cordial reception." He had a craggy face, a large nose, and held a cane and gloves in his left hand when he spoke in public. Germany, he said to cheers, "had failed to achieve every one of her aims. It was difficult to understand how any man of ordinary sanity, even for a single moment, doubted that in the end the British Army would be successful in this great struggle." While the Germans were fighting Russia and France as well, everyone present, he said, "knew very well that we were the true objective, that it was Britain that Germany was out to crush."[12]

William Paterson of Edinburgh University rose to propose a resolution: "That this meeting of Edinburgh citizens, in view of the European War, and the momentous issues therein involved, records its belief that it is the duty of all to assist in this national crisis, and in particular to aid in securing recruits for the armed forces of the Crown."[13]

The resolution was, not surprisingly, successful, and bagpipers and drummers from the Fourth, Sixth, and Ninth Royal Scots began to play. McCrae rose to speak, to a floor-shaking ovation that McCartney later claimed had nearly knocked him over. Sir George wore a khaki officer's coat and a glengarry cap. His mustache was nearly as wide as his face; his large eyes scanned the Usher's twin balconies as he walked to the front of the stage. Gold-leafed plaster relief sculptures of famous Scots lined the cream-colored walls. The jostling crowd filled every red velvet seat and lined every passageway.

The Hearts men sat behind him, along with members of the team's board, and John McCartney.

"Well done, Sir George!" a man shouted from the crowd. McCrae corrected him: "This is not a night for titles," he said, and continued:

> I stand before you humbly as a fellow Scot. Nothing more and nothing less. You know I don't speak easily of crisis, but this is what confronts us. I have received permission from the War Office to raise a new battalion for active service. It is my intention that this unit will reflect accurately all the many classes of this famous capital, and that it will be characterized by such a spirit of excellence that the rest of Lord Kitchener's Army will be judged by our standard. Furthermore, with the agreement of the authorities, I have undertaken to lead the battalion in the field. I would not—I could not—ask you to serve unless I share the danger at your side. In a moment I

will walk down to Castle Street and set my name to the list of volunteers. Who will join me?[14]

About three hundred men that night alone, as it turned out. Hearts fans were eager to serve next to their sporting heroes.

On Saturday, December 5, Hearts played their first home game since they'd enlisted, a holiday-season "derby" match against Hibernian. Hearts' directors circulated an invitation the day before to recruits saying anyone who had joined would be admitted for free. "Sir George McCrae will be glad if you will 'fall in' at the foot of Ardmillan Terrace at 1:45 PM," it read. Underneath gray and threatening skies eight hundred men showed up before kickoff and took the field alongside the team. Twenty more men joined during the game, taking their medical examinations in the club's boardroom and being sworn in on site by a justice of the peace.

Hearts destroyed Hibs, 3–1. They even scored their rivals' only point, an "own goal" by Archie Boyd, who tried to clear a corner kick and "had a stiff lesson in finding the ball in the net from his save," the *Edinburgh Evening News* wrote the following Monday. Low scored the final goal as rain and hail pelted the field and thunder roared overhead. Hibs "defended stubbornly and attacked with pluck," the *Evening News* wrote, but Hearts "took matters very seriously, and during the game never showed a tendency to lapse into over-cleverness."[15]

Football finally had some breathing room. But Saturdays were never going to be the same.

When the Empire is in danger, and we hear our country's call,
The Motherland may count on us to leave the leather ball.
We've hacked our way in many a fray, we've passed and gone for goal,
But a bigger field awaits us, and we're keen to join the roll.

So it's right wing, left wing, front line, and goal;
Half back and full back, every living soul;

Sound o'wind, strong o'limb, eager for the fray,
Every soul for the goal—
"Hearts!" "Hearts!" "Hearts," lead the way!

—"Hearts, Lead the Way," a song by T. M. Davidson and David Stephen, printed in the Dundee *People's Journal*, March 13, 1915

2

THE SCIENTIFIC GAME

Oil shale is a rock that burns. It formed three hundred million years ago in the Carboniferous period, when Scotland sat at the equator, attached to North America and Greenland, and algae bloomed in coastal lagoons. After the landmass that's now Britain began to drift northward, the lake beds eventually turned dry and fine-grained rock stuffed full of kerogen remained.

Prehistoric humans learned they could dig up those sharp gray rocks and burn them for warmth, but it took a man born in Glasgow in 1811 to figure out how to squeeze wealth from the streaky stones just below the cold Scottish earth. James Young trained to be a carpenter, like his father. Then he discovered chemistry and began taking evening classes at Anderson's University. He excelled at it and followed his instructor Thomas Graham to London and eventually moved to the market town of Newton-le-Willows in England, where he pursued a career in practical science at James Muspratt's chemical plant. Muspratt used an environmentally extravagant process to make soda ash, an alkali vital to the textile and glass industries. After five years as Muspratt's manager, Young moved in 1844 to Charles Tennant's chemical plant in Manchester. There, he realized that oil that seeped from a coal mine in Derbyshire could be distilled to make oil for lubricating looms, and went into business on his own. But the coal mine eventually went dry, and Young had to look for another way to dig up money.

He found it in the rocks back home. Others had realized they could heat cannel coal, or oil shale, until it released gas; Young tuned the process until it produced paraffin oil, as well as solvents to make paint and linoleum. Later on, his method was adapted to make "motor spirit," which eventually became known as petrol or gasoline.

Shale lay in great quantities below the ground of Linlithgowshire, a region between Glasgow and Edinburgh now called West Lothian, so Young moved back north. On December 30, 1865, Young formed his Paraffin Light & Mineral Oil Company, with a plan to establish works at a place called Addiewell. The little town's name practically took up more space on a map than it did, but Addiewell had a superb location, with a connection to a railroad line as well as a long agricultural road that runs north of the Pentland Hills into Edinburgh. The hamlet's green spaces would soon be menaced by his plant, a blackened vapor-spouting monster fed by rocks dug up nearby and discarded in great red piles called bings when they were spent.

Many Victorian-era capitalists took a paternalistic influence in the lives of their employees. Inspired by the ideas of a movement called "muscular Christianity," these bosses exercised control over the lives of their workers on and off the clock, steering them away from the complications of a life lubricated by alcohol and toward associations and amusements that enriched their meager lives—and not coincidentally, kept them from showing up to work hungover.

Young was not especially concerned with his employees' moral well-being. But he did recognize that they needed shelter, and the nearby town of West Calder didn't have enough housing for workers. At their first meeting, on January 1, 1866, Young and his board talked about how the company would house employees at Addiewell, which had few houses of its own. But he had to move quickly: "Time was of so much value," Young said.

Like the city fathers of Edinburgh a hundred years before, Young decided to build a "new town." Noting the cold of a Scottish winter, Young decided against using cheap materials to build 360 houses made of bricks he discovered he could form from local clay. The houses were built in squat rows of ten with peaked roofs and chimneys. A single apartment was 178 square feet with high ceilings; a double had 143 square feet for a kitchen and another room that measured 9½ by 11 feet. Those were called "but and bens," a Scots term for a holiday home, and they were for people with families. Young laid out the streets straight—no winding medieval roads in this monument to progress—and named them for notable Scots like James Watt, Michael Faraday, and the medical missionary David Livingstone, whom Young had befriended at Anderson's. There was a school, a reading room, two churches, and games rooms workers could use for one penny a week. "The houses were more than adequate," Young's great-great-granddaughter Mary Leitch wrote a century later, "as it was reported that the employees were 'exceptionally well off for house accommodation.'"

"Well off" was a relative term. The school and the other modest amenities were mostly where the similarities ended between Young's village and worker villages like Bournville, a model town the Quaker-owned chocolate company Cadbury built for its workers around the same time. While George and Richard Cadbury wanted their workers to live with light and good sanitation, Addiewell's residents had "shunkies" fifteen to twenty yards from their houses. A shunky was a structure poorly enclosed on three sides. People threw ashes and refuse into a privy midden on the open side and used the other as a latrine. They were "a positive pestilence in the summer time, and at all times a danger to the health of the community," the Scottish Shale Miners' Association stated in evidence it submitted to the Royal Commission on Housing for Scotland in March 1914.[1]

Four years earlier a correspondent for the socialist newspaper *Forward* visited to catalog the town's grim amenities. "The household washing has to be done in the houses," the paper's reporter wrote. "Water for domestic use and for drinking purposes has to be carried in pails from pumps, of which there were two in each street. To the woman upstairs who has a big household to look after, this means a great amount of inconvenience and hard labour that could be quite well done without." The water pipes froze in the winter, forcing people to walk half a mile to a stream called Scolley Burn. They disposed of wastewater in open brick-lined channels called "schouchs" that ran along the streets.

Workers coming home from the mines or factory covered in sticky coal dust had to wash outside. And the fact that the houses had belonged to Young for four decades, the *Forward* wrote, "leads us to assume that the people who have survived the horrible conditions have paid in rent the value of the houses three times over."[2]

In such a dour environment escape generally took one of several inexpensive forms: spiritual, carnal, or violent. Some may have even resorted to adventurous combinations thereof, especially when abetted by alcohol. The *Falkirk Herald and Linlithgow Journal* reported in 1877 that in Addiewell it was "no uncommon thing for workmen to spend Saturday afternoons in drinking together, and then issue forth, ready for any brawl, and dangerously forward, when any disturbance does take place, to arm themselves with ugly pieces of the sharp-edged shale which is scattered plentifully about the village."[3]

One person who learned the hard way about the bountiful stone, the newspaper reported, was a fellow named James Pattison, who walked up Campbell Street after a pleasant evening with friends. There "he stopped at the door next the house where he had passed the evening and asked for a drink of water from a woman, with whom he is said to have been pretty well acquainted." There the time line grows fuzzy, but not long after Pattison stopped for his water a man named Kitchen noticed "a couple of men behaving in what seems rather an odd way" and then one of them making a sudden acquaintance with the ground. It was poor, unfortunate Pattison dead in a pool of blood. His face was bruised above the eye and there was "an ugly gash immediately above the right ear, evidently inflicted with a sharp piece of shale picked up close to the body, in a tell-tale, bloody state."[4]

Athletics were a somewhat safer diversion. Around 1882, locals, many of them Catholics who'd come from Ireland looking for work, formed a soccer team at Cuthill, just north of the town center. They called it Addiewell Shamrock, and its matches later moved to a park on Campbell Street, where Young's company had built the easternmost row of houses.

Patrick James "Paddy" Crossan was born to Addiewell, arriving at his parents' home on Baker Street on May 21, 1891. He was the second child of Bridget and Edward Crossan, who worked as a foreman at the oil works. Edward was born in Ireland, Bridget in Linlithgow. By the time of the 1901 census, the family, which now included six children, had moved to larger accommodations on Simpson Street, one row of houses away.

Baker Street was named for Sir Benjamin Baker, the man who built the Forth Bridge, a mile-and-a-half-long cantilevered marvel that connected rail from Edinburgh to Fife. It is so large that Scots use the phrase "painting the Forth Bridge" to describe a task so large that by the time you finish it, you have to start all over again.

That feeling would have been familiar to any member of Scotland's working classes at the turn of the century. Life was hard, repetitive, and short—life expectancy was around fifty for men, fifty-three for women. By the time Paddy was twenty, thanks to famine and the evictions that forced Highlanders off their land, twice as many Scots worked in manufacturing as in agriculture.

Paddy would never settle for an ordinary life. He was strong and solidly built with thick black hair he parted on the right and slicked down. But his most striking feature was his stare, his dark eyes tending to fix upward at some point above his observer, somewhere on the horizon. It suggested he could take care of himself if necessary.

Crossan was a natural athlete: lithe and fast, with an excellent spatial awareness that helped him excel as a defender in football. The game was almost entirely focused on offense when Paddy began playing it. A right back like Paddy would have been one of three players on his team charged with preventing goals rather than making them. It required intimidating forwards, maneuvering them into spots where they were less likely to score, and clearing balls before they sailed beyond the goalkeeper's reach. It was a tough position in a rough game.

For a boy from Addiewell, football was played on hard-packed dirt or slippery mud. Players had to make do with a corrugated surface on a park on Campbell Street. Paddy played alongside a boy named Johnny Hanlon, as well as children from the Meechan and McGinty families. When Addiewell Football Club took the field, the playing area would be roped off, with spectators cheering and threatening players only a few feet away from the action. Most towns had at least one team, and many had two, one for Scots players and another for the Irish, with names like Celtic or Shamrock or Hibernian. The separate teams reflected the separate lives Irish workers led outside work, with their own parts of town or sometimes their own sides of the street. Football may have looked like a game, but it was really a way for people to identify with their tribe. Fans were on one side or the other, and rarely did the lines cross.

For players, though, divisions were a bit looser. Football matches followed the rail lines from tiny town to tiny town: Seafield, Broxburn, West Calder. A good player could and did switch teams often, following his fortunes from one squad to the next. (Some towns eventually combined their sectarian teams to prevent bigger clubs from poaching their players; those squads were termed "united.") The games were violent, and defenders often took kicks to their stomachs. The *Edinburgh Evening News* once wrote about Broxburn Football Club's "peculiar country style." It quoted a player from Glasgow's Celtic, which had been unfortunate enough to play another West Lothian team. "They don't play much football themselves," he said, "but they don't allow others to play it at all."[5]

There were headbutts, broken bones, shins bruised and bloodied by kicks and falls, and fights. And more often than not, anyone injured played through the pain.

The Scottish Football Association was founded in 1873 with eight clubs. The association standardized rules of the game and offered a way to organize orderly tournaments. Its first cup competition drew sixteen teams. Over the next decades dozens more began to fight for the right to qualify in the early stages of the cup. The first West Lothian teams entered the Scottish Cup in 1881. There were no professional players yet in these clubs—that would have to wait until 1893, after Scottish teams got tired of losing players to English teams, whose league began allowing professionalism in 1885. Players would work hard in mines or factories, then lace up their boots on Saturdays. The clubs had their own goalposts, which they removed and stored after every match. Their athletes changed in pubs or hotels; local merchants—tailors, grocers, ironmongers—sometimes helped sponsor teams to pay for equipment and train fares. If a club couldn't afford to get to another town for a match, the game was called a "walkover," and the home team moved on in the competition. The only other income was from the "gate"—the fees fans paid to watch. It was rarely much money. If you were lucky, you'd make enough to pay for your players' tickets home.

As competition got fiercer, so did the hunt for talent. Some players were professionals in all but name. A club would arrange a job for them, usually in a pub. If you lost your position on a club's "first team," its starters, you'd lose your job as well. The league played a frustrating game of cat and mouse with these secret professionals, vacating victories and suspending clubs that used them, until it gave up and allowed teams to pay players. But inequities of scale continued. Clubs in cities had bigger fan bases and more money and began picking off good players from small-town squads. They'd meet them in matches that required the city clubs to venture out to the mining villages.

On October 13, 1888, Heart of Midlothian left Edinburgh by train to visit Broxburn, whose team played in their namesake oil shale village on the Union Canal between Edinburgh and Falkirk. Eight hundred Hearts fans accompanied their team on "football special" trains from the capital. More than a thousand local fans were waiting to greet them. The gate was one of the most spectacular in the history of Broxburn, the home team taking in ten pounds, according to the *West Lothian Courier*. "There was little in the town to attract the admirers of the Heart of Mid-Lothian," the *Edinburgh Evening News* reported, so all the spectators headed to the football field, dismal as it was. "The grass on the field was hardly worthy of the name," the *Evening News* sniffed, noting the pitch's substandard narrowness as well. "The surface was baked like a turnpike road, and a very bad and irregular thoroughfare it was."[6]

Broxburn's style frustrated Hearts—they'd kick the ball a long distance, then race toward it, elbowing or knocking over anyone in their way. They scored two goals in the first nine minutes, drawing a huge cheer and toots from their band, but Hearts forward James Reid got the visitors on the scoreboard before the end of the first half, and Jimmy Wood tied the score in the second. The game was rough, the *Evening News* reported—Hearts' John Sneddon "was on one occasion smashed against the dressing box"—and the refereeing "hardly satisfactory," but the biggest trouble came after the final whistle blew. "Everyone will take exception to the conduct of some spectators at Broxburn," the Edinburgh paper huffed. Two Hearts players were attacked: "One of them was severely kicked, while another dodged a stone or two. Even long after the match, one impudent fellow desired an apology from an Edinburgh back for something said in the village seasons ago. Not content with this, threats were frequent, and one or two of the Edinburgh players were in fear and trembling when leaving their hotel through the threats of loudmouthed village roughs."[7]

The games in Addiewell were also likely to end in brawls. Addiewell Football Club was the first West Lothian team to compete in the Scottish Cup but bounced out after substantial defeats from Hearts and Hibernian, another big Edinburgh team.[8] If Paddy was going to earn a proper job playing football, he'd have to do so outside town. He began seeking playing time in other West Lothian clubs like Seafield Athletic, a few towns away. In 1911 Paddy, who worked during the summer as a boilermaker's laborer at the oil works, found a spot at Arniston Rangers, a junior team that played thirty miles away, across the Pentland Hills in a town called Gorebridge.

The term *junior* is a peculiarity of Scottish football. It refers not to players' ages but to their semiprofessional status—often they'd be stocked with young players hoping to break into the bigger clubs or former professionals eking out a few last years on the pitch.

In Arniston, Paddy met Willie Wilson, a left winger from Edinburgh's Dalry neighborhood. The two made an immediate impression on their team, and bigger teams began sniffing around. In November 1911 the Dundee *Courier* reported that Hearts had acquired Crossan, who stood at 5'9½" and 160 pounds—a big man for his day, perfectly sized to intimidate a spindly forward heading toward the net.

New players on big clubs like Hearts had to prove themselves first on the reserve team and hope for a chance among the starters, or "first eleven." Such an opportunity was likely to come in a less important match—a "friendly" against a nonleague team, or a minor cup competition, which tended to come toward the end of the season and whose matches would often be played within a day or two of league games. While the star players rested, the reserves would get a shot.

Football is a winter sport in Scotland, and the cold months of 1911–1912 were the second full season for John McCartney, who'd been hired as manager for five pounds per week in January 1910 after the disappointing tenure of James McGhee, a former player for hated crosstown rival Hibernian. McGhee had suspended Bobby Walker, the club's biggest star since he joined in 1896, in a dispute over discipline. Fans were furious, and the board intervened to put Walker back on the field. Stung, McGhee resigned in December 1909.

McCartney's first months on the job were not much more auspicious. On February 19, 1910, Hearts met Hibs on their home grounds on Easter Road in the third round of the Scottish Cup competition. Afternoon sun had burned off the morning rain, but it was windy and the grass was slippery.

Between twenty-six thousand and twenty-seven thousand fans had made their way to the game, and just before halftime the crowd broke through the palings and began invading the field. The referee, J. B. F. Stark, kept the match going, occasionally stopping play to shoo the fans behind the playing area, but with twenty-five minutes to go ordered the players off the field for good, at which point thousands of fans pushed onto the pitch, taking down about a hundred yards of fencing and sending one man to the Royal Infirmary with a broken collarbone.

McCartney was charged with rebuilding this demoralized and chaotic squad, whose roster seemed to change weekly and which didn't even have a trainer. Professionalism had landed unevenly on teams in the Scottish Football Association. Glasgow had nearly three times Edinburgh's population, and its football clubs were perennial league winners. McCartney was born in Glasgow and played for one of its biggest clubs, Rangers, before eventually moving down to higher-paying teams in England. He retired from the Yorkshire club Barnsley and began pursuing a career in management, moving back north in 1904 to run the Paisley club, St. Mirren.

At St. Mirren, McCartney tuned his approach to managing a team, adopting a tactic American baseball fans might recognize: he looked for bargains. McCartney would scour small clubs for good underpriced players and signed players from teams he felt had overlooked their talents. (When Crossan was signed in November, he was already the third junior player McCartney had acquired that season.) He even brought on two English players, to the collective gasp of Edinburgh fans: Percy Dawson, whom he obtained from North Shields Athletic for a hundred pounds, and Lawrence Abrams from Stockport County for the astonishing sum of £650. McCartney also hired Tom Brandon to be the club's first trainer, imposing a heretofore missing physical discipline on the team.

McCartney played a "scientific" game. He stretched out the field, making it harder for defenders to predict where a scoring attempt would come from, and forcing them to divert resources to defense. The press called Hearts' fancy play "cleverness" and noted the forwards' "carpet-weaving" style. "One had difficulty at times in telling where the half-backs ended and where the forwards began," a correspondent for Glasgow's *Daily Record* wrote in 1914 about a game in which Hearts tied Queen's Park.[9]

Bob Mercer's tenure at Hearts preceded McCartney, but he quickly became the engine of the new manager's machine. He played, as the name of his position suggests, right in the middle of the field, pivoting from defense to attack. Mercer was also big—over six feet tall. It was his job to turn the ball around if it was going the wrong way and get it to a halfback or forward. It was one of those incredibly important jobs that few notice unless someone does it badly—and Mercer was terrific at it.

Hearts finished their first season under McCartney in twelfth place. Scottish league football is organized under a simpler structure than the playoff system common in North American sports. Teams earn points depending on the outcome of a game—two for a win, one for a tie, none for a loss. A "league table" keeps track of the teams by order of points earned; the team with the most points at the end of the season is champion.

Separately, the teams take part in cup competitions, which are usually shorter than the thirty-eight-game regular season and earn the winners a trophy. Cup games are called "ties," a term confusing for anyone from North America, where a tie usually means a draw. The competitions are usually shorter than a regular season and often draw from a bigger pool of teams, allowing smaller clubs the opportunity to compete against bigger squads. Cups were a way to secure local bragging rights, but they also played an important economic role—they kept fans paying to see football matches. As the sports historian Matthew McDowell puts it, when demand for the product you're manufacturing is elastic, you make more of it.[10]

On Tuesday, January 2, 1912, Hearts played a Northeastern Cup semifinal match against Falkirk. They were home in Tynecastle, their stadium on Edinburgh's west side, and ten thousand people celebrating the New Year were in attendance. Hearts had played twice in the preceding three days, which meant the Falkirk game was a good opportunity for players on reserve squads to get some playing time. That day, one of them was Paddy Crossan, who made his first-team debut substituting for Mercer at center.

The weather was rainy and overcast, and the ground at Tynecastle was so wet that running felt like wading, but the players were charged up when they took the field. Abrams was "unceremoniously bowled over" by the visitors at the beginning of the game, the *Falkirk Herald* reported. The referee granted him a penalty kick, and he neatly potted a goal. But then Falkirk's Jock Rattray scored once to tie up the match, and later put his team ahead with a shot that faked out Hearts goalkeeper Tom Allan.

Crossan immediately made an impression on the Tynecastle fans by taking a pass from William Macpherson and sending it hurtling toward the Falkirk goal. One of Hearts' "prettiest efforts," as described in the *Herald*, it caromed off the goalposts, just missing the net. None of the Hearts players actually paid to score goals managed any further offense, and Falkirk ended up winning 3–1.

Paddy finally got his first league match the next month, when Scotland's national team played England's in Middlesbrough, taking Mercer out of the lineup and allowing Paddy to again take his place. Three other Hearts players—Percy Dawson, Peter Nellies, and Tommy Murray—were out with injuries, and the Hearts team that traveled north to Fife to play Kirkcaldy's Raith Rovers in Stark's Park only slightly resembled the group that trounced Hibernian in a midweek Scottish Cup match.

It showed. Hearts were "soundly thrashed," the Dundee *Courier* wrote the following Monday. Raith Rovers' forward line ran all over the Edinburgh team, and it was all Paddy and his fellow halves could do to prevent another 3–1 smackdown.

After yet another losing appearance the next month, Paddy finally got a little good news: Hearts had signed Willie Wilson, his old teammate from Arniston Rangers. They played a losing game together in early April and joined again against Motherwell on April 22. Wilson created some offensive chances and Paddy helped thwart the other side, and Hearts prevailed 2–1. The season was nearly over, and Hearts were stuck in fifth place in the league table, so McCartney played his young signings again the next week, when Hearts beat Partick Thistle 2–1 for the last game of the regular season. Paddy snatched the ball from a Thistle forward and shot it to Abrams, who along with Dawson provided both of the day's goals.

The next month Hearts traveled to Norway and Denmark, whose football association had struck up a friendly relationship with several British clubs and paid them to come over in early summer to help stoke interest in the game. Hearts received £220 to make the journey.

The games weren't just moneymakers for the club, though: they also served as a reward for a long season. While in Denmark, Hearts were entertained by their hosts at a hotel near the Tivoli Gardens, toured the Carlsberg Brewery, and even saw King Frederick VIII's funeral. (He died May 14, delaying one of their matches.)

Hearts more or less had their way with the Norwegians. On May 12 they thumped Kristiania Kretslag 9–0, with Dawson scoring four of those goals. Two days later they blew out Grenland Kretslag 6–0. The Danish team they faced next was a select squad, comprising mostly middle-class men from Copenhagen's four big clubs, Københavns Boldklub, B93, Frem, and Akademisk Boldklub. They surprised Hearts with a draw on May 19, and Crossan and Wilson got to play together the next night; the home team beat the invaders 2–0.

Over the summer, the players often returned to their civilian occupations. McCartney also ran two cinemas, the Salon Picture House in Leith and the Tivoli in Gorgie, and the income from that helped him save Hearts money—he took a voluntary pay cut to one pound per week. Wilson, who grew up in the shadow of Tynecastle on McLeod Street, was a tinsmith. In addition to his work at the Addiewell works, Paddy, the historian Jack Alexander notes, took part in professional footraces using fake names.[11]

Summers were tremendously important to Scots of all classes, offering rare respite from toil. While the upper and middle classes quit town by steamship or headed to villas by the sea, the working classes tended to make do with day trips to Dalkeith Park or street picnics in Gorgie where mothers organized games and children jumped ropes or swung from trees.

Hearts' 1912–1913 campaign opened on Thursday, August 15, when Hearts met St. Bernards at the Old Logie Green in Edinburgh in the first round of the Dunedin Cup. Before the end of the first half, they had a rotten bit of luck—one of St. Bernards' forwards fired off a ball that hit a Hearts defender and ricocheted into their goal before goalkeeper Tom Allan could respond. The game ended in a draw, so under cup rules it had to be replayed. The rematch came five days later at Tynecastle in abysmal weather. Willie Wilson pounced on the opportunity, running through St. Bernards' defense as if it weren't there and scoring five goals. A couple of times he came close to making it six. A regular place at the front of the team followed.

Four days after that rout, Wilson took part in a league game at home against Queen's Park, the only team in the first league that still held out against professionalism. It, too, was a turkey shoot. Hearts forward William Macpherson had three goals. Bob Mercer and Bobby Walker each got two. Nellies and George Sinclair scored, and Wilson added to the visitors' humiliation.

On September 21 the actuarial table caught up with the Bobby Walker era. Walker was thirty-three and the game against Rangers at their home ground, Ibrox, was his 379th appearance with Hearts. This was supposed to be his last season. He'd announced his retirement before the season started. Fans started a "testimonial fund" that eventually raised money from the Scottish Football Association, the famous entertainer Sir Harry Lauder, and the comedian "Wee Georgie" Wood, among others.

Walker joined the club when he was seventeen and playing for Dalry Primrose, a junior team from Edinburgh. Hearts were very interested in the tall thick-necked young man with sleepy eyes, a Roman nose, and a prominent cleft chin, but tried not to show their hand by arranging a trial alongside two other young players in a match against the English team Sunderland. Walker played in a loping, seemingly easygoing manner, but after he suddenly wrested the ball from Sunderland and narrowly missed a goal, Hearts signed him. He'd been a fan favorite ever since and was Scotland's "most-capped" player, meaning he'd been selected for the national team more than any other man. He was a quiet man—in 1901, as Hearts faced a Scottish Cup final against the heavily favored Celtic, Walker's teammates asked him to make a speech. "Gentlemen, you must excuse me," he told them. "I would rather play than speak." After falling behind Celtic 3–1, Walker led Hearts back to beat them 4–3. "Bobby, you're the best player in Europe," his awestruck teammate Charles Thomson told him repeatedly on the train ride home.[12]

Fifteen minutes into the Rangers' game that September, Walker wrenched his back and had to leave the field for a physical examination. He returned but reality beckoned, and he left the game not long afterward. Minus their superstar, Hearts rallied, thumping Rangers 4–2. Wilson got one goal, George Sinclair two, and Jimmy Low, an agriculture student at Edinburgh University whom McCartney had signed in August from the Highlands club Inverness Caledonian, helped finish off their hopes. One account of the game praised the forwards' production but noted they were freed to attack by a defense that blunted Rangers' hopes and consistently turned the ball toward the front of the team. In the back of the field that day were Bob Mercer, a journeyman defender named David Taylor, and Paddy Crossan.

Walker sat out the games that fall when Hearts, for the first time in years, contended. They were undefeated until October 5, when Falkirk took them down 2–0. They managed a couple of additional blowouts, thumping Kilmarnock 5–0 on October 26 and Partick Thistle 4–0 the following week. Wilson scored three goals in that game.

Scotland woke up to frost-covered ground on Saturday, November 30. Rugby's powers that be examined the playing fields and declared them unplayable. Association football had no such qualms. The ground was slippery and frozen hard at Tynecastle, where Raith Rovers were visiting. As soon as they took the field, the players had trouble staying on their feet, but Dawson and Wilson found scoring opportunities. With ten minutes left in the game, Wilson slipped and injured his shoulder so badly he had to be helped off the field. It was an injury that would haunt him for years to come.

Throughout December, Hearts, Celtic, and Rangers fought for the top of the league table, with only a point or two difference between them. But Hearts' inconsistency began to make it unlikely that the league championship would leave Glasgow for the first time in a decade. Even without Bobby Walker, McCartney had built a respectable side that would play four forwards at away games and launch a fearsome whole-squad attack at home. Inconsistency remained a problem, however, especially when Hearts played small teams with fewer resources.

By Christmas Eve, Celtic was four points ahead of Hearts, and the lead was beginning to look unassailable.

Christmas and New Year's in Scotland are known as the "festive period," a time to give your house a special cleaning and to greet visiting relatives with a drink and some hot soup. But for football players at the turn of the century the season was anything but restful, as clubs alternated cup competitions with league matches to draw more fans. Between December 28 and January 4 Hearts played four games in a sport so physically demanding that players usually required a week's rest between engagements. That was often good news for players on the reserve team, who like Wilson and Crossan the season before, got a chance to prove themselves.

This was the case for Duncan Currie, a lad from Kilwinning all the way on the other side of the country in northern Ayrshire. Currie was a twenty-year-old hairdresser whom Hearts signed for two pounds, two shillings from Kilwinning Rangers. His brother Bob also played for Hearts. Duncan played in defense with Mercer and Taylor again on New Year's Day when Hibs edged Hearts by one point on New Year's Day to win the Wilson Cup, but they roared back the next day to shut out Falkirk in front of seventeen thousand at home.

Another new player started getting regular spots in the team's lineup in late December: Alfred Ernest "Alfie" Briggs, a twenty-four-year-old Glaswegian who had built machines at the Singer factory and played for a local junior team until he was picked for the Scottish junior international team in October 1912 for a game against Wales at Tynecastle. McCartney signed him the same month.

As a rule, fans had to use their imaginations when they looked at recaps of matches in newspapers. The *Scotsman* shunned photography, apparently preferring dense, reassuringly spare columns of text. Dundee's newspapers, on the other hand, had begun running illustrations of the previous weekend's matches on Mondays, and Glasgow's papers ran photographs. The January 13 editions of the *Dundee Evening Telegraph* and the Dundee *Courier* carried drawings of a Hearts–Hamilton Academical match the previous Saturday, played on a snow-covered field that a caption described as "more like a curling pond than a football pitch."

Bobby Walker returned to Hearts on February 1 for a home game against Aberdeen. By this point Hearts' championship hopes were all but squashed. Celtic was eleven points ahead on the league table, and Hearts had slipped to fifth place. In early March they defeated Celtic 1–0 in front of a record sixty-five thousand people in a Scottish Cup match in Glasgow. It was a "narrow, but brilliant, victory," the *Scotsman* recorded. The game's only goal came from Wilson, and Celtic's grinding offense failed to get past Mercer, Crossan, and Taylor. Paddy, the paper noted, was "in the wars now and again," but his line held.[13]

His team's league dreams gone, McCartney could reasonably now hope for a cup victory. It wasn't to be. On March 29 Hearts and Falkirk met at Ibrox for a semifinal. The play was chippy. Falkirk forward James Anderson Croal fell headfirst after a collision with Crossan that concussed both men. Croal left the field, returned to loud cheers, scored the game's only goal, and then had to be helped back off after what one newspaper called "contact with Nellies."[14] Falkirk managed to end Hearts' Scottish Cup campaign with only ten men. Even the Rosebery Charity Cup eluded the exhausted side, who finished their 1912–1913 season with a 0–2 loss at home to Hibernian.

Over the summer McCartney began taking steps to improve Hearts' attack. In May he signed James Speedie, another insurance clerk from Edinburgh, as a backup to Wilson. The next month, he signed Harry Graham from Raith Rovers for £200 to replace Walker. Graham was twenty-six and had trained as a dentist, but unfortunately for local oral hygiene he had great skill as an inside forward, a position then mostly used to make opportunities for the wingers to score. Graham distinguished himself by scoring lots of goals as well. He grew up with asthma, but it didn't get in his way much: after going senior at St. Bernards he played two seasons in England before Raith picked him up.

In August, McCartney signed Harry Wattie, an insurance clerk who played for Tranent Juniors. He saw a successor to Bobby Walker in the unassuming, quiet twenty-year-old from Marchmont, an Edinburgh neighborhood just south of the great green park called the Meadows. Wattie was "in the first flight of players—in fact, an artist," McCartney wrote years later. Like Walker, he would feint and swerve on the field; off it he had little to say but was "rich in snatches of dry humour."[15] He and Paddy quickly became close friends.

McCartney's ideal side was emerging. He was building a balanced machine whose front line would bamboozle defenders with interlocking unpredictable attacks, whose center would rob other teams of momentum, and whose defense would come down hard on anyone unlucky enough to get close to Hearts' net.

Hearts opened the 1913–1914 season with a 3–1 victory over Airdrieonians at home. It was the second league game for Robert Malcolm, a lantern-jawed utility player from the reserve team, and the first for James Speedie, who scored twice.

Harry Wattie had a similar debut the following month against Rangers at home, notching two goals in inclement weather before 15,500 soggy fans. He played again a few days later, when Hearts thumped Celtic 2–0. Soon he was a regular sight in the first eleven, which by early October was atop the league table and packing them in at Tynecastle, whose faithful could sense something special was beginning to happen with their heroes.

Hearts remained undefeated until November 1, when St. Mirren blanked them in a match into which a "good deal of forcible play and some bad temper crept," the *Scotsman* wrote.[16] They avenged the loss two weeks later playing against the same team in heavy rain; Dawson scored four times in the 6–0 walloping. But Celtic had crept up behind Hearts and was two points ahead on the league table after the Edinburgh team drew with Dundee the next week. "Wattie is a capture," a sportswriter for the Dundee *Courier* enthused. "Fancy Bobby Walker's place being filled by a junior!"[17]

By the end of the year, Hearts were still winning, but so were Celtic. The Edinburgh team just couldn't claw back over the Glaswegians standing athwart the league table. The December 29 edition of the Dundee *Courier* carried a drawing of Mercer checking Airdrieonians'

James Greig Reid, the top scorer in Scotland that year, on a field covered in snow. Twelve days later they were playing Aberdeen, whose left half George Wilson collided with a teammate in a game played under what the Scotsman called "wretched weather conditions." Both players were taken off the field to be examined, and the doctor, Ellis Milne, quickly decided to take Wilson to the Royal Infirmary, where it was discovered that the player's kneecap was completely severed. Under the circumstances, the *Aberdeen Evening Express* reported two days later, Wilson was "wonderfully cheerful."

Hearts won that game but lost the next week at Dumbarton. Bad luck struck in the seventh minute, when Dumbarton forward James McDade fired a missile into Hearts' net. Goalkeeper Tom Allan expertly punched it out, but the ball hit McDade's teammate John Rowan and rebounded into the net. The tough breaks, draws, and close losses were adding up: Hearts slipped to third place on the league table, and the promise of another season began to evaporate. The team had gelled in a remarkable manner—during one game, a Glasgow sportswriter wrote, they "were practically playing eight forwards," but they couldn't close the deal.[18]

In late February, papers all over northern Britain carried remarkable news: Hearts had transferred Percy Dawson to Blackburn Rovers for a fee of £2,500. With the title appearing ever more out of grasp, the team began to seek new blood. Speaking anonymously, team directors put out the word that "only a decided change in the team will stop the over-elaboration which cost the club much recently."[19]

There was another more pressing reason: Hearts needed the money. Dawson received £500 for the trade, and the team banked the rest to help it build a new stand. Football grounds were still rough places in 1914; Hearts had nevertheless been steadily improving Tynecastle since the turn of the century. It added rush-resistant turnstiles in 1901, a new stand and press box in 1903, and brick walls around three sides in 1906. The cycle track that used to help the team make money on off days was removed; in 1911 it opened the "Iron Stand," which held 4,500. In 1913 Hearts decided it needed a new main stand and hired

Archibald Leitch to design it. Leitch had designed Rangers' grounds at Ibrox, and, despite a collapse there in 1902 that killed twenty-five and injured more than five hundred, his career had flourished. He designed and improved stadia all over Britain, including at West Ham in London, Celtic Park in Glasgow, and St. James' Park in Newcastle upon Tyne.

Sobered by the Ibrox disaster, Leitch set about making stands safer. There were few seats for football fans at the time. You stood on a slope, on terraced boards if you were lucky, behind steel crush barriers that afforded the tired a place to lean. Leitch's design for Tynecastle called for a redbrick exterior, skylights, electric lighting, and up-to-date restrooms. The cost, he told Hearts in February 1914, would be around £8,000. Hearts had about £4,000 in the bank before the team transferred Dawson.

As the season wound down into another mediocre finish, Currie, Alfie Briggs, and a center named Walter Scott began to get more playing time as McCartney tested combinations for the next season. They finished the season with a rousing game against Rangers at Ibrox where bad luck again landed on Hearts when Crossan missed a kick, leaving an opening for Alec Smith to fire in a goal. Rangers won 3–2, and the league season ended with Hearts in a distant third place.

On June 3 Boyd, Crossan, Currie, Briggs, Mercer, Nellies, Wattie, Gracie, Graham, Wilson, and others joined McCartney, club president Elias Fürst, and trainer Jimmy Duckworth on another visit to Copenhagen. They played two games there, the second on June 9 against the Danish national team squad. Twelve thousand people came out to see Hearts play, and the team was feted by Danish officials, who threw a banquet for them on June 7 and invited the Hearts brass to a special soiree with King Christian X.

It was all quite wonderful, and everyone involved with Hearts felt things were finally in place for a brilliant season. They returned home on June 14 full of optimism. Two weeks later, Gavrilo Princip shot Franz Ferdinand. Hearts' next trip to Europe would be under very different circumstances.

3

THE SPORT IN WAR

After the Usher Hall meeting, all of Edinburgh invested in Sir George's goal to fill the battalion in record time. Its newspapers breathlessly kept track of the climbing total of recruits, which seemed to increase by a hundred men every day. The recruiting drive was part political campaign and part marketing stunt—in other words, it was classic George McCrae.

McCrae, Sir James Leishman, and two MPs, Charles Edward Price and James Myles Hogge, began barnstorming Edinburgh, speaking at any dinner meeting, union hall, or meeting of sportsmen that would have them. By the morning after the meeting, five hundred men had signed up.

At a meeting of city big shots at the Carlton Hotel on Monday, November 30, McCrae told those gathered he was pleased that so many potential recruits had asked him, "What will my mother get if I go?" He said that demonstrated not only that they were attracting the type of men who cared about their families but also that the government was doing its part by providing financial support to the wives (both formal and common-law), mothers, and sisters of those who served. Few women in Scotland's working classes worked outside the home, and men often provided most of the income for large family units.

The Edinburgh and District Trades Council met in Melbourne Hall on December 1 to discuss ways it could help send men to McCrae's.

The group's executive committee had proposed dividing trades into four groups to speed recruitment: printers, builders and furnishers, engineers and metal trades, and a catchall group for all other occupations such as bakers, coopers, and shoemakers. Those men would funnel into a "brotherhood company" in the battalion; the Hearts players, McCrae had decided, would seed a company of their own filled with other athletes and fans. There would be another company for students.

Council chairman James Campbell suggested that the first men to go should be those who weren't the primary means of support for their households. Price agreed and channeled the mainstream belief that conscription would be a "disaster" for Britain—the country should set an example for other countries by raising armies of volunteers. Even if Britain weren't "bound by a sense of honour to defend the neutrality of Belgium," he said, if Germany took over the country its long coastline would make a "constant menace."[1]

Leishman also spoke at the union meeting, noting that twenty thousand Edinburgh men had already left for the front, and said criticism in the press against "shirkers and cowards" was regrettable. "Very many young men were willing to go, but the circumstances kept them back," he said.

The newspapers reported messages of support arriving from all quarters. "I am glad to see you have 'roped in' some of the Hearts," Col. A. S. Blair of the Ninth Royal Scots, a former president of the Scottish Football Union, wrote to battalion headquarters. "I hope their example will be as contagious as was the Rugby epidemic."

Hearts chairman Elias Fürst's father, Rabbi Jacob Fürst of the Jewish synagogue, wrote, "The supreme law of loyalty demands sacrifice and self abnegation on the part of every man fit for service."[2]

"The fire you are trying to kindle in Edinburgh is a holy fire," Father Power of the Jesuits wrote. Mr. MacFarlane, Edinburgh's former bailie, also sent a message: "For every man capable of bearing arms who neglects his country in her hour of need there will be a hell in his conscience for as long as he lives."[3]

In that day's papers, Fürst and John McCartney had placed a notice encouraging Hearts fans to tell their recruiting officer they specifically wanted to join the Hearts company. "Now then, young men, as you have followed the old club through adverse and pleasant times, through sunshine and rain, roll up in your hundreds for King and country, for right and freedom," they wrote. "Don't let it be said that footballers are shirkers and cowards. As the club has borne an honoured name in the football field, let it go down to history that it has also won its spurs on the field of battle."[4]

Fürst was a watchmaker and jeweler with a shop on the South Bridge and had been an avid Hearts fan since his family arrived in Edinburgh from Russia. His father was so determined for his children to assimilate into local life that he took them to football games on the Sabbath. Elias grew up to become a member of the club and a contributor to their coffers, but by 1904 the team organization was in serious trouble. English teams, unconstrained by agreements with their northern neighbors, had poached three of their best players, paying Hearts nothing. A fire forced the team to replace its south stand, putting it dangerously in debt. It owed its creditors and the taxman £1,450 and had to pay wages of £60 per week. Close to insolvency, its managers decided they had no choice but to sell three more players to Chelsea.

Working with Leishman and George Wilson, who owned most of the *Evening News*, Fürst reorganized the club's finances. Previously a members' club with dues, in 1905 they turned it into a corporation whose new shareholders injected £5,000 in new capital into the team. When Hearts won the Scottish Cup in 1906 the team allowed Fürst to display the trophy in his shop window.

Sir George was not above the occasional display himself. The December 1 *Evening News* included a photo of Sir George with his sons, who were all serving. Second Lt. Kenneth McCrae of the Seventh Cameron Highlanders, Capt. George McCrae of the Fourth Royal Scots, and Lt. W. R. McCrae of the Lowland City of Edinburgh Royal Garrison Artillery flanked their famous father. The next day's paper included a letter from someone complaining about "inquisitive and interfering nobodies" who harassed men in public about enlisting. "H" said he'd seen a woman harangue a fellow on the street. The man asked her if she was referring to him, removed his glove, and placed a wooden hand in hers, explaining he'd lost it in a different war. She didn't even have the decency to apologize, H marveled. "I really don't think that that type of fighting will advance recruiting or kill Germans," he wrote.[5]

While busybodies used the same message on any unfortunate soul who happened into their sights, Sir George tailored his pitch to his audience.

On Tuesday morning McCrae and Price visited McEwan's Brewery in Fountainbridge for a breakfast-hour meeting. Managing director William Younger informed McCrae and Price that 40 percent of his employees were already serving. When he spoke, McCrae acknowledged the brewers' sacrifice and said he hoped they had a few more men left to offer. He explained that he hoped to fill the battalion with "men of an extra good physical type."

McCrae was also keen to attract more people from what he called "the sporting interest." He didn't have to wait long. Word of Hearts' grand gesture was already bringing football players from around Scotland to sign up. Six members of Falkirk's football team joined on Wednesday—Alexander Henderson and John Morrison from the first team, and Robert Godfrey, Michael Gibbons, Robert Wood, and Andrew Henderson from the reserves. Their club agreed to pay them full wages if they were able to continue playing while training and half wages if they couldn't take the field. Their manager, William Nicol, came along, telling a reporter he thought a few more men would join.

The same evening five players from Raith Rovers—James Todd, James Logan, William Porter, Jock Rattray, and George McLay—enlisted. Their manager, John Richardson, accompanied them to Edinburgh from Fife and stood next to Fürst in a photo showing McLay signing his name while his teammates watched.

And following a postgame address by Hogge at Inverleith Park on Wednesday, eight members of the junior Edinburgh Nomads—James Baigrie, Andrew Millar, William Easton, James Barbour, Alexander Cameron, Adam Moyes, William Hadden, and William Roxburgh—grabbed their things and followed him to the recruiting office, where they enlisted in the battalion's Hearts company.

After the brewers' meeting, McCrae asked Price when he'd see him again. "Well," Price replied, "I'm speaking for you in the afternoon, and again at night."[6]

On Wednesday, December 2, Hearts players Tom Gracie and Walter Scott joined McCrae at a meeting of more than four hundred people at Tynecastle Parish Church hall. McCrae had another meeting to go to, so he spoke first, saying that if Edinburgh (and, of course, everywhere else) sent as many men as they could to the front, "it would bring the war to a decisive issue."[7]

Lord Arthur Dewar spoke next. Dewar hadn't followed his brothers into the whisky business founded by their father, John Dewar Sr., but instead studied law and eventually entered politics. Standing to speak, Dewar got the crowd laughing about the "old degenerate days" when he and his friends passed many happy nights in the hall. Then he turned serious: "Scotland had few, if any cowards, and some of the thoughtless young women who were offering the white feather were probably wounding and insulting the wrong men," he said to applause.

McCartney stood to speak near the end. An *Evening News* reporter recorded the speech, in which the manager relayed that "as much as had been said that night about what the Heart of Mid-Lothian players had done, he wished to assure them that it was not from any point of view of the showman that the step had been taken. It was purely and solely an act of patriotism and duty on their part."[8]

On Thursday morning the *Evening News* reported the battalion had 779 recruits, including 20 young men from the town of Penicuik, which had already contributed 300 to the war. Across the country, newspapers were now celebrating every footballer who enlisted. John Bow of Bo'ness Football Club had also signed up, joining 130 more from the West Lothian coastal town who were at war. The tiny town of Spott had also provided a significant response; in that East Lothian village, not a single man stayed behind.

A week into recruiting, McCrae's battalion stood at almost nine hundred men. The student company was full, the brotherhood company was on its way, and the Hearts company, the executive committee reckoned when they met on Friday, would be full after the battalion's first public appearance, which they set for Tynecastle the next day. They made arrangements to sign up recruits directly in the pavilion. If any other athletes wanted to fight alongside the Hearts men, McCrae said at one meeting, "they had better hurry up."

December 4, 1914, would have been a perfect day for Scottish football. There was heavy rain, wind, and even some snow. That evening McCrae hit three gatherings, at Newington United Free Church Hall along with Hogge and others, at South Morningside School, and in the Oddfellows' Hall on Forrest Road. The last was held to appeal to sportsmen.

Elias Fürst chaired the meeting; John McCartney sat on the dais, as did several of the Hearts players, including Tom Gracie. Andrew Macbeth Anderson, the senior senator of the College of Justice, was the featured speaker. Lord Anderson was himself an athlete, and in 1883 his team at the University of Edinburgh defeated Hearts 5–2 in what was then known as the Edinburgh Shield cup competition. He continued to play after he joined the bar until an injury at a game in Falkirk ended his playing days. He remained a keen spectator of Edinburgh football and went to matches in the city frequently. He was also a curler, a fisherman, and a golfer.

Lord Anderson lit into the "lucubrations" of people who, he said, hadn't fully considered "the propriety and wisdom of stopping the game." As many as fifty thousand people depended on professional football to make a living; football clubs were businesses just like theaters.

Anderson noted there had been no drumbeat of calls to close theaters, which drew just as many men through the week as attended Easter Road or Tynecastle on a Saturday. Where, he asked to laughter, was the "suggestion that the picture houses should be shut up, the theatres closed, and that we should go to our houses, drawn down the blinds, put on black gloves, and sit like a nation of undertakers"?[9]

It wasn't just young men who attended football matches, Lord Anderson said. Shutting down the sport didn't mean the army would automatically get the men who were able to fight but chose not to—"If they did not recognise their duty now while the game was being played, they would not recognise it if football stopped to-morrow."

The motto of Scotland should be business, and pleasure, as usual. "If we could show other countries that we could carry on our affairs, picture-houses, theatres, and football matches, without worrying much about the great task we had on hand, we could show them that we could fasten on to that task and deal with it without excessive worry."

Sir George knew how to make an entrance. He came in near the meeting's end to an "enthusiastic reception," a *Scotsman* account related. He told the crowd a doctor had told him, "I have been doing this sort of thing since the beginning of mobilisation, and I have never seen anything like those men. They are beautiful men, well developed, and fit to stand any strain."[10]

In the neighborhood of Morningside Sir George said he expected recruiting to wrap up not just the battalion but a reserve company as well by the following Monday.

On Saturday, December 5, the battalion assembled down the road from Tynecastle, where Gorgie Road meets Ardmillan Terrace. They weren't in uniforms yet, since the battalion didn't have them, and the professional athletes who'd joined all had to work on Saturdays. Led by McCrae and the band and pipers of the Ninth Royal Scots, the battalion marched to the stadium, where Hearts were planning to play Hibs in a league game. Despite high winds and cold, twelve thousand people turned out to cheer the local heroes.

Hibs knew they couldn't win the crowd over, so they tried to silence it early. They opened aggressively in an attempt to rattle Hearts and signal that they'd be in charge. But then they lost the ball. Hearts quickly fed it up the field to Low, who set up a surgical goal by Wattie.

The score was still 1–0 at halftime, when the Hearts players joined their fellow soldiers for a loudly cheered march around the field, and a call for more recruits. Nine fans joined on the spot, and more waited for the end of the game to head up to the recruiting office on Castle Street.

They made a good choice by staying. Crossan and Currie frustrated the Hibs forwards, and Graham fired the ball into the net fifteen minutes into the new half. Five minutes later Hibs finally earned the right to hope when they earned a corner kick. Smith took it, warming Archie Boyd's fingers as the ball sailed into Hearts' goal. But that was the extent of the visitors' luck. Their defender Robert Templeton hurt his leg and played with a limp until the pain was so great he had to be carried off the field in the seventy-fifth minute. Then even the wind betrayed Hibs, helping a Jimmy Low shot curve past Allan and into the net.

It was over. The score might have been even higher if not for a Hibs defender named Sandy Grosert, who stymied Wattie for much of the game.

Traditionally if they lost to Hearts in a league match, Hibs could look forward to a do-over in the Scottish Cup. But that competition was suddenly in danger. A group of representatives of Scottish football had been called to London to meet with the undersecretary of state for war, Harold "Jack" Tennant. In a September conference with representatives of all British football associations, when the cries to stop the sport during wartime were getting loud Tennant had proposed keeping clubs' regular seasons intact but scuttling cup and international matches.

After Hearts enlisted, the loudest noises about ending football had been quieted. But they and the other countries' association had publicly put themselves at the disposal of the War Office, so after a six-and-a-half-hour meeting on December 3, England, Wales, and Northern Ireland voted to go along with the plan to end cup competitions anyway. The Scots asserted that they weren't bound by the vote, and sought a meeting with Tennant on December 5 to sort things out.

Tennant was a Scot and Prime Minister Asquith's brother-in-law. He was a "well-meaning man with the faintest idea of what the playing of football implied," an account of the meeting read.[11]

Tennant was also unburdened by knowledge of the effect of Hearts' enlistment on public sentiment about ending football. He repeated to the

Scots that, as one account put it, "he did not think the full programme of amusement was in accord with public sentiment at this moment."[12] In other words, everyone had to appear to be doing something, no matter how empty the gesture. The delegation left to the sound of Tennant's expressions of delight that the other associations had seen things his way. They told him they'd think about it.

It would be financially disastrous for many Scottish clubs to go along with the plan, but at a meeting of the Scottish Football Association Celtic chairman Thomas White supported it—the associations had already committed themselves to the war effort, he argued. If they went along with the cup ban, they could say the regular season had the War Office's blessing. Eventually, the other directors acceded in a 10–7 vote.

To soften the blow, the association voted to allow them to cut wages to players and staff by 20–25 percent. That was hardly enough to offset the loss of the cup matches, the smaller clubs argued. Only by cutting wages by 60–70 percent could they make it. Their objections were overruled, and the association went ahead with Tennant's harebrained scheme.

Wages weren't clubs' only cost. They also had to furnish equipment, which could be quite expensive. A player for a professional club didn't have to provide for his own gear. Off-the-shelf shoes, known as "boots" in Britain, cost a guinea, just a shilling over a pound.[13] Custom shoes could cost twice that. Clubs could go through dozens of pairs of boots each season, replacing them whenever a player found them "the least uncomfortable or reliable," a member of one team's management wrote in the *Evening News*.[14]

Jerseys were also expensive—the good wool ones could cost as much as fifteen shillings. Clubs needed home and away jerseys, and had to keep them laundered and in good shape. They needed sweaters, socks, and underwear for practice. Good-quality football undergarments could be had for five shillings, but those "hemmed and braided in the artistic fashion beloved by some club managements," the team person wrote, could cost much more. As it turns out, "the wear and tear on knickers are very considerable."[15]

Balls, too, cost more than one might think—between eight and twelve shillings apiece—and clubs preferred new balls for each game, so they didn't lose their shape.

Celtic and Rangers both voted for the resolution. The big Glasgow clubs were the largest in the association and could better weather the loss of income. Neither was playing as well as Hearts, nor had they made much of an effort to recruit players for the war effort. "Possibly, Edinburgh is to blame in the matter," the *Evening News*'s sports columnist "Diogenes" mused in a tongue-in-cheek column. "Glasgow is not used to taking a lead from Edinburgh in anything," he wrote, "and I am afraid that Glasgow resented Edinburgh's lead in regard to recruiting." Perhaps, he wrote, "What Edinburgh should have done should have been to go West, cap in hand, and offer to take a lead from Glasgow. Edinburgh committed an unpardonable breach of the conventions as between the two cities."[16]

Hibernian was one of the clubs whose players had to that point mostly sat tight instead of joining Kitchener's Army. But before the Hearts-Hibs derby on December 5, word began to circulate that Hibs' star defender Sandy Grosert had joined McCrae's. It became official the next week.

Recruiting was slow in other cities' clubs, too. Certainly the clubs were trying. The Woolwich Arsenal Club, which had officially shortened its name to the Arsenal the year before, had offered to make up the amount of wages any player lost by enlisting. Other clubs had followed suit. But there just weren't that many players available to fill the army; there were 306 professional footballers in London in 1914. Fifty-six of them were already with the colors, and 156 were married—so all that noise by the local outrage industry was effectively landing on only ninety-four single men.

"The topic of the week has been Sir George M'Crae's Battalion," the *Evening News* wrote on December 5. "No corps raised for the war have received more vigorous 'booming.'" An article on a different page agreed: the battalion, it said, had "been worked up in quite American style."

In fact, the speed with which the battalion came together stirred memories of the City of London Imperial Volunteers, raised at Christmastime 1899 to fight the Second Boer War. The CIV's time at war resembled the brief adventure many Britons joining Kitchener's Army were expecting in this war—the battalion left for Africa at the beginning of the year and was home by October.

Some were jealous of the resources on which Sir George had been able to draw, "an Observer" noted, before slamming the door on such carping: "As for jealousy, all that needs to be said is that certain corps were on the ground for months before Sir George M'Crae got to work. What did they do? Much of the machinery used with such great effect during the last few days was at their disposal." When "Sir George took off his coat," the paper wrote, "his example became slightly infectious," and the "big drum Sir George thumped so vigorously awoke several of our influential Territorial Rip Van Winkles."

The McCrae effort had even revived the old-fashioned recruiting meeting, where speakers put forward the case for their country and urged men to come along on what "an Observer" called the "great adventure." Those meetings frequently brought together political enemies to illustrate the comity needed for the task: "One certainly rubs his eyes to see men on a common platform whom only a miracle have brought together, but this common bond of fellowship is one of the rewards of this period of national trial."

When eight members of the Mossend Swifts joined McCrae's, it made the papers. The football team from a tiny West Lothian shale-mining village near Addiewell was legendary for games so rough and wild they were nicknamed the "cow-punchers." They'd changed their name to the West Calder Swifts in 1903 after amalgamating with another club, but their former name was the one everyone remembered them by, an "old terror to the 'city clubs,'" as the *Evening News* described them at the turn of the century.

The Swifts thrived on the underdog feeling that came with playing bigger clubs who clearly felt above engaging county teams, and they became a familiar sight at disciplinary hearings at the East of Scotland Association's general committee meetings. Two of their players had gone on to represent Scotland in international competitions, an unheard-of achievement for a scrappy mining-town team, and they'd given Hearts George Hogg, a turn-of-the-century star. Their games tended to be blowouts, whether they won or lost. With this crew, it was all or nothing.

Dunfermline Athletic halfback David Izatt, who worked as a plumber when he wasn't playing football, joined the same day as the Swifts. That evening, December 7, the *Scotsman* reported the battalion's Hearts company was "more than full." Anyone who wanted to help fill out the battalion's remaining places would do so at a slight remove from the local heroes of sport.

On December 8, there were a few last recruiting meetings. By 10:00 PM, the battalion had more than 1,300 recruits. The battalion officially reached full strength the night of December 9. Two clergymen were among the last recruits—the Reverend William Urquhart of a small village called Kinloch Rannoch, and the Reverend Alfred E. Warr of Hamilton, just outside Glasgow.

They'd also managed to land Harry Julian, the tallest man in Kinghorn. He was 6'6", and known locally as the "Big Chief." Julian was the scoutmaster in the seaside Fife town; he'd trained with Boy Scouts founder Baden Powell. He was a teacher, and Kinghorn's school board agreed to hold his job for him while he was away and also to pay him seventy pounds per year.

That day the Army Council gave the battalion a proper name: the Sixteenth (Service) Battalion, the Royal Scots (Second Edinburgh). It would share a motto with the venerable cavalry regiment the Royal Scots Greys: "Second to None." People in Edinburgh shrugged and continued to call it "McCrae's."

Sir George sent a letter to the *Evening News* on December 10: "I beg to convey to the citizens of Edinburgh my grateful thanks for the prompt and remarkable response made to the appeal for recruits for the new service battalion of the Royal Scots." He continued:

> The original demand was for a battalion 1000 strong.
>
> In opening the campaign I "appealed with confidence to the patriotism and generous enthusiasm of my fellow-citizens." They have honoured the demand with interest.
>
> The further call of the War Office that the battalion should stand 1350 strong has been complied with in record time. This happy result has been achieved by the hearty cooperation of all classes in the community.
>
> The Committee desire me to express our obligation to the press for the powerful aid so freely given, which has done so much to enable them to carry the enterprise to a successful issue.

That Thursday, Sir George arranged for a few hundred members of the battalion—mostly those who had already left their jobs—to assemble at Castle Street for a route march up Lothian Road to the Blackford Hills and back again. A large crowd turned out to watch them, and "commented in favourable terms on the appearance of the recruits," the *Evening News* reported.

On Friday evening the Liberal Association of East Edinburgh met at Picardy Place Hall. Hogge spoke and told the gathering that some people had thought Sir George "had got his political coffin" when he left national politics and took up a post at to the Local Government Board. "If that was so," Hogge said to laughs and applause, "then Sir George had had a most glorious resurrection."[17]

The battalion's mobilization orders arrived. The men would officially fall in at 11:00 AM on Tuesday, December 15. As long as the weather was agreeable, they would assemble on George Street, march to Waverley Market for dinner, and sleep that night in quarters.

And so it was that on a cold and cloudy Tuesday in mid-December 1914, eighteen days after Sir George's speech at the Usher Hall, McCrae's became a real battalion. As if to emphasize how much of Edinburgh's mental space the men had occupied over the past few weeks, McCrae and his officers planned their debut to maximize public attention. They lined up four deep on George Street in the New Town, stretching a half mile from Charlotte Square to Hanover Street. A large crowd greeted them, standing in front of the stately soot-blackened Georgian sandstone buildings along the parade route, cheering raucously. "Good old Hearts," people shouted whenever they recognized a member of the team. An *Evening News* reporter noted that one particularly tall soldier of approximately six and a half feet "caught the eye." The city's swells turned up—politicians, clergymen, leaders of other military groups. Elias Fürst and John McCartney represented Hearts.

Sir George was on horseback at the front of the line, accompanied by his sons George and Kenneth. The procession was so long two bands of bagpipers were required. The first, from the Ninth Royal Scots, was up front, next to a brass band. The second, from the Fifth Royal Scots, blasted martial airs halfway down the line.

The men weren't in uniform yet—they marched down Charlotte Street and then Princes Street toward Waverley Market in their work clothes, carrying suitcases and underwear wrapped in paper. That morning they'd been grocers, tradesmen, students, and athletes. Now they were all soldiers, about to leave their everyday lives, if not yet their city.

They halted at Waverley, where Sir George addressed the battalion:

> Men of the 16th Battalion, Royal Scots, you have to-day been mobilised as part of the oldest regiment in the British Army, a regiment with glorious traditions of service in the field and of general good conduct, and I ask every man here to remember that the honour of the Royal Scots is entrusted to him, and that we as a battalion will do our very best to maintain those great traditions and to prove ourselves worthy of the great name we bear. I welcome you here, and I do so with confidence that

we will be able to give a good account of ourselves whenever we are called upon to defend our King and country.[18]

The men cheered heartily. Hugh Jamieson, the doctor who had examined many of them, got up and asked them to give Sir George three cheers. He got them.

After lunch, five hundred of the men marched to their billets at Sir George Heriot's Hospital, while nine hundred stayed behind in temporary quarters at the market.

The arrangements for where the battalion would sleep had finally been settled the day before, at a meeting of the governors of the trust that oversaw Sir George Heriot's Hospital, which despite its name was a school with a grand turreted gray sandstone main building, and a large square situated between the Grassmarket and the Meadows.

Heriot's had from the start of Sir George's campaign offered its facilities as billets. Its examination hall could accommodate five hundred men, and McCrae requested the use of an unused former brewery it owned for the rest. A temporary gangway would connect the two buildings. The battalion would put the brewery in order, McCrae assured the board.

The governors had originally agreed that the men could use only the school examination hall, drawing classrooms, "swimming bath," and gymnasium after school hours; that only officers could use the library and the chapel; and that the battalion would pay three pence per night per man. They would only be allowed to enter via the Vennel Gate, which connects with Keir Street and the steps coming up from the Grassmarket. In this way, the men "would not have to go through the Grassmarket, and would not be tempted by public-houses."

"Who suggested that?" asked a member of the Heriot's Trust. Councillor John William Chesser told the room he couldn't remember, but "if they were to rely on men to serve their country who would be tempted by a public-house, God help them."[19]

The final arrangements were more generous: the board dropped the price it would charge to one and a half pence per man per night with no charge for the use of the brewery. Sir Andrew McDonald asked headmaster John Brown Clark about the inconvenience of having a small army take up residence in the school. "I am perfectly patriotic, gentlemen," Sir Andrew said to laughter, "and I want to do all we possibly can, but it's ourselves first." On a more serious note, Sir Andrew reminded the trust that people paid good money to send their children to Heriot's, and that this affair had been "humbugged and bamboozled" from the start.

Clark replied anxiously that he expected the staff and students would be "subjected to very considerable inconvenience," but that he thought that in the spirit of patriotism, everyone could work around it. Some parents might object, but he and his staff could muddle through.[20]

Those first two nights in Waverley Market were not optimal—there weren't enough mattresses, but "the men accepted the situation with little grumbling," an *Evening News* reporter wrote later in the month. The nine hundred in temporary quarters at Waverley then moved to George Watson's College, nearby on Archibald Place, where they waited for the brewery to become a barracks.

It took two weeks to turn the former Castle Brewery into "most comfortable billets," as a 1921 history by the school's executive committee put it. John Anderson, the superintendent of works at Heriot's, oversaw the operation. The building had been constructed in 1875 and had been empty for twelve years. Heriot's bought it and a ruined tenement next door for £1,250 in 1912 with the intention of turning it into laboratories for the school of mining in nearby Heriot Watt College, which the trust also ran.[21]

Despite the brewery's long desuetude, it was dry as a bone inside. The ground floor became a dining room that could accommodate 500 men, and the three floors above it became dormitories, each holding 250 men. The beds were wooden trestle models with straw mattresses. It was better bedding than the stuff many troops got, but hardly luxury accommodations.

The building had many windows (some with ropes to be used in case of fire) and was well ventilated; Anderson used strategically placed wooden screens to prevent it from becoming drafty. The brewery was wired, with lights above the dining tables, and it had indoor plumbing, with sinks and flush toilets. They used lime wash to freshen up the walls.

One of the most thoughtful features was a drying room, made in a space with an old kiln. Stoves and hundreds of pegs and racks offered the men places to hang their wet gear after training in the rain. Even the wettest coat took only an hour to dry in the hot room.

The brewery had its own cooking and dining facilities and was connected to the main buildings by a temporary bridge made of wood. On Heriot's playgrounds, the battalion built temporary storerooms for meat and bread.

Edinburgh had just given 1,400 of its men to the colors, but to scolds around town that was merely a start. Writing under the name "Constant Reader," a letter writer told the *Evening News* that he had watched McCrae's men march to Waverley the day before. "I think they are a nice lot of fellows, but Edinburgh could do with a lot more. Look at the young fellows in public-houses and other shops. They will not join, because they would lose money and their nights off with their sweethearts. They are what I would term truly 'swankers.'" The letter closed with the obligatory statement that if the Constant Reader were younger than his fifty-nine years, he'd of course "been off [himself]."[22]

In the waning days of December a clergyman from Leith gave Sir George a revolver. The letter accompanying the gun expressed "the hope that it would account for some of the 'modern assassins,'" The *Scotsman* reported.[23]

The Hearts players got uniforms before many of their comrades. They needed to look good. On December 19, they left for Glasgow dressed in khaki for a match against Queen's Park.

The match came at an existential moment for Queen's Park. The Glasgow team had resisted professionalism and was the only remaining amateur member of the first division. It was the first association team in

Scotland and mostly drew its players from Glasgow's middle classes; even today its motto is *Ludere causa ludendi*—to play for the sake of playing.

The team had dominated Scottish football and even played in the English league for a couple of years in the 1870s, but its almost religious adherence to amateurism had begun to cost it. The team was at the bottom of the league table that Saturday, with only eleven points.

Two Queen's Park players, Thomas Haydock and John Roberts, were with the colors, but many in the crowd of seven thousand at Hampden Park were there to see the soldier-footballers of Hearts.

For the first thirty-five minutes, Queen's Park gave Hearts a game. The Edinburgh team was having trouble finding its stride, its play at the top of the field lacking "the snap or click that should characterise the play of forwards so skillful," the Glasgow *Daily Record* wrote in a recap two days later. Then Willie Wilson beat three defenders to whiz the ball to Tom Gracie, who banged it into Queen's Park's goal with his left foot. Queen's Park's goalkeeper, Gordon Kerr, injured himself trying to stop it and had to leave the field. Their defender James Wilson took his place just as Hearts found their gear and Harry Graham scored another goal.

Kerr returned, obviously in pain, only to see Wilson deftly weave the ball through his defenders and set up another goal by Graham delivered with such force that the keeper had no chance to stop it. He left the game with twenty minutes to go, as did James Wilson, who had "incurred the displeasure of the referee," as the *Daily Record* put it. Willie Wilson finished the pasting with a fourth goal.

Three of the four first-division teams who'd given players to McCrae won that Saturday. "Who said barrack life was going to have an injurious effect upon the players?" the *Daily Record* asked.[24]

On Sunday the whole battalion paraded to church at the United Free Church's assembly hall, piped in by their own band as well as Heriot's. The men attended in civilian dress and were addressed by the Reverend Dr. Thomas Burns, recently named chaplain to the battalion, and Sir George, who read the lesson from 2 Timothy 2:3–4: "Thou therefore endure hardness, as a good soldier of Jesus Christ. No man that warreth entangleth himself with the affairs of this life; that he may please him who hath chosen him to be a soldier."

But the affairs of this life still beckoned. Christmas Day 1914 was pleasant, with crisp air perfect for exercising outdoors. Troops stationed around Edinburgh observed the holiday with marches and dinners. The Fifth Royal Scots celebrated where they were barracked at the Marine Gardens. Before the war it was a popular spot for dancing that also featured a skating rink, ornamental gardens, and something called a "human zoo," in which people from Somalia lived in mud huts and conducted fake spear fights. The men of the Fifth got an extra dinner, and the officers' children put on entertainment, including a magic show.

The Fourth Royal Scots got a special dinner that included turkey, and the Highland Battalion of the Royal Scots, whose sergeants and officers feasted the night before, had a route march followed by what was reportedly an excellent meal.

McCrae's battalion got proper uniforms for Christmas, and they celebrated with a march around town, from Lauriston to Tollcross, down Lothian Road, along Princes Street, over the bridges, back to headquarters via Buccleuch Street, Bristo Street, and Teviot Place. Sir George rode in front, still appearing more comfortable in his khaki and crisp glengarry hat than many of the men, some of whom looked slightly bewildered by how quickly they'd become soldiers. The battalion pipe band marched, too, the skirl of its pipes and the crackle of their new boots echoing off the sides of hard sandstone buildings.

Edinburgh's citizens turned out all along the route to admire the battalion, who "created a favourable impression among the onlookers," the *Scotsman* observed on December 26. When the march finished, they formed again at Watson's College, where Sir George addressed the men. They already looked like trained soldiers, he said, and Edinburgh would be proud of them. He announced he was going to give them Christmas dinner, including plum puddings donated by local lawyer and historian William Moir Bryce, and then they were at liberty until 10:00 PM to enjoy Christmas with their families.

At dinner the townspeople presented them with presents. One parcel included a knitted scarf and a note: "Would you please give this small gift to your first recruit, as I have taken a great interest in your battalion. I am sorry indeed I am a girl, or I would have been one of your battalion also. I shall send a few more comforts for your brave men later on. Wishing you and your lads a Merry Christmas and a happy New Year."[25]

4

IN SUNSHINE AND
IN SHADOW

Sir Douglas Haig was mortified.

It was October 28, 1915, and His Majesty King George V had come to La Buissière Castle near the northern French town of Béthune to inspect troops under Haig's command. Haig was fifty-four years old and a major general. Through hard work, luck, and careful cultivation of connections, he had risen further in the British Army than most men could have ever hoped. He was an architect of the fighting force that had stymied German ambitions for more than a year in France and Flanders and had overseen the writing of the book at the heart of British military organization, 1909's *Field Service Regulations*.

And on this October afternoon, he had hoped to bolster his king's notion that he deserved to rise a little higher and replace his friend and mentor Sir John French as commander in chief of British forces in France.

Haig provided the king with a horse, his own chestnut mare. He had exercised the horse regularly for more than a year, taking her out almost every afternoon. In Picardy's rolling fields and small dense woods he'd inhale the pastoral scenes just a few miles from the grinding carnage of the front lines, cataloging their beauty with a poet's eye and pondering questions of command. That very morning, he'd seen that the horse was specially exercised in anticipation of His Majesty's visit.

And then, as so often happened in Haig's life, unforeseen disaster undid all his careful planning. While the king was inspecting a small group of officers and men at Hesdigneul, an officer ordered them to cheer. The noise startled the horse, who reared. The king fell; the horse lost its balance and fell on top of him.

George V was not in prime condition under the best of circumstances. Like Haig, he had breathing problems. Haig's were caused by asthma, which bedeviled him all his life; the king's were associated with the lung condition pleurisy and aggravated by his heavy smoking. That evening, as George recovered, the royal master of the household Sir Derek Keppel telephoned Haig to reassure him. "His Majesty knew very well that the mare had never done such a thing before and that I was not to feel perturbed at what had happened," Haig wrote in his diary.[1]

Haig's journal was another refuge from the stress of command. He wrote in a field service notebook every evening after dinner and before his bedtime, invariably 10:45 PM. He even risked national security to keep his musings organized—he made carbon copies of his writing, and every few days he would send them back to England, where his wife, Dorothy, would type them out and store them. Had any of the pages fallen into the wrong hands or Lady Haig mentioned to someone with loose lips what she had learned, the effect on his career—not to mention the war—could have been devastating. It was a tribute to Haig's trust in her, and the King's Messenger service by which he sent the pages, that no secrets ever leaked.

The diary was also a place where Haig, a man who was often tongue-tied in public, could express himself fully, often cattily. He noted that he had no doubts about the military ability of Second Division commander Sir Charles Monro, but that his years with the territorials, Britain's reserve force, "has resulted in his becoming rather fat." British Expeditionary Force (BEF) chief of staff Maj. Gen. Archibald Murray, "in some respects," Haig wrote, "seemed to me to be 'an old woman.'"

He saved his cruelest observations for Sir John French, the first commander of the BEF and Haig's superior when he first came to France. "Sir John's French was not fluent," Haig wrote after a meeting with French generals in October 2014. "I could with difficulty restrain my laughter at some of the language."

French was also one of Haig's few close friends. Neither fit the image most had of a British cavalryman of that period: a tall, thin, dashing, witty, dauntlessly brave aristocrat. In battle these brave gentlemen enforced their moral superiority with *armes blanches*, the swords and lances with which they shocked and scattered their enemies, breaking through their lines and always, always serving as the tip of victory's spear. Haig was tall and broad shouldered, with thick hair he parted above his prominent forehead and wide eyes that made him look like someone constantly at the moment of realizing that he'd stumbled into the wrong room. French was short and stocky, with striking blue eyes. Both sported the large mustaches fashionable among the upper classes of their time.

They'd met in cavalry camp in India, where one of French's most remarkable qualities became evident—his attractiveness to women.

French was raised by women. His father, John Tracey French, was a retired navy officer who lost an eye during the Portuguese Civil War and died when he was two. His mother, Margaret (née Eccles), suffered from mental illness and was removed from the family when French was ten, leaving him in the hands of his six sisters.

French was born September 28, 1852, at Ripple Vale, Kent, near the Dover coast. His grandfather Fleming French moved to England from Roscommon, Ireland, thirty-four years before, and the Frenches always considered themselves Irish.

The orphaned French was drawn to the military. He first saw naval service at thirteen, when he joined the crew of the HMS *Britannia*. Eventually, the sea lost its hold on young John and he resigned from the navy, hoping to become a cavalry officer instead.

Cavalry officers were the most flamboyant members of Britain's army, almost entirely stocked with the children of aristocrats who loved the horse-based service's pageantry and pomp but weren't necessarily ambitious. French ended up in the Nineteenth Royal Hussars, a slightly less fashionable unit but one that was just as expensive as Britain's others—officers' pay was not much more than it was in the seventeenth century, and they had to provide and care for their own horses and pay for their dashing uniforms.

A cavalry officer at the end of the nineteenth century needed around £500 a year to make up the shortfall. French's share of the proceeds from the sale of his family's home should have sufficed, but he had a chronic inability to manage his finances. In his whole life, he never lived within his means. Even the windfall he reaped from investing in the Muir Mills Company of India, an opportunity his brother-in-law Gavin Sibbald Jones introduced him to in 1874, couldn't fill the hole he'd dug himself into.

His other weakness was women. While not classically attractive, French was charming, giving, and attentive—features not especially cultivated among many of his upper-class male peers, and perhaps an explanation of how he ended up romancing so many of their wives. French was on his second marriage by the time he began accompanying the Hussars overseas, going to Cairo in 1884 to help suppress an uprising in Sudan. His brother-in-law John Lydall helped him out of a secret marriage he'd entered into as a young officer in 1875. (Lydall also paid off his debts more than once.) By the time he made it to India he'd been married for four years to Eleanora Selby-Lowndes, who grew to tolerate his indiscretions.

In India he first got to know Haig, who served in the Seventh Hussars and couldn't have been more different than the magnetic, reckless French. Haig was a Scot and always had a little bit extra to prove because of it. Many of his English colleagues looked down on him for his roots in "trade"—his father, John Haig, had built a distillery at Cameron Bridge in Fife, next to the river Leven. John Haig and five other liquor makers had formed the Distillers Company, which sold grain whisky under the Haig name, including the popular Dimple brand. Douglas grew up at his family's country house in Fife, his childhood mostly escaping his father's notice. Douglas and his mother, Rachel, were particularly close, and she raised him to be a devout Presbyterian.

Haig loved the cavalry and was an excellent horseman—he played polo, a sport he'd taken up at university, in interregimental polo tournaments, often helping guide his teammates toward victory. But socially he was a disaster, an extreme introvert who found most interactions excruciating and struggled to come up with even the wrong thing to say.

It was also in India that French had an affair that nearly ended his career. He began seeing the wife of a fellow officer, who sued for divorce and named French in the papers. That was a scandal even the cavalry couldn't turn a blind eye to, and when the Nineteenth returned to England in 1893, French was placed on the half-pay list. It was a dark time in his career—he had no command, and he could no longer afford to keep horses. He took up cycling as an alternative way to get around, even though he never quite got the hang of getting aboard his machine. He "would disappear into the distance hopping wildly alongside his machine, but failing to get astride it," his biographer Richard Holmes wrote.[2]

A year later, things began to turn around, career-wise, at least. After doing well commanding a brigade during maneuvers, he was tapped to write a drill book for cavalry and made a colonel. In 1897 he got command of the Second Cavalry Brigade at Cambridge, and the following year he took over the First Cavalry Brigade at Aldershot, the most prestigious command in the army, where he was temporarily made a major general.

At Aldershot he reunited with Haig, with whom he'd maintained a friendly relationship for several years. Haig became his brigade major. He helped French a little with his book and visited him at his house on the base. Things seemed happy for French, who had three children with Eleanora by this point, but by 1899 the wolves were again at the door. His debt had ballooned during his year of half pay, and, worse, he'd made a bad investment in South African gold mines. Lydall was no longer interested in helping his brother-in-law out. The army would not tolerate another scandal. If French couldn't find a way out of the situation, his career would end.

Enter Haig. The Scotsman was very careful with money and offered to help out his boss. He lent French £2,000, and it's not clear whether French ever repaid him.

That same year Haig and French departed for South Africa, where Britain wished to quell a rebellion by the Boer settlers. It was the type of small mobile engagement the British Army was built for. While its navy was a world power, Britain's army was notably small for a major nation. It had 227,000 regulars and 81,000 reserves. Apart from the odd foreign policing operation, service was not particularly demanding. "We all thought that we received half a day's pay for half a day's work, and all but a few enthusiasts acted upon this principle," the Rifle Brigade officer Charles à Court Repington remembered.[3]

In South Africa, French really made his name at Elandslaagte, a tiny town near Ladysmith. Boers under General Johannes Kock had seized a train and Elandslaagte train station. French sent in squadrons of the Imperial Light Horse and cleared the station before Boer artillery drove them back out. French received reinforcements from Ladysmith and attacked on October 21, 1899, following an intense bombardment of Boer lines with a cavalry charge that took place amid a thunderstorm. Kock was mortally wounded, and the Boer force was decimated.

Elandslaagte was a very minor engagement in the scheme of things—the British didn't even bother to hold it—but it was a nice victory in a war that was not going according to plan, and French became a darling of the London press.

Haig got something different out of the war. He was French's chief of staff, and the war gave him an opportunity to see how dysfunctional the British Army could be. He was chagrined to learn the war minister didn't even read intelligence reports, and that they rarely inspired action. Various fiefdoms in the government and the military closely guarded from one another information that could have helped speed an end to the conflict. There was no easy way for a commander in the field to make a reasoned criticism of strategy to a general. "I think we would have better generals in higher ranks and the country would not have passed through such a period of anxiety, had honest criticism, based on sound reasoning, been more general in reference to military affairs during the past twenty years," Haig wrote to a friend.

The British outlasted the Boers; Haig proved particularly adept at translating French's wishes into action and drew notice from higher-ups. After the war finally ended, Haig returned in 1902 to Britain, where he threw himself into making the Seventeenth Lancers one of the best-run regiments in the army. French and Kitchener came home celebrities. While French found he very much enjoyed speaking with journalists, Kitchener despised journalists, calling them "drunken swabs."

At Aldershot Haig reunited with French. There, French gave his friend a gold flask with the inscription "A very small memento, my dear Douglas, of our long and tried friendship proved 'in sunshine and in shadow' J. F."

In 1903 Haig was promoted to inspector general of cavalry in India. He was forty-two; the job usually went to an older commander. But Haig's superiors had begun to take notice of the Scottish-born lieutenant colonel. The king himself, Edward VII, asked Haig to report to him directly on the Indian cavalry.

Haig's connections to the royal family only deepened after that. While on leave in England during Ascot Week in June 1905, he met Dorothy Vivian, who was one of Queen Alexandra's maids of honour. They married the next month. When one of Haig's friends noted how quickly Douglas and Dorothy had cemented their relationship, Haig replied, "Why not? I have often made up my mind on more important problems than that of my own marriage in much less time."[4]

Haig's career took another broad step forward in 1906, when the new secretary of state for war, Richard Burdon Haldane, chose him to help reform the army. Many in the establishment believed a land war in Europe was imminent, and Haldane knew the British were ill prepared to fight it. Unlike the French and the Germans, the British didn't have large land armies made up of conscripts.

The societies in both those countries, in fact, were organized around what was beginning to be known as "total war," the conflation of everyday civilian life with a nation's ambitions. In Britain the military was mostly tucked away from view, run by aristocrats.

Haig and Haldane were both from moneyed backgrounds, but they were hardly idle. Both were Scots—coincidentally, they'd both been born on Edinburgh's tony Charlotte Square, Haig at No. 24 and Haldane at No. 17.

In London, Haig began swiftly implementing Haldane's ideas. He helped organize an "expeditionary force" that could be deployed to the European mainland, and also helped organize a volunteer force to supplement it. Because of his success in South Africa, French was tapped to lead the expeditionary force. The Territorial Army, however, suffered from the same snobbery Haig encountered; for instance, Field Marshal Frederick Roberts, the last commander in chief of British forces before the reorganization, believed it would be disastrous to let citizen soldiers anywhere near artillery.

Thanks to Haldane and Haig, Britain had an expeditionary force of 130,000 men, and a reserve force of 120,000. That would be adequate if financial experts were correct that no nation would be foolish enough to conduct a long war. Haig suspected any conflict that drew Britain onto European soil would prove them wrong. "Great Britain and Germany would be fighting for their existence," he wrote in his diary at the beginning of the war in 1914. "Therefore the war was bound to be a long war, and neither would acknowledge defeat after a short struggle."

Before the territorials, the British Army drew almost exclusively from the upper and working classes. Men from the middle classes tended to avoid military service, as the pathways to advancement there were often clogged with the children of elites. The territorials offered middle- and even working-class men a route to commissions, an opportunity that broadened considerably as the Great War dragged on.

Haig returned to India in 1909 as chief of staff to Gen. Sir Garrett O'Moore Creagh, and he tried without much luck to reform the office there. He returned to England in March 1912 to take over the Aldershot

Command, which included the First Cavalry Brigade, First and Second Division, the Royal Field Artillery, and most of the Royal Engineers. It would later form the backbone of the British Expeditionary Force.

But first Haig had to convince his fellow officers he was the right person to lead it. His personal awkwardness didn't help; it was only through a series of intimate dinners with his subordinates that Haig began to win them over.

At Aldershot, Haig worked on incorporating modern technology like aircraft into traditional British warfare. His views on the role of cavalry had changed during the Boer War—they needed to be able to fight well while dismounted, a combination of infantryman and horseman. With improvements in heavy artillery and machine guns, Haig reasoned a versatile mobile force would be key to breaking through enemy lines.

When war finally came, French was appointed commander in chief of British forces. He thought the war would be quick, a view not shared by his longtime nemesis Lord Herbert Kitchener, Britain's secretary of state for war.

On August 11, 1914, King George V and his wife, Queen Mary, motored down to Hampshire to inspect the lines at Aldershot. In private, George asked Haig what he thought of French's appointment. "In my own heart, I know that French is quite unfit for this great command at a time of crisis in our Nation's history," Haig wrote in his diary that evening. "But I thought it sufficient to tell the King that I had 'doubts' about the selection."

In truth, neither French nor Kitchener possessed the military minds the moment required. French was prone to feuds (he especially hated Lt. Gen. Horace Smith-Dorrien, who took over Aldershot after him and got a lot of credit for remaking the base with more recreation facilities), he could let minor slights turn into career-threatening ultimatums, and his personal life continued to be a catastrophe. Kitchener was imperious, distrustful of democracy, consistently overstepped his authority, and was annoyed that he had to, as he said, "reveal military secrets to twenty-three gentlemen with whom I am barely acquainted."[5] Kitchener called for a new army made up of pals' battalions in part because he, too, had an inbred aristocratic distrust of the territorials.

But both men were skilled at another type of warfare.

The British decision-making process was convoluted and subject to sabotage by political enmity. Prime Minister Herbert Henry "H. H." Asquith had a cabinet committee devoted to the war, but its decisions weren't binding, and members could force any issues it had worked on before the full cabinet, where they would be relitigated. Asquith was a Liberal whose government was constantly teetering, especially after a crisis over Irish home rule that had also roiled the army. Its war planning was, as Haig biographer Robert Blake wrote, a "system of aristocratic anarchy" better suited to the eighteenth century.

Kitchener powered through this chaos with bluster and sneers; French was quieter and instead made allies within and without the government. He was particularly close with Repington, who, after his army career ended because of a longstanding affair with another aristocrat's wife, had chosen a career well-suited to scoundrels: journalism.

Repington was thin, balding, and handsome, with wild eyes and a mustache that floated like a *W* contemplating escape from underneath his narrow nose. He wrote for the *Times* of London and had brilliantly covered the Russo-Japanese War, which was fought from 1904 to 1905. In contradiction to conventional wisdom, Repington had come to believe he didn't need to be stationed on the front lines to report on war; he felt he got a clearer picture at the head of the snake, skulking around the halls of power where he could find out what was really going on. (In many ways, he was the first national security analyst.)

When the conflict that he later named "the First World War" came, Repington preferred to remain in London, working his connections and filing devastating scoops from information he'd wheedled out of his sources. He *hated* Kitchener, a sentiment "K" returned fully.

In the fall of 1913 the army conducted maneuvers around Aylesbury. Haig and Gen. Sir Arthur Paget were corps commanders while French commanded the exercise. The general opinion around the army was that Haig bombed, the second time in two years that he'd blown a war game. Haig, however felt *French* had blown it, an opinion Repington amplified, much to French's annoyance.

In the years just before World War I, the cavalry was convulsed with the army's growing sense that cavalry was outdated.

It's difficult today to comprehend the widespread and almost mystical belief in the power of dashing men to crush the enemy's spirit under the hooves of their horses, but the fact that it still animated much of French's and later Haig's planning for war is instructive. Both believed in the "cavalry spirit," a power that flowed primarily from the cavalryman's *armes blanches*. French wanted his cavalry to carry firearms, but as a secondary weapon; indeed, he wanted the army to develop a better sword. French believed in the "moral power of the cavalry." The cavalry were trained in "shock action," a tactic that dated to the middle ages and the Crusades. Without it, and the sword, French believed, the cavalry's "spirit" would deflate and its moral power would be lost.

By the time Britain declared war in 1914, these questions had largely been settled in French's favor. But he had different problems as he prepared to fight the Germans, including a remarkably unclear set of instructions from Kitchener, now the secretary of state for war, on how to cooperate with the French Army. Sir John, who'd received the first of his four knighthoods thirteen years earlier, was not under the command of the French, but he was to "coincide most sympathetically" with their plans. The British kept these instructions secret from the French government, which believed it was in charge of the British Expeditionary Force and ordered it to work in a small triangle in the north of France, between Le Cateau, Maubeuge, and Hirson.

Haig had no patience for these intrigues. He was now a lieutenant general and commander of I Corps and was once again charged with putting French's plans into action on the battlefield. One hundred and twenty thousand members of the BEF left for France in the second week of August, preceded by nineteen battleships. The operation took place in absolute secrecy; the Germans weren't aware they'd even landed.

French arrived in France on the cruiser *Sentinel* on Friday, August 14. On August 20, the BEF assembled at Maubeuge in the north of France near the Belgian border. That same day the Germans entered Brussels following a swift campaign through Flanders that saw thousands of Belgians flee from the conflict. Meanwhile in Morhange, a tiny town in the northern province of Lorraine, France's early plan for the war was disintegrating. Plan XVII called for a lightning offensive against the Germans that would cause them to fight on multiple fronts; part of it called for French troops to sweep into the portions of Alsace and Lorraine France had lost during the Franco-Prussian War forty-three years earlier.

In Morhange on August 20, the Germans routed the French Second Army. Retired general Alfred von Schlieffen had devised Germany's war plan, which German Army chief of staff Helmut von Moltke revised. Germany had to fight wars on two major fronts on opposite sides of the country. Before it could turn its attention to defeating Russia, Germany hoped to neutralize the French by sending a large force through Belgium and a smaller one through Lorraine to envelop Paris.

Gen. Joseph Jacques Césaire Joffre had written Plan XVII. The son of a cooper, broad of beam and fond of a good meal, Joffre was born near Perpignan, in French Catalonia. He hadn't attended Saint-Cyr, the traditional training school for French cavalrymen and infantry officers. Instead, he went to the "X," the Ecole Polytechnique, a training school for engineers. What he lacked in personal dynamism (he was so imperturbable the historian Basil Liddell Hart referred to him as a "national nerve sedative") he made up for in *cran*, the French word for grit.

On August 22 British soldiers outside the Belgian city of Mons, thirty-two miles north of Le Cateau, spotted German soldiers near the village of Casteau and fired on them. The next day was a drizzly Sunday, and the Battle of Mons began in earnest. On Monday French learned to his shock that French forces were falling back all around them, badly exposing the British. He reluctantly ordered a retreat south to the French border. Two days later Smith-Dorrien's II Corps engaged the advancing German troops at Le Cateau.

The early conception of the BEF as a force commanded by French was quickly melting on contact with Germany. Communications between corps were slow, and individual commanders took most of the initiative in the war's first days. Haig declined to help Smith-Dorrien at Le Cateau, an acceptable choice for the "man on the spot" within British military doctrine at the time. He continued the retreat.

In early September the British attacked at what would become known as the Battle of the Marne. There, Joffre saved the French from catastrophe, building a new army from the parts of others and famously transporting men to the front from Paris by means of taxicabs (which arrived with their meters running). The British also prevailed but didn't press their advantage, and the Germans and Allies eventually dug in, at points only a few hundred yards from one another.

This was essentially the end the mobile phase of war on the Western Front and the beginning of a stalemate that would fester for years. Martial technology, particularly that found in machine guns, and tactics had improved so much that lines were very difficult to breach. Technology could take men no further, however, and until the introduction of the tank a year later the Allies and the Germans found themselves clawing away at one another's defenses, wrestling for small advances in what quickly became a war of attrition. The British command, in particular, had trouble accepting this new reality.

French thought this conflict was simply a larger version of the Boer War. Haig, like French and most of their colleagues, had studied the battles of Napoleon and the US Civil War and believed that bolstered by the correct assaults by infantry and artillery, cavalry could break through German lines and roll up their flank much like Napoleon did at Jena and Auerstedt in 1806, Grant did at Petersburg in 1865, or French did at Klip Drift in 1900. Over the next year, the British began throwing tens of thousands of lives at this illusion.

The British needed more men and better equipment. The troops Britain had sent to France were among its best, and Germans at Mons reportedly thought they were meeting machine-gun fire rather than crack troops equipped mostly with Lee–Enfield rifles. British artillery, in particular, was slow to adapt to the grueling requirements of trench warfare.

Communications were another serious problem. Any success in breaking through enemy lines needed to be followed quickly with reserve forces. But to remain in contact with their subordinates, generals needed to be near a telephone in a building beyond the range of German artillery. On October 31, 1914, the First Division commander Lt. Gen. Samuel Lomax was in a grand steepled château in Hooge, near the front line in Belgium. Haig had moved out of the château two days before, and German aerial reconnaissance spotted officers' cars parked outside while Lomax met with Monro. That afternoon gunners targeted the house, severely wounding Lomax, stunning Monro, and killing several other officers. Lomax later died of his injuries.

British commanders also used telegraph, signal flags and runners, and even carrier pigeons to communicate with the lines. Radio technology was primitive and unreliable. The army had never fought a war on this scale and had no real plan for its various weapons systems to work in concert.

It was in these muzzy conditions that the British greeted 1915 and a war that stubbornly resisted predictions of ending before Christmas. There would be no frolic to Berlin, just days on end in flooded ditches in the cold French and Belgian earth with bullets for any man who stood up in sight of the enemy and ever more bales of concertina wire between them and the pockmarked span of ground that separated them from their equally miserable counterparts a few hundred yards away.

Everyone was stuck.

5

RARE SPORT, MY MASTERS

When Rangers scored their fourth unanswered goal, it looked as if the Hearts were finally beginning to crack. For six weeks after the New Year, the Edinburgh team had managed to keep adding points to their lead in the league table while most of its members trained to go to war. That meant squeezing in practices around exercises, drills, and late-night "route marches" that took them all over Edinburgh and the Lothians. Now it was Saturday, February 20, and the price of that training was becoming higher every time a ball whooshed past Archie Boyd.

A little more than a week before, the battalion had a misadventure in the Pentland Hills south of town, where a march turned life-threatening. Regimental sergeant major Fred Muir, a coal miner who had served in the Gordon Highlanders and who was in charge of discipline and drills, led them up for what was supposed to be a routine tramp through the countryside. But then the wind began blowing hard, and soon it began snowing. Very quickly, and despite the officers' affectations otherwise, the men soon realized they were completely lost. Two soldiers who worked as gamekeepers in the area were able to take over navigation, and they got the troops safely to Straiton, a village about five miles south of town.

Hearts came back to score three goals against Rangers that Saturday, avoiding a rout but still losing. Harry Wattie didn't knock in any goals. Like many of his teammates he had spent the early months of the year fighting illness. A bout of the flu had kept him for a week at his parents' house, where Paddy Crossan had lived with him before they'd enlisted. Paddy, who was felled by the flu a week before Harry and had to return to Addiewell to recover, had begun dating Harry's sister Mary Alice when he was on premises, and still got up to the house in Edinburgh's Marchmont neighborhood to see her when he could.

Harry had joined Hearts in 1913 after a junior career at Tranent. In contrast to Paddy's dark inscrutability, Harry was fair and wide eyed, with a broad forehead, a prominent nose, and a mouth constantly on the verge of breaking into a grin. He played up front for Hearts, often creating chances for Jamie Low or Tom Gracie or scoring himself. Hearts brought him on with the idea that he'd eventually replace Bobby Walker. Harry was the youngest member of the Wattie family and Mary Alice's favorite.

Hearts' twenty-five-year-old assistant trainer, Alex Lyon, died from the flu on February 14. The day after he was buried, C Company soldiers got their second typhoid shot. The typhoid inoculation in those days was administered in two parts and was voluntary, though strongly encouraged by the authorities, especially Lord Kitchener. It helped protect the men against a disease spread by what's gently known as the "fecal-oral route," a real concern on the battlefield, where sanitary conditions were nonexistent. The vaccine could weaken its recipients for as long as a day—two to five hours after administration, they might develop pain in their groins and armpits or even collapse, followed by fitful, fevered sleep.

That same day, Germany declared that British waters were legitimate hunting grounds for its U-boats. The war, for months an abstraction to the British public, was knocking on its door.

By the time Rangers came to Tynecastle, Hearts had managed to stay on top of the league table since the New Year, winning most of their games and tying three others. But those ties were costly. Celtic, which had yet to send a single player to the war effort, was now only four points behind Hearts on the league table and had an easy spell in its schedule. And Rangers, too, were beginning to stir.

Founded in 1872, Rangers were traditionally Glasgow's Protestant team and fiercest rivals of Celtic, the Irish Catholic squad. They'd had a remarkably successful run under their longtime manager William Wilton, who led them to an undefeated season in 1898–1899. Hearts had beat Rangers 2–1 in their September meeting at Rangers' home ground, Ibrox. Now with Willie Reid at forward, Rangers had overcome an early-January swoon to win four of their last five matches. And like Celtic, Rangers' players were lightly burdened by the demands of military service.

Twenty-three thousand people came to the match at Tynecastle that day. It quickly began to look like a fiasco. Reid drew first blood, scoring a clean goal in the seventeenth minute that whistled past Archie Boyd. One minute later, Scott Duncan fired another shot at Boyd, who knocked the ball down—right in front of Rangers forward Tommy Cairns, who knocked it into the net. Fortune was no less a stranger to Hearts' offense. The fans groaned as Graham hit a strong header that bounced off the crossbar of Rangers' goal. Their hopes rose when Wilson took a Hearts penalty kick awarded after defender Henry Muir shoved Wattie, but it, too, pinged maddeningly off the goal's frame.

Celtic were playing Dumbarton at home that week, and beating the team from the other side of the river Clyde convincingly. At halftime, there was a celebration when the scorekeeper put up the halftime results of the Hearts-Rangers match—if the loss held, Celtic would trail Hearts on the league table by only two points.

After halftime, Rangers' defenders continued stretching out Hearts' attack, on the theory that it would strain the Edinburgh team's intricate passing game. The gamble worked, and the ball remained mostly on Hearts' half of the field. Despite his health struggles that week, Paddy was in top form, clearing ball after ball. His partner on defense, Duncan Currie, however, was having an inconsistent game. Rangers got four corner kicks—awarded when the ball rolls out of play after being touched by a defender—before Hearts managed their first.

Twenty minutes into the second half, Reid scored a beautiful goal on a pass from Scott Duncan. With fifteen minutes to go, Reid ripped the ball from Nellies and scored again. Hearts fans began to leave the stadium.

But with eight minutes left to go, Rangers center Peter Pursell got called on a handball. Gracie took the penalty shot, and this time it went in. Four minutes later, Wilson got Hearts' second corner kick, which he placed directly in front of Low, who hammered it home. Two minutes later, Wilson faked out goalkeeper Herbert Lock and sent the ball caroming off the crossbar into the net. There were two minutes left in the game, and the fans who'd stayed began to allow themselves a pinpoint of hope—could Hearts at least finish the match as a draw? The crowd grew uproarious, but Hearts could not squeeze any more fortune out of their pluck. They were still down by one when the whistle blew.

That evening, Hearts trainer Jimmy Duckworth visited battalion headquarters to complain. He couldn't very well produce results without consistent training, he said. The battalion granted his request—henceforth, the Hearts men could go to Tynecastle two nights a week to work on their game.

It was one of the few times the battalion acknowledged the Hearts' players' special circumstances. Many of the men supported Hearts, but they were largely unsympathetic to the strains of playing football and training.

Life in the Heriot's barracks was loud and strenuous. The men lived in a large room where members of the regimental band practiced bagpipes and wet clothes hung all over the exposed rafters to dry. For many who grew up sharing sleeping quarters in Edinburgh flats, having a bed to one's self was a novelty, even if the mattresses were filled with straw with the uncanny ability to move exactly where it was least needed. Company Quartermaster Sgt. Donald Gunn wrote accounts of the training that ran in the *Edinburgh Evening News*, describing a tough routine. Reveille, followed by drilling in the dark, plentiful but unappealing food, exercise, more drills, route marches.

There were no stars in the barracks. Gunn marveled that the Hearts players' platoon was under the care of Annan Ness, who was only on the reserve team. "Imagine a man whose football talent is practically

unrecognised by the powers that be in the football world superintend-
ing the pipe-claying of a stairway and the scrubbing out of a room,
with some internationalists and several candidates for 'caps' wielding
the scrubbing brushes and pipeclay."[1]

The other men were unsympathetic to the Hearts players' exhaustion; they were all doing the same amount of activity. Fellow soldiers
took every opportunity to berate the footballers when they felt they
hadn't acquitted themselves well on the field. One Monday morning,
Paddy was shaving in the washhouse when a group of critics of his
performance the Saturday before descended on him. He smiled, "realis-
ing that it was all in the Army game," Gunn wrote. A journalist who'd
spent time in America, Gunn went on to tell the story of one Hearts
player who broke his food plate and, rather than wait for one of his
fellow soldiers to finish with theirs, returned to his bunk and emerged
with an octagonal biscuit-tin lid. He "dared the torrent of jeers from his
football companions at his misfortune, and lined up to the cookhouse
with his improvised plate," Gunn wrote. "It may have been an undig-
nified position for a prominent footballer to be in, but, again, dignity
vanishes at the rack-room gate."[2]

Sir George had a flexible definition of dignity himself. A few weeks
before the Rangers game, the battalion attended the pantomime at the
King's Theatre, a grand venue with a red ashlar sandstone exterior about
ten minutes from their billet at Heriot's. "The panto" is a British tradition that brings fairy tales, slapstick, popular songs, and audience participation to the stage over Christmas and New Year. They were there
to see *Jack and the Beanstalk*, a production that had been resodded with
allusions to the battalion for the evening. During a performance of the
1914 hit "Sister Susie's Sewing Shirts for Soldiers," the actor Jack Edge
bolted on a new verse, "Molly's making mittens for McCrae's men." And
midway through the performance, when Jack rapped his magic sword
on the gates of the Giant's castle, they opened to reveal Sir George,
accompanied by lieutenants Warr and Fowler.

Sir George took the opportunity to break the fourth wall and
give a speech. He told the men something he said would have been

inappropriate when they were on parade before him earlier in the month: he was proud of them. They'd mobilized just six weeks earlier, but they looked like men who'd trained for three months, he said to cheers. Sure, he said to laughs, there were one or two men who originally "thought that they were out for a picnic," but the veteran soldiers among them had straightened out those slackers. He hoped they were enjoying relaxing that evening, especially following their inoculations, he said to more laughter. The battalion would be ready by the time it was needed, Sir George said, and at that time would go forth, as Jack was instructed by the fairy in the play, "with a will to do and a soul to dare."[3] The men rewarded him with raucous cheers. *Jack* picked up where it left off, just in time for the giant killer to triumph.

Only nine days earlier, German zeppelins had bombed Great Yarmouth and King's Lynn in England, killing twenty people. The war was no longer bounded even by the British coastline. And for many with sons, fathers, and brothers abroad, its proximity was becoming unbearable. Newspapers were careful to underreport casualties suffered by British troops who'd fought in the first battle of Ypres, in Belgium, and who were digging in along the western part of the four-hundred-mile front between the North Sea and the Alps. But by looking at death notices in the same editions, locals could see that the British Expeditionary Force was losing men at an alarming rate. There simply weren't enough men yet to replace the professional soldiers who each did the work of three men when holding the line against the Germans. Nor was there enough matériel to equip the replacements—for all their training, the men of McCrae's still had no guns.

Meanwhile, on any given match day, eight or nine of Hearts' starting eleven really could have used the day to rest instead. The midseason slump brought on by military training coincided with a time of increased financial peril. When Hearts' new stand at Tynecastle finally opened in October, it was an expensive marvel that ran the length of the field, with a redbrick exterior, electric lighting, modern restrooms for fans, and plenty of space off the pitch for the players and the referees. If the team won the league flag that year, Fürst reckoned, they could swing all the payments to contractors who'd built it.

Things weren't working out that way. By March someone in the organization was worried enough about its finances that they put out the word to newspaper reporters that Hearts were down £1,500 over the previous year. Normally, in a year when the team was playing so well they would expect revenues to rise by about 20 percent, but a lot of the young men they could have drawn to the stadium were away with the military. At least the games continued—before the Hearts players saved the football season for the Scottish league (and probably the English league as well), the team had faced the prospect of having an expensive stand but no season to play.

The other teams in the league were doing no better. Most were £1,000 to £6,000 behind the previous year's revenue, and many had put players on half wages.

The war continued to creep closer to football. In March, despite reports of U-boat activity in the Irish Sea, Scotland's national junior team traveled to Belfast to play their Irish counterpart. Fortunately, their passage was without incident, though they drew the game 1–1.

The Saturday after their loss to Rangers, Hearts drew against Hibs at Easter Road before a record crowd of sixteen thousand. That same day the *Evening News* speculated which Hearts players might be chosen to represent Scotland for its international game against England on March 20. Leaving aside the question of whether McCrae's might still even be in Edinburgh by the time the match rolled around, the match represented a harder truth for the national team. Whereas Hearts' entire lineup could have easily represented the nation a few months before, now none were in good enough form to represent Scotland.

The draw against Hibs put Hearts in a precarious position—just one point ahead of Celtic, which beat Partick Thistle in an away game. Math now became Hearts' enemy. To keep the flag, Hearts would have to run the table *and* drive up the score for each win, so if there was a points tie at the end of the season, they'd win on goal difference.

The Hibs game was a "rare old hammer and tongs affair," the pseud-onymous sports columnist Donovan wrote in an account in the *Daily Record* a couple of days afterward.[4] Both teams went after each other hard, but fatigue was doing its work. Paddy tried to head out a shot from Hibs center forward Robert Lennie; both he and Boyd looked on helplessly as it sailed into Hearts' goal instead. Thirty minutes later Paddy missed a kick, and Currie cleared the ball, defusing the immediate threat posed by Lennie but giving Hibs a corner kick. Lennie fired it to John Robertson, who headed the tying goal under the bar. "It has been a case of too much work and too little play making the Hearts men dull boys," another columnist wrote.[5]

Hearts had allowed as many goals in the first ten games since New Year's Day as they had in the previous twenty-one. The next week they were at home against Dumbarton, and they pounded the visitors 4–1. Gracie scored three goals, and Harry Graham got the other. For a week, Duckworth felt like his extraordinary efforts to train his players around their military duties might just pull out the season. But the miserable winter continued for Wattie. His father, William, died the week before the game, so he skipped the match to attend the funeral. Led by Paddy, his teammates wore black armbands in his honor. Celtic also won that week, leaving the league table unchanged.

Harry returned the next week as Hearts played Airdrieonians on their home field, Broomfield Park. Celtic had the week off league play, so they hosted the Belfast team Glentoran at Parkhead for a "friendly"—an exhibition match that kept the team in form and, even more important, the fans buying tickets. Hearts knew that if they won against Airdrie they'd go two points ahead of Celtic. Nine minutes of furious play after the opening whistle, Hearts were up 2–0 on goals from Harry Graham. The first was off a pass from Wattie, the second off a sneaky deft pass from Nellies. Graham eluded two Airdrieonian defenders and then zinged out an angled shot that hit the high top corner of the goal.

Then, disappointingly, Airdrie summoned some grit. They attacked relentlessly in waves until their forward James Grieg Reid finally found purchase on a ball Boyd threw out of the goal. Reid returned it to sender, delivering it to the back of the net like a cannonball. Hearts tried to rally, but their tempo was off. Their forwards couldn't quite find the rhythm that had once suited them so well. Low missed repeated passes. Gracie and Wattie kept getting outrun by the ball. Four minutes before the end of the half, Low went around Airdrie defender George Gane and put the ball between the goal and Harry Graham. Graham took a hard kick, and . . . struck the crossbar.

The second half was better for the Hearts' attack, but then a freak incident in the seventy-fifth minute dampened their spark. Moments after Airdrie goalkeeper James Brown stopped a shot by Low, the home team's forwards made another push at the other end of the field. Reid was flying toward the goal when Paddy intervened, not stopping him but pushing him off his line. The ball rolled toward the net, but Boyd momentarily turned to try to help Crossan, losing sight of it. Paddy desperately ran to try to stop the ball and even made contact—in a most unfortunate manner. The ball dribbled into Hearts' net.

It was a 2–2 draw. "We saw a manly game played in a manly fashion," *Daily Record* sports writer Brigadier wrote. "Rare sport, my masters, and may we see more of the like." Hearts didn't share his connoisseur's view of the proceedings. The tie meant they had gained only one point, leaving Celtic one game away from sharing the top spot on the league table.

It was difficult for many people to concentrate on the football standings, though. On March 11 the German submarine *U-27* sank the HMS *Bayano* about ten miles west of Corsewall Lighthouse, on Scotland's west coast. The *Bayano* was a banana boat that had been converted into an armed merchant ship. Of the 220 men aboard, 194, including the captain, died; their bodies began washing up in Ireland the next day. Four days later George Llewelyn Davies was killed in action in Flanders. As a boy in London, George and his brothers Jack, Michael, Nico, and Peter played in Kensington Gardens, inspiring their neighbor, the Scottish writer J. M. Barrie, to write stories about boys who never grew up. George reportedly inspired the author to craft the character Peter Pan. After their father died, Barrie supported the boys. George joined the King's Rifle Corps as a second lieutenant, and was shot in the head while in a trench. He was twenty-one.

The Western Front was at a stalemate, grinding down the armies on both sides. But it was far from the only place the war was being fought. On March 18 six British and four French battleships steamed into the Dardanelles, a narrow strait in Turkey that separates Asia from Europe. Turkey had allied with Germany and fortified the strait, but Kitchener and the first lord of the Admiralty, a forty-year-old Winston Churchill, believed that the overwhelming show of force would force the Turks to surrender, and that they could then perhaps even take Constantinople with no ground troops. That would open up naval supply lines to Russia, and possibly bring Greece, Bulgaria, and Romania to join with the Entente. In the long term, a victory in the Dardanelles could open up a new front against Austria-Hungary, relieving pressure on Russia and France.

The Entente navies had bombarded Turkish forts at the opening of the strait and swept mines across its entrance before the attack. They'd identified all the remaining lines of mines, or so they thought—a Turkish ship had laid another twenty-mile line that the Entente didn't know about. The oversight birthed a disaster. Two British battleships, the *Ocean* and the *Irresistible*, and the French battleship *Bouvet*, were sunk, and two more ships were heavily damaged. Bad weather scuppered plans to attack again the next day. A breakthrough on the sea was proving as elusive as the one Britain hoped for on land.

Britain did have one naval success that day. In the fast tidal waters of the Pentland Firth north of Scotland, the HMS *Dreadnought*, an outdated ship that had been transferred out of the Grand Fleet, rammed the German submarine *U-29*, sinking it. It was the first and last time any ship would sink a sub that way.

On Saturday, March 20, Hearts played Partick Thistle before a crowd of only eight thousand at Tynecastle. It was a cold and wet day—"They tried to play their pretty game in the mud," the *Evening News* wrote of Hearts.[6] Pretty or not, Hearts won 3–1. Peter Nellies and Willie Wilson weren't with them. Both were in Glasgow representing

Scotland in an international game against England played at Parkhead. General admission was six pence, though soldiers and sailors in uniform could get in for half price. Anyone who paid two shillings, six pence for a reserved seat probably soon questioned the wisdom of the decision, as it was played in what the Scotsman called "Blinding showers of sleet" from the west, and Scotland lost 4–1.

Wilson was the first player to represent Scotland while on active duty. He had become a fan favorite as a utility player, equally comfortable on the outside attack and at center forward. He was fast and an excellent shot, though his shoulder was still giving him trouble. He'd dislocated it two more times thanks to falls and hard hits from defenders.

Hearts trudged on without Wilson the next week. They were again home at Tynecastle, hosting Clyde, another team from the west. Clyde had had a tough year, too—their grandstand burned down the previous September, moving them to Celtic's grounds for practice and home games, and they'd already started sending players to the war. They were reeling even more than Hearts that week, even though the Edinburgh military men had undergone another round of vaccinations earlier that week, and Currie, Briggs, Low, and Wattie felt terrible. William McAndrew, a corporal in the Seventeenth Highland Light Infantry, tried to rally his Clyde teammates from midfield, but the forwards were effectively AWOL. Hearts won 2–0. Had Hearts' players felt better, this would have been an ideal game to run up the score, in case they tied Celtic on the table. But they just weren't up to it.

Hearts were now only barely ahead of Celtic. Even Glasgow papers were rooting for them to finish the season on top. "Let us hope they will yet manage to finish first," the *Sunday Post* wrote. "The Maroons, if only for what they have done in a military sense, would be extremely popular champions."[7] The other Scottish teams didn't feel obliged to help with this project: Aberdeen's management offered its players a bonus for their upcoming games against Hearts on April 3 and Celtic the following week, two pounds for a win, one pound for a draw.

That Saturday, the Rosebery recruiting committee held a "free gift" auction sale at Gorgie Mart in Edinburgh. A soldier bought two Great

Danes for one pound each, telling the *Evening News* he intended to offer a handsome black one to McCrae's to be its mascot. They named him Jock. The same morning, Hearts traveled to the northeast of Scotland to play Aberdeen at their stadium, Pittodrie, but the scheduled referee, a Mr. Dougary, apparently didn't expend as much effort. Fifteen minutes after the game was scheduled to start, he still hadn't shown up, and the *Daily Record* reported the clubs drafted "a local knight of the whistle" named Montgomery to officiate.

The knight oversaw a grim affair. "Seldom have I seen a game in which there was less shooting," the *Daily Record*'s "Viking" wrote.[8] Not until seventy minutes had passed was there a decent attempt at goal, by Aberdeen's Joseph Walker. He missed. Aberdeen couldn't score, but it could prevent Hearts from scoring. Gracie was out sick, and Low was feeling bad but played anyway. Wattie "was the essence of trickery," the Dundee *Courier* observed, but aside from an unsuccessful header, he never gave Aberdeen's goalkeeper much trouble.[9] When the whistle blew, neither team had scored, and Hearts had only one point between them and Celtic. To stay ahead, they'd have to win every remaining game, and Celtic would need to lose at least once.

On April 5 the *Dundee Evening Telegraph* ran a cartoon showing an airplane marked "League Flag." "Where Will It Drop?" the cartoon wondered. On one side stood a Celtic player next to "Parkhead Air Cushions"—"Come on down at the old spot!" he admonished the pilot. "No place like home." On the other side a Hearts player standing above "Tynecastle Feather Beds" addressed the sky, "Have a bit of a change this time."

Another change was in the air. The shortage of working-age men wasn't affecting only football clubs. Seventy thousand had left Glasgow for the colors, leaving only the indifferent and the indispensable. Men were so in demand for vital trades like shipbuilding and weapons manufacturing that a worker could make as much as seven shillings a day, far more than before the war. They could work as it suited them, which meant that especially on weekends, some men chose to drink away the days altogether. An *Evening News* editorial in early April pondered a radical step—whether Sunday work should stop altogether.

———

Hearts' miracle season was now in need of a miracle itself.

On Saturday, April 10, Celtic were at home, hosting Aberdeen. Hearts, on the other hand, had to travel to Cappielow Park, just steps from the south bank of the river Clyde, to play Greenock Morton. Tom Gracie used to play for "the Ton," and he was finally feeling well enough to take up his usual spot. Willie Wilson was out, but the team that took the field that afternoon almost represented John McCartney's perfect side.

Archie Boyd in goal. Paddy Crossan and Duncan Currie on defense. Alfie Briggs, Walter Scott, and Peter Nellies in midfield. Jimmy Low, Harry Wattie, Harry Graham, and Tom Gracie up front, with George Bryden filling in for Wilson.

Greenock Morton was a small club, but it caused Hearts outsized problems. Of their previous nine meetings, five had ended in draws. Hearts opened slowly, and Gracie had trouble finding his rhythm. The forwards nevertheless tried to get their intricate passing game going, hoping to bamboozle the Greenock Morton defense.

But something was off. Several of the men had been out on a march the night before and didn't return to their barracks until early Saturday morning. Crossan was the first to show rust—in the twentieth minute, referee Tom Robertson awarded Morton forward James Stark a free kick from twenty-five yards away from Hearts' goal. He shot a wild ball at kicking height, and Paddy, inexplicably, missed it. Had he not been in the way, Boyd would have probably cleared it. As it was, the home team was up by a goal.

The scientific game was just not gelling. But then, after one attack, Robertson blew the whistle on Morton defender George Ormond for a handball, giving Hearts a penalty kick. After some discussion with Gracie, Nellies reluctantly took it. He tried shooting it past goalkeeper

John Bradford, firing it at an oblique angle toward the corner of the net. It went wide.

"Oh, Peter," some in the crowd murmured. If Hearts couldn't take advantage of their luck and win an easy penalty point, what chance did they have with the rest of the match? At the interval, the fans paused for a cup of tea and a laugh as a bizarre recruitment gag took the field—a stuffed soldier mounted on a prop horse.

Hearts were no better after the half. Morton continually interrupted their attempts at offense, and then, with fifteen minutes to go, luck smiled briefly on the Edinburgh team. Robertson called another penalty, and this time Nellies urged Gracie to take it. His shot was straight and true; it was also far too softly kicked, a "sorry-to-trouble-you" ball, as another *Daily Record* columnist described it.[10] Bradford had little trouble making a stop.

As the clock ran out, Hearts' season was slipping away. Two minutes before the end of the game, Robertson called yet another penalty, and Morton chose their forward George Stanley Seymour to take it. His shot landed squarely in the net. Over in Parkhead, Celtic were victorious, beating Aberdeen 1–0. Hearts had no chance to hold on to the top spot in the league now. Their hopes for a championship, so bright the previous autumn, were fully extinguished.

The stands were filled with men in khaki, many—even the locals—hoping to see Hearts continue their run at the flag. "Most people feel that they deserved to succeed after their sacrifices, yet, after all, a League championship is a small thing compared with the bigger issues in which the Hearts' players have set themselves to take a part," Brigadier wrote afterward. "I should not wonder if this be remembered as the Hearts' Year."[11]

———

Thomas Carr was leaving his job at the Swan Hunter shipyard in Wallsend, England, at 8:30 PM on Wednesday, April 14. He was clambering up a bank toward the train he'd take home when he heard what he later described as a "curious sound" that he reckoned must have been a tramcar, even if he'd never heard one that sounded like that before. As Carr continued toward the train station he heard a loud crack. He turned toward it, and saw a tower of flame twenty yards long erupt to the east.[12]

It was another zeppelin raid. When the Romans occupied Britain, Wallsend was at the easternmost point of Hadrian's Wall, built by the invaders to keep out barbarians to the north, or perhaps just impress them. The zeppelin *L9* had entered Britain in a manner the Emperor Hadrian could scarcely have imagined, floating under power over the North Sea and making landfall over Blyth, about fourteen miles north of Wallsend, which is just east of Newcastle. Its captain, Heinrich Mathy, wired back to Germany seeking permission to bomb England. He got it.

Mathy and his crew first surprised C Company of the Territorial Force's Northern Cyclist Battalion, whose stunned men fired unsuccessfully on the looming ship. It continued east, trying to drop bombs on mining works but mostly hitting fields (one device fell in the village of Choppington, breaking a hotel window). It wasn't until *L9* turned south that Mathy found any purchase, raining thirteen bombs on a railway but causing very little damage. In Wallsend he had his greatest success, finding the roof of the house where Margaret Robinson was giving her baby and seven-year-old, Eddie, a bath in the bedroom. All family members escaped with minor injuries. *L9* dropped three more bombs, causing only minor damage with one, before floating away back over the sea.

Wallsend is about one hundred miles south of Edinburgh.

The morning of the zeppelin raid, the Sixteenth Royal Scots laid their first comrade to rest in Piershill Cemetery, in the shadow of Arthur's Seat. Lance Cpl. J. W. Campbell of A Company had died the previous Sunday from double pneumonia. His coffin, covered in a Union Jack and topped with his glengarry cap, belt, and bayonet, arrived on a gun carriage on loan from the Royal Field Artillery's Thirty-Sixth Battery. Pipers preceded Campbell playing "Flooers o' the Forest" and "Lord Lovat's Lament" as the procession approached his grave. All the members of his company were there, as was Sir George. The Reverend J. R. Sabiston of Abbey Church led the ceremony, and a party from the Sixth Royal Scots fired a salute before "Last Post," the British Army's traditional bugle call at day's end, was played.[13]

Three days later, Celtic clinched the championship at Cathkin Park, spanking Third Lanark 4–0. Hearts were nearby at Paisley, playing St. Mirren in the last game of the regular season. The wind was strong and the ground was as hard as a Scottish winter. Hearts played a new ball. Their players were downcast. They were visibly tired. And they were unlucky—in the second half, Gracie broke a muddle in the center of the field and shot the ball up to George Bryden, who fired it directly into goalkeeper Willie O'Hagan's hands. The match continued scoreless until the very end, when St. Mirren forward John Clark headed in a lovely goal. "Such is football," the *Daily Record* wrote.[14]

Hearts still had several local cup matches to go. On Monday, April 19, they pounded Leith Athletic 6–1 in the semifinal of the East of Scotland Shield, which they won the next week by beating Hibs 1–0 at Easter Road. A week later, they played St. Bernards in the semifinal of the Rosebery Charity Cup. The match was played at Tynecastle "in depressing conditions before a mere handful of spectators"—just two thousand people showed—the *Evening News* reported. Willie Wilson returned, and James Frew filled in for the still-injured Walter Scott. If Hearts won, it would have been the second year in a row, at least, that they'd won all local trophies. Harry Graham got two goals, but Archie Boyd was hurt toward the end, so Paddy Crossan had to don his sweater and fill in at goal.

St. Bernards won 3–2. It was the last time this Hearts team, the best the club had ever fielded, would ever play together.

The war inched ever closer. On April 30 the German submarine *U-20* left Emden, Germany, and began skulking around the waters of the British Isles. The Germans had intelligence that suggested Britain was planning an invasion of Germany, and Kapitänleutnant Walther Schweiger had orders to navigate around Scotland to an area between Liverpool and Ireland to sink troop transports. *U-20* was no stranger to Scottish waters; its previous captain, Otto Droescher, had even sailed her into the Firth of Forth along with another sub but fled to the North Sea after they were spotted.

The next morning, the ocean liner *Lusitania* left New York City with Capt. William Thomas Turner at its wheel. She was headed home to Liverpool with 1,959 passengers and crew aboard.

Schweiger had a frustratingly quiet trip around Scotland but found better hunting on the southwestern Irish coast, sinking a schooner and two freighters. May 7 was a Friday, and Schweiger decided to return home; he was low on fuel and had only three torpedoes left. It was a stunningly beautiful day, with calm and green seas. On the *Lusitania*, Turner had heard reports of U-boats in the waters nearby and decided to enter the St. George's Channel near the Coningbeg light vessel in hopes of evading them.

U-20 spotted the *Lusitania* at 1:20 PM on May 7. At 2:10, just as the big ship's second-class passengers were eating lunch, *U-20* fired a G6 torpedo at the giant ship. Seaman Leslie Morton was in the fo'c'sle and spotted what he later described as "a big burst of foam about 500 yards away."[15] Passengers watched helplessly as it bored through the still water toward the vessel. It hit the *Lusitania* on its starboard side, blowing a hole forty feet wide into its hull. Open portholes on that side let more water through. Many of the lifeboats were launched clumsily, killing more people. Only six of twenty-two boats got away. Some passengers simply stepped into the water and tried to swim for it. Eighteen minutes after the torpedo hit, the *Lusitania* was gone. In all, 1,198 people aboard died.

The sinking appalled the British. "The verdict of the world would be that the Germans' action amounted to no less than cold-blooded murder," Sir James Leishman declared that evening, while presenting a trophy in the shape of a shield to Captain Warr of the Sixteenth Royal Scots' A Company, which had prevailed over its fellow companies in an efficiency competition.[16]

Nine days later Lord Kitchener issued a proclamation, saying Britain needed three hundred thousand more troops to fight the German scourge. "Those who are engaged on the production of war matériel of any kind should not leave their work," Kitchener wrote. "It is to men who are not performing this duty that I appeal."

Sir George was ready to respond. He'd already begun planning, with War Office approval, to add another company to the Sixteenth Royal Scots. It would have four platoons, one specifically for university men, and a second pipe band. He had McCrae's march around Leith and held meetings in Lasswade, Bonnyrigg, Newtongrange, and Dalkeith. At the Dalkeith Corn Exchange, McCrae said, "We must see that the Germans get such a beating that never again would the world see what it had had to witness lately."[17]

He hadn't lost his touch. Men began streaming into the recruiting office on Castle Street. Meanwhile, the Fifteenth Royal Scots, an Edinburgh pals' battalion that had been overshadowed by McCrae's, campaigned at Tollcross. They needed one hundred men to be at full strength, said its leader, Sir Robert Cranston. The Fifteenth marched around town and held a rally at the post office on May 16. Three thousand people came and heard the Reverend Father Power of the Church of the Sacred Heart invoke Belgium and the *Lusitania*. "It was the same spirit which trampled on Belgium in the first month of the war that sank the *Lusitania* in the tenth month," Power said.

If Sir George was sympathetic to the Fifteenth's problems getting over the finish line, he had an unusual way of showing it. Over the weekend, his plan to add another company to McCrae's battalion expanded—why not, he decided, answer Kitchener's call with another entire battalion? Edinburgh's city fathers, however, did not greet this new plan with the same enthusiasm they had mustered in November.

There simply weren't enough men to become officers, and Edinburgh needed more men for the battalions it already had. The Royal Scots' Fourth and Seventh battalions were about to leave for the front, and it had few reserves. The Fifth Royal Scots had just sailed for Gallipoli via Egypt. The Thirteenth was in Chiseldon, England, preparing to move to France. There was also the question of poaching men from surrounding country districts that were trying to raise battalions—a practice grudgingly overlooked when McCrae raised his first battalion and likely to become an open grievance if a new glamorous battalion sucked the oxygen out of all other recruiting.

On May 21 the treasurer's committee of Edinburgh's town council agreed to give McCrae the use of Usher Hall and Portobello Town Hall to hold meetings, in addition to a route march from Heriots to Portobello. This was extraordinary, according to the *Evening News*, because Sir George's plan hadn't yet been sanctioned by military authorities. The Royal Scots' existing battalions needed no fewer than 1,300 men, "and Sir George's proposal is regarded as directly inimical to the interest of these battalions."[18]

That evening, Sir George addressed the contretemps when he spoke at Portobello. Citing his experience in parliament, he said to applause that he didn't want to get dragged into a controversy. But he was clearly rankled by the loss of the *Evening News*' support. "This is not a time for petty jealousies—for discussions on things that did not matter," he said. Referring to 1 Corinthians, he said, "It is not the time to say 'I am of Paul,' 'I am of Apollos,' 'I am of Cephas.'" The situation was too grave, too momentous, and everyone in the country needed to face the situation: men were needed, and Sir George was out to get them. The day before, two of his sons had left for the front with his blessing. Another son was going in June—he had no idea which of them would be at the front first. Back in the Usher Hall last fall, the overwhelming need was for fresh men to replenish the ranks of the BEF. Now Britain needed men to advance upon the Germans and win the war. It was now or never, McCrae said to growing applause.[19]

The *Evening News* spit back fire at McCrae the next day. "Sir George M'Crae was evidently a trifle excited when he delivered his recruiting speech at Portobello last night," an editorial read. "When Sir George M'Crae raised his original battalion we gave him ample assistance." Since then, "things have altered." If it wasn't the time to say "I am of Paul," "neither is it the time, to our mind, to say, 'I am of M'Crae.'" Edinburgh, the editorial noted, "did great things even before Sir George M'Crae appeared on the field at all. The city will continue to do great things, even if this famous offer be withdrawn."

The dispute had become unexpectedly nasty. But that morning, May 22, an event that would complicate it had occurred too late for the *Evening News'* deadline. At 3:45 AM, about five hundred men from the Royal Scots' Leith-based Seventh Battalion got on a train for Liverpool, where they'd sail to fight in Gallipoli. The carriages they traveled in were wooden and lit by gas stored in canisters below the cars.

At 6:30 AM, George Meakin was nearing the end of his shift as signalman at the Quintinshill signal box near Gretna Green, a Scottish town one mile from the English border. He controlled a pair of passing loops that allow multiple trains to share two tracks safely.

Against the rules, Meakin and his replacement, James Tinsley, were in the box with three other railway employees, who were looking at newspapers that had just come off the train that brought Tinsley to work. Two trains were parked in the loops. As the Quintinshill staff had done before, Meakin shunted a local train from Carlisle onto the wrong side of the tracks to let a Scotland-bound sleeper express move forward. Had Meakin signaled ahead to the next box, placed a safety collar on the signal lever so it couldn't be moved, or even adequately described his plan to Tinsley, all would have been safe.

But he employed none of those safeguards. The signalmen apparently forgot about the local train, and one of them, probably Tinsley, pulled a lever clearing the troop train for passage. At 6:49, it collided with the local. The gas canisters beneath the troop train exploded, instantly creating a crumpled inferno. A minute later, another sleeper express on its way to Scotland slammed into the flaming wreckage.

It took twenty-three hours to quell the fires. One eyewitness said mangled bodies protruded from all parts of the train. A local carpenter assisting the rescue had to use his saw to cut off a man's leg to free him from a wheel. Other improvised amputations saved others. There are reports some soldiers shot their fatally trapped colleagues out of mercy.

Of the 500 troops on the train, 230 died and 246 were injured. Photographs in the *Evening News* the next day show a saloon car from the sleeper turned into little more than a wheeled platform with charred timbers reaching for the sky, its engine and coal car jackknifed atop a bed of tangled iron and steel.

That Saturday, as rescue efforts at Quintinshill grew more desperate, Sir George led a procession of automobiles plastered with recruiting posters in a tour of West Lothian, leaving from Charlotte Square and driving around Broxburn, Uphall, Bathgate, Armadale, Addiewell, and West Calder. There were speeches and music from pipe bands. At the last stop, a few audience members fortified by drink began to interrupt the proceedings with critical notes; the police removed them from the area. Then McCrae's crew returned to Edinburgh and held rallies at movie theaters around town.

By Sunday, the enormity of the Quintinshill disaster was evident. But at the Usher Hall, Sir George infused his message of sympathy with the spirit of recruiting. He'd said he'd be "very much surprised if for every man taken away there should not be ten others who would step forward to take their places."

The *Evening News* editors were exasperated, writing about Sir George's "strange mission" the next morning. McCrae, they wrote, "possesses a personal magnetism that is a big asset, but those other assets of November and December, the press, the Heart of Mid-Lothian, and the host of M.P.'s who were commandeered to rush up a battalion in a fortnight, are no longer available. With the new requirements of the Leith Battalion added to existing wants, Sir George M'Crae is simply courting failure. We may leave him there for the time being."[20]

On Monday the soldiers' bodies came to Leith; the civilians killed were brought to Glasgow. Leith's theaters closed on Monday, May 24, to honor a mass funeral held that afternoon; detachments from all of Edinburgh's units lined the road for what was treated as a military funeral. Sir George sent a telegram to Leith's provost, Malcolm Smith, offering to make his meeting there the next week an appeal to refill the Seventh. It was the least he could do.

The following Saturday the War Office could no longer countenance Sir George's apparently boundless enthusiasm. "Army Council thank you much for your offer to raise a second battalion, but regret they cannot accept it at present," it wrote in a telegram. If Sir George was daunted, he didn't show it at the bandstand in Leith's Victoria Park, where he tempered his empathy with a dark picture of what life would be like under conscription. "God help the man who had to be dragged to his country's defense under such circumstances," McCrae said.[21]

A little after 11:00 PM on the evening of May 31, German Army zeppelin *LZ38* appeared over North London, having left its base at Evere in Belgium, crossed the North Sea, and entered English airspace at Southend. It was a terrifying machine, 536 feet long, that made a low throbbing noise as it passed by two miles overhead. Its thirteen-man crew dropped their first incendiary bomb on 16 Alkham Road in Stoke Newington and continued south, raining death from above on the terrified citizens of the capital. One bomb it dropped in Stoke killed three-year-old Elsie Leggatt.

London was all but unprotected, with no searchlights or any sort of organized antiaircraft guns. As the zeppelin continued over London skies, the Royal Naval Air Service flew fifteen sorties against the invader, but only one pilot could manage to locate the dirigible, and his plane developed mechanical trouble that took it out of commission. One plane crashed while attempting to land.

In all, seven people died and another thirty-five were injured. It was the eighth zeppelin raid on Britain but the first to strike London. By order of the War Office's press bureau, reports of the raid eliminated the names of neighborhoods struck, lest the Germans gather any information about the success of their routes. The next morning rioters looted shops whose owners had names that sounded even slightly German.

On Saturday, June 5, fifty thousand Edinburghers attended a grand military tattoo in the Meadows. There about three thousand troops had gathered among the trees under bright sunshine, rare weather in Scotland even in the middle of summer. There was patriotic music from the battalions' brass and pipe bands. McCrae and Cranston were there, among local luminaries who organized the event and delivered speeches.

Lord Provost Inches wore khaki and spoke first. He asked the crowd to imagine what might happen if the Germans entered Edinburgh and treated it like they'd treated cities in Belgium. But it was the Reverend Dr. Wallace Williamson who gave the day's most memorable speech. Williamson had just returned from a ten-day tour of the trenches on the Western Front, and he had just one question for the crowd: Were we going to win this war? "Hear, hear!" people shouted in affirmation.

This, he said, was not a war to muddle through. The Germans were standing against the "great principles for which Scotland stood— patriotism and freedom." The "simple, strong men" in the trenches were quietly prepared to make all sacrifices necessary: "Were we worthy of it?" he asked to more cheers.

Williamson invoked Sir Walter Scott's epic poem *Marmion*, asking a question the great author had put into the mouth of one of the characters. Gesturing to the Meadows' spectacular surroundings, with Edinburgh Castle to the north and Arthur's Seat to the east, he asked, "Who would not fight for such a land?" It was a romantic allusion, though perhaps not the best—the battle Scott wrote about was Flodden Field, a romantic, futile clash in 1513 with the English that cost Scotland thousands of men, including King James IV, grandfather to Mary, Queen of Scots.[22]

On Friday, June 18, McCrae's battalion left Edinburgh. With their pipers playing before them, they marched down Lauriston Place and Forrest Road, across George IV Bridge, past St. Giles' Cathedral, and down the Mound to the grand glass-ceilinged Waverley Station, singing as they went. They left in two groups, the Hearts players on the first train departing at 11:00 AM. Elias Fürst and John McCartney were there to see them off, as were a great number of family, friends, and fans. As the train left the station, some cheered and waved cloths; others wept.[23]

The departure of the battalion's second half was a bit less picturesque. While the first group left in an orderly, high-spirited manner, the boarding of the second train happened in a rush, overwhelming the police who tried to control the situation. Sir John Spencer Ewart, the officer commanding in Scotland, the lord provost, the town clerk, and other civic dignitaries had come down to make of the leave-taking a more or less ceremonious affair, but they were simply engulfed by the three-thousand-strong crowd, hundreds of whom apparently hoped to say goodbye to Sir George personally. Eventually the battalion made it through the boisterous masses onto the train, and as it pulled out of Waverley, the men sang from the windows.

They were headed south to Ripon, England, to complete their training. They had signed up for a war but thus far stayed in familiar surroundings. From here on out they would no longer be hometown heroes but just another battalion on its way to the front. The day before they'd been tailors, grocers, and professional footballers in uniform. Now they were soldiers.

6

GET THE DEVILS
ON THE RUN

At 5:00 AM on September 25, 1915, Douglas Haig and his aide-de-camp Alan Fletcher walked outside First Army headquarters at Hinges, France. It was a calm, cool morning. Fletcher lit a cigarette, and he and Haig watched the smoke drift slowly to the northeast.

It was Haig's last chance to decide whether to attack the Germans with a weapon still unfamiliar to commanders and soldiers on both sides: gas. The wind was gentler than he liked, but after watching Fletcher's little clouds drift by, he gave the order to "carry on."

Zero hour was 5:50 AM; a whistle would blow for British infantry to go over the top of their trenches at 6:30 AM. Here, among the slag heap–covered fields and muddy mining villages of northern France, the British thought they could finally break through Germany's defenses.

Germany's early plan to neutralize France while it fought Russia and Austria-Hungary on its eastern borders had changed—it was now fighting a primarily defensive war on the Western Front. Thanks to constant engagement with the French and British offenses at Aubers Ridge, Neuve-Chapelle, and Ypres, the Germans had learned to fortify their defensive lines so any attack would be expensive in lives and matériel.

Their positions had evolved to a series of trenches—a forward position behind a hedge of barbed wire, a more fortified second trench with reinforced underground rooms to withstand bombardments, and a third position for command, support, and artillery operations. Any attack would have to cross a no-man's-land pockmarked by shell holes and easily raked by machine-gun fire, then clear all three before gaining any ground.

It takes a system to beat a system, and the British hadn't yet figured out how to synchronize their offensive weapons. British commander in chief Sir John French still believed that under the right circumstances they could turn this stalemate into a mobile war where cavalry could "get the Devils on the run," as French wrote to his new mistress, Winifred Bennett, in May. "How I should love to have a real good 'go' at them in the open with lots of cavalry and horse artillery and run them to earth," French wrote.

French's best idea for breaking through the stalemate was high-explosive shells, which he thought could flatten German defenses and make an offensive that followed a kind of clean-up operation. But those shells were hard to come by.

Britain was also fighting in Turkey, where "Easterners" in the British War Office like Chancellor of the Exchequer David Lloyd George and First Lord of the Admiralty Winston Churchill wanted to draw Germany into conflicts in satellite territories, fatally distracting it from the fronts where it fought Russia, France, and the British. French and Haig were "Westerners"—they believed Germany could only be defeated if it lost in northern France and Belgium.

Somewhere in between was Lord Kitchener. On March 31 Kitchener warned French over breakfast that if he and Joffre couldn't produce a breakthrough, as French recorded in his diary, "the government should look for some other theatre of operations." Yet French felt Kitchener was starving him of troops and ammunition. Getting more troops was a matter of time and logistics—as "New Army" units like McCrae's were forming all over Britain, training with broomsticks and wooden guns in many cases, but shells were another matter.

Earlier in March, the British had tried a big push at Neuve-Chapelle, where they overwhelmed German defenses and gained 1,200 yards before a lack of shells stymied any further progress. In May, cheered by reports that the Germans had diverted forces to the Eastern Front, they tried again for a breakthrough at Aubers Ridge, where French watched machine guns mow down his infantry as artillery failed to support them. For reasons lost to history, French told Kitchener before the attack that "the ammunition will be all right."

It wasn't. There weren't enough shells, and many of the ones the British did have were duds. French decided it was time to make a move against Kitchener, using an unpredictable weapon: Repington.

On May 12 Repington sent a telegram to the *Times* saying that at Aubers Ridge the "want of an unlimited supply of high explosive shells was a fatal bar to our success." It was important, when trying to understand what happened, Repington wrote, "to realize that we are suffering from certain disadvantages which make striking successes difficult to achieve."

The *Times* published its article on May 14. In it, Repington tipped his hat to his benefactor: "The men are in high spirits, taking their cue from the ever-confident and resolute attitude of the Commander-in-Chief." He even used the same term French used to describe the German defenses to Bennett: "It is certain that we can smash the German crust if we have the means. So the means we must have, and as quickly as possible."

The article caused an immediate scandal. Alfred Harmsworth, better known as Lord Northcliffe, owned the *Times*, and blamed Kitchener's parsimony with shells for the death a few days earlier of his nephew Lucas King near Ypres. The *Times* and Northcliffe's other newspapers, the *Daily Mail* and the *Daily Mirror*, began a drumbeat of outrage against the government.

Repington's attack missed its target. On May 17, Asquith's Liberal government fell and was replaced by a coalition cabinet. Churchill was out, and Lloyd George was given the newly created cabinet post minister of munitions. Kitchener, much to French's dismay and despite a continuing campaign against him in the *Daily Mail*, remained. French may have gained himself some more ammunition, but he lost even more support with his boss.

Britain burned through summertime in France, planning and stocking up for a big push in the fall. On July 14 Haig visited King George V at Buckingham Palace. The king said he'd "lost confidence in Field-Marshal French," Haig wrote in his diary. George was also dismayed by the role French played in the shells crisis. "I pointed out the time to get rid of French was immediately after the retreat," Haig said. He then went to visit Kitchener at the War Office's headquarters on Pall Mall. "K" asked Haig to begin writing him in confidence: "He would treat my letters as secret, and would not reply, but I would see my proposals given effect to and must profess ignorance when that happened!"[1]

Back in France, Joseph Joffre wanted a breakthrough as well. The French commander in chief felt that if things broke his way, he could push the Germans back across the Belgian border. The month before Haig's visit home, French asked him to survey the area around a mining village called Loos, and report to him whether it would be a good place to attack. Haig took a look and replied that it wouldn't. But Loos was where Joffre thought the British should go, and Sir John didn't need any more enemies. Further, Kitchener and the War Office were worried that the French, weary of the martial stalemate, might sue for a separate peace with Germany.

The Russians were not making a lot of progress against the Germans on the Eastern Front. The Dardanelles campaign had been a failure, with Turkish forces fighting far more effectively than the British expected. The country needed a success somewhere. French began to plan for an attack at Loos.

Haig was eager to avoid the problems of Neuve-Chapelle and Aubers Ridge. He wanted the British to throw everything they had at the German lines and have reserves ready for a breakthrough. French wanted to take more care with his reserves—he was worried Haig might waste them before the Germans were sufficiently weakened. He wanted to hold the Cavalry Corps, the Indian Cavalry Corps, and a New Army unit called XI Corps for the battle's second day. The decision infuriated

Haig, but he was unable to change French's mind. The battle was fixed for Saturday, September 25.

The night before, French left his château at St. Omer and moved to a command post near Lilliers, where he had no direct way of speaking to Haig at Hinges. French considered the battle planned and wanted to stay out of Haig's way while he fought it.

Artillery had pounded the German lines since September 21, and following Haig's orders early Saturday morning, the British fired gas at German lines before its infantry, wearing primitive gas masks that some soldiers called "Ku Klux Klan helmets," went over the top of their trenches to attack. The gas clouds were yellow and white and moved slowly. In some places they blew back on the British troops, who moved through them with various degrees of success, often fighting hand to hand with German soldiers.

As grim as the fighting was, by 7:00 AM the British had advanced enough that Haig decided it was time to send in the reserves. As he was unable to reach French by phone, he drove to Lilliers to ask. French agreed but didn't directly phone XI Corps' commander, Lieutenant General Richard Haking; for some reason, he drove to see him and issued the order in person.

XI Corps was made up of two untested divisions, the Twenty-First and the Twenty-Fourth. They were Kitchener's New Army men, almost all of whom had been civilians when the war broke out. Their approach to the front took hours, and German artillery began to successfully target them. By the time its first battalions began to reach the front, it was late afternoon. Haig managed to deploy two battalions, one of which, the Eighth East Yorkshires, mostly from the market town of Beverley, had landed in France only sixteen days before. They got confused during a push toward a strategic hill and lost many men to machine-gun fire.

Other parts of XI Corps got to the front line by 7:30 PM, far too late to make a fresh attack. As far as Haig was concerned, the opportunity had already been lost.

The Battle of Loos raged on for several more days. On September 28 the Fourth Grenadier Guards, formed just that summer in Marlow,

England, attacked the same hill the Eighth East Yorkshires had tried to find three days earlier.

The British press reported Loos as a triumph. "Splendid Anglo-French Advance on Whole Line," the *Daily Mirror* crowed on September 27. In reality, Whitehall and Westminster were seething. On the first day of battle alone, the British suffered eight thousand casualties. By the time operations drew to a close in mid-October, 59,247 men were killed, wounded, or missing. British gains were minimal; the Germans retook a key defensive point known as Hohenzollern Redoubt in October.

While Haig held command of the operation, fury about its outcome landed on French, who tried to absolve himself by writing a dispatch that ran in the *Times* on November 2. Rather baldly, he claimed he'd released reserves to Haig at 9:30 AM on September 25. Haig was livid: "It is too disgraceful of a C. in C. to try and throw dust in the eyes of the British people by distorting facts in his Official Reports," he railed in his diary. Haig wrote general headquarters two days later asking for the report to be corrected and helpfully enclosing telegrams that proved French was lying. A meeting between the two men on November 10 went nowhere: "I gather that no one of importance takes much notice of Sir J. French when he goes to London, and that he feels his loss of position," Haig wrote afterward. The friendship was over.

On November 23 Asquith decided to sack French and sent Reginald Brett, the second viscount of Esher and a Liberal fixer, to ask him to resign. They offered him home command and a peerage in return; French joked with Esher that his name should be "Lord Sent-Homer." French attempted to use his removal as one last lever to oust Kitchener, subtly implying he would not frame his departure as a resignation unless a civilian replaced his nemesis. On December 4 Asquith, weary of French's antics, telephoned him and ordered him to resign immediately. He did, and in his letter recommended that Sir William "Wully" Robertson, the first man in the British Army to rise from private to general, replace him as commander in chief. The government announced French's resignation on December 17 and named Haig his replacement the next day.

Now the war was Haig's to win. "I am sure that you fully realise that you can rely with the utmost confidence on the whole-hearted and unswerving support of the Government, of myself, and of your compatriots," Kitchener wrote to him in a set of instructions on December 28.[2] It was almost word-for-word what he'd told French two and a half years earlier.

7

IN SEARCH
OF ADVENTURE

On a cold day in early December 1915, Paddy Crossan, Harry Wattie, Duncan Currie, and Alfie Briggs made their first appearance at Tynecastle since April. They didn't come to sit in the stands and wave to the crowd; they were there to try to help John McCartney beat Aberdeen.

The last few months had been trying for Hearts. Celtic had again risen to the top of the league table while Hearts' players were training in England. Meanwhile, the decline in play from the "soldier-players" as they trained was noticeable. They weren't bad; they were just . . . not great.

Crossan's kicking "was not so crisp and sure as of yore," a sportswriter for the *Evening News* gently wrote the following Monday. Anyone hoping to see Currie score "must have been sadly disappointed." Wattie "began well, but faded away."[1]

Aberdeen beat Hearts 2–1; none of the military men scored.

An earlier plan to get the original eleven back together had foundered when Sir George decided it wouldn't be fair to the lads from other teams. Hearts were middling, but Raith Rovers hadn't won a game since the beginning of the season. Falkirk was also mired toward the bottom of the table, having won only four matches.

And Sir George had other things on his mind, anyway. His son Capt. George McCrae died fighting at Gallipoli with the Fourth Battalion of the Royal Scots on June 28, the first anniversary of Gavrilo Princip's fateful shot in Sarajevo. Captain McCrae commanded two companies, and at 11:00 that morning was supposed to take two lines of Turkish trenches. They charged but met with enfilade fire. McCrae was shot in the leg but rallied his men by shouting, "Do you see that trench there? Well they've got to be put out of that. Come on boys!"[2] As he climbed over the parapet of the British trench, he was shot in the head. He left an estate worth £481, including furniture, an insurance policy, and shares in McCrae Limited, to his wife, Mima.

Three months later, McCrae's son Kenneth, who served with the Seventh Cameron Highlanders was wounded by a trench mortar at Noeux-les-Mines, France, just before the Battle of Loos.

After leaving Edinburgh in June, the battalion traveled to Ripon in Yorkshire, where they camped at a site called Studley Royal, near a ruined twelfth-century Cistercian monastery called Fountains Abbey. Over two weeks in July, a writer identified as "a Wandering Scot" tormented readers of the *Edinburgh Evening News* with a two-part series of overwritten reports on the camp:

> The approach to the Royal Scots camp is superb. There is no other adjective meets the case. It is a royal way through a glorious English park. I was directed to a break in the hedge which marked the entrance to the Royal Scots' ground, and the acting military policeman with the iron-grey hair and the soft Lowland Scots accent directed me to the guard tent, where further instructions could be obtained. The St. Andrew's flag floated on the breeze, and as I made my way up the hill I could almost imagine I was treading again my native heath.[3]

Once there, Wandering Scot settled down a bit, describing the bread and butter and jam he ate ("I declare on soul and conscience I tackled that simple and excellent fare with a relish I never felt in the daintiest tea shop in Princes Street") and quoting a "famous Hearts' player" who wasn't as enthusiastic about the food in camp: "There's one thing we have learned in this life, and that is we won't quarrel so much about our meals when we get home again."[4]

The Sixteenth Royal Scots were assigned to the 101st Division alongside the Fifteenth Royal Scots, also from Edinburgh, the Tenth Lincolnshires, better known as the Grimsby Chums, and the Eleventh Suffolks. All were New Army battalions and had received a similar amount of training—which is to say, hardly enough to go to war.

"My mother was very upset," Private William Rowse of the Grimsby Chums remembered after the war. Rowse had asthma. "She was afraid the army life would be fatal. 'It'll kill him,' she'd say." He was in the third year of a five-year apprenticeship to a gents' outfitting firm in Grimsby, making fifteen pounds per year. The battalion was originally independent of the War Office, but once the government took it over he and the other members began making a shilling a day—"quite well off, really, considering what we'd been getting before," he said.[5]

Most of the Hearts players were making four pounds per week before they joined—an unimaginable salary for most members of the working classes. Paddy Crossan had become a "rigid disciplinarian" while in camp, Wandering Scot reported, but was still as "great a favourite in the Royal Scots Camp as he was at Tynecastle." Crossan would shout at the men to look sharp: "I want to see every man on parade with his tunic buttons and cap badge rigidly fixed!" the *Evening News* correspondent noted. "If Paddy keeps this up, he may some day become the sergeant-major of one's dreams."[6]

In camp the battalions went on ever-longer route marches, carrying all their equipment over a dozen miles or more. They moved to Strensall Camp, about thirty miles away, in August to begin firing training with the Short Magazine Lee–Enfield Rifle Mk III. The weapon was dependable and easy to use, a big advantage for the often green troops who would be deploying them.

Recruits of the "Grimsby Chums" in 1914, a "Pals'" battalion from Lincolnshire town. They were later given the official name of the Tenth Battalion, Lincolnshire Regiment.

Collection of the Imperial War Museum

The Lee–Enfield took an eighteen-inch bayonet, a weapon meant to be deployed up close in one-on-one combat. To use it effectively, soldiers were taught to twist the bayonet as they withdrew it; otherwise, their opponent would bleed only internally. They learned to use grenades, called bombs, as well. Trench warfare renewed the need for these weapons, which could be used to clear a part of a trench during an attack.

By July the Hearts' men's teammate Jimmy Speedie was already in France with the Seventh Battalion, Cameron Highlanders. He wrote McCartney telling of his "first experience under shell-fire, and the demolition and carnage inside their shelter. Of the accuracy of snipers, etc.," McCartney wrote in a remembrance after the war. Still, he noted, Speedie's "optimism was pronounced."[7]

Toward the end of August, the division moved south to Salisbury Plain for its final training. They were 250 miles from Ripon, and a world away from Edinburgh (400 miles). The whitewashed cottages with their thatched roofs looked so different from the sandstone buildings they knew and were a clear signal that they were getting nearer to an even more foreign land.

Ludgershall, where they detrained, was one of the Wiltshire towns that had experienced an unexpected renaissance with the troops that flooded in. The region's wool industry had declined in the nineteenth century, thanks in part to industrialization in the north, and the War Office's turn-of-the-century purchase of forty thousand acres of land for training became a local bonanza when the government started warehousing recruits there before shipping them across the channel.

The locals pounced. The Tyneside Irish, who arrived around the same time as McCrae's, remembered photographers encouraging servicemen to come into their shops in the village for portraits; they also visited camp to make pictures that soldiers could send home.

On Salisbury Plain's chalklands the route marches continued—a summit above the villages known as the Deverills called Cold Kitchen Hill, whose summit rises 257 meters above sea level, figures in many doleful remembrances—as did training that dated back to the Boer War. Troops would practice advancing across open country, dropping when an officer shouted "Down!" "The last 50 yards you charged and everybody shouted, 'Hooray!'" Second Lt. Malcolm Hancock of the Northamptonshire Regiment remembered. "Whether that was supposed to frighten the enemy to death I don't know, but it must have been absolutely suicidal."[8]

In late September the entire 101st division moved to Sutton Veny, near Warminster, where the Sixteenth Royal Scots settled at No. 2 Camp, Green Hill. There the Hearts men received some terrible news: Jimmy Speedie had been killed on September 25, the first day of the Battle of Loos. The Seventh Battalion of the Queen's Own Cameron Highlanders were to help take a fortified German position on Hill 70 and suffered horrific casualties. Stopping at a ruined house on their way back to the lines, the Camerons took an informal roll: "There were 4 officers and 75 other ranks present out of 20 officers and 827 rank and file who had started off so proudly 24 hours earlier," the battalion history reads.[9] Stragglers later bolstered those numbers, but the damage was almost beyond belief.

Sutton Veny had a rifle range for training and amusements that could help the soldiers forget the war's growing proximity. There were two pubs, a YMCA, and three cinemas. The historian John Sheen tells the story of a cinema run by a Sutton Veny woman who habitually charged soldiers to see a movie, then claimed the projector had broken. A Tyneside Irish battalion was in attendance at the cinema on what proved to be the last occurrence of this innovative business model. They asked for a refund, but she said that was impossible, because the money was already deposited at the bank. The troops were due to depart for France the next morning. They burned the place down, singing "Keep the Home Fires Burning" as it turned to ash. The authorities did not pursue any further remedy.[10]

On October 23 Tom Gracie died in Stobhill Hospital in Glasgow. To his teammates, it seemed his health had never recovered from the early days of training, but in fact he'd been diagnosed with leukemia in March. He'd told no one but McCartney and been admitted to the hospital in mid-September. There, his obituary in the *Edinburgh Evening News* reports, he learned his brother John Gracie had died at Loos on September 28, serving with the Fifth Battalion, Cameron Highlanders. That day Hearts played Greenock Morton wearing black armbands in honor of Gracie and Speedie. They won 2–0. Gracie was buried at Craigton cemetery in Glasgow, not far from Rangers' home ground of Ibrox, three days later. McCartney and Bob Mercer attended to represent the club and his teammates.

Gracie's death reverberated beyond the players and supporters of Hearts. In Merseyside, where he'd played for Everton and their crosstown rivals Liverpool, the author of the "Bee's Sports Notes" column said he was "one of nature's gentlemen, and his sudden demise causes me to lose a true friend." The *Evening News* said he would be "remembered by the football public as a man who never committed an unfair act even under provocation."[11]

Tom's mother, Harriet, wrote the *Echo* in November, thanking the paper for its kind words about her son, "Only God knows what I have lost in my darling boy, and when I state that another loved son of mine fell in battle on September 28, only three and a half weeks before Tom died, you will understand what my loss is, and how much I appreciate any little words of praise, especially coming from such an unlooked for source as yours did. They who have gone left pleasant memories behind them to others outside their own private circle."[12]

The day after Gracie's funeral Sir George returned to Edinburgh for another quick recruiting blitz. At an open-air meeting in front of the Castle Street office, he gravely intoned that "even the most Socialistic" man in the crowd had to give serious consideration to the crisis facing the nation. He needed another 250 men "because the wastage of war under modern conditions must be very great." Still, he said, if those in the crowd could have seen the calmness of the men of the Sixteenth Royal Scots in the trenches, as bullets flew and shells exploded nearby, they would realize why he could not understand anyone hanging back. He repeated the question he had asked of the original recruits: "Will you come with me?"[13]

The following week the *Evening News* reported "a considerable accession to the numbers" of the battalion, aided in part by a postcard McCrae distributed that bore "the appeal to chivalry and patriotism on one side and a portrait of Sir George on the other."[14]

Time was, in fact, running out for any man who hoped to choose where he'd serve. Despite the turnout to pals' battalions, Britain still didn't have enough men. Conscription was looming. In early December, on the same day Crossan, Wattie, Currie, and Briggs tried to help Hearts best Aberdeen, Sir George visited Edinburgh's King's Theatre, where he spoke alongside the famous illusionist David Devant. Devant, one of the most famous entertainers of his day, the man who popularized the rabbit-from-a-hat trick, promised to "present small tokens of his regard to any man who wrote him saying he had been in the King's Theatre and had joined the 16th Royal Scots."[15]

It was still unclear where the 101st Division would take recruits, new or old. In December they were issued tropical kit and told they were headed to the Dardanelles. But plans to reinforce the troops there fell victim to the same upheaval that cost Sir John French his job and put Haig in charge of the British Expeditionary Force. From now on, Britain's land forces would put most of their effort toward winning the war on the Western Front. In late December, the 101st Division was given mobilization orders.

On January 8 the Sixteenth Royal Scots traveled by three trains to Southampton, where at 5:15 PM all but one hundred of its men boarded the *Empress Queen* for Le Havre. The rest arrived on the SS *Courtfield*. The *Empress Queen* was a swift paddle steamer, the fastest of its time, that in peacetime took Liverpudlian holidaymakers to the Isle of Man. The

Sir George McCrae and his "Soldier Footballers" a year after enlistment: Standing, from left, Sergeant Cecil Neill, Jimmy Todd (Raith Rovers), Alfie Briggs (Heart of Midlothian), Paddy Crossan (Hearts), Andrew Henderson (Falkirk), Annan Ness (Hearts), George McLay (Raith Rovers), Sergeant Frederick Muir. Seated, from left, Jimmy Boyd (Hearts), Harry Wattie (Hearts), Captain Frederick Fowler, Lieutenant Colonel Sir George McCrae, Lieutenant Cuthbert Lodge, Robert Wood (Falkirk), Jimmy Scott (Raith Rovers). Front: Duncan Currie (Hearts).
Edinburgh Evening News, November 27, 1915

crossing took about six hours; at 7:00 AM they disembarked (the battalion's war diary is silent on the reason for the delay) and marched to a rest camp.

A member of a different battalion who arrived via *Empress Queen* wrote home to describe the arrival in Le Havre, "I should think we went through all the worst streets of the town, for filthier roads I have never seen." There were no men around, just women who "looked as if some soap would not have hurt them."[16]

Before arriving in France all men were given an order from Kitchener in their Army Service Pay Book. "You are ordered abroad as a soldier of the King to help our French comrades against the invasion of a common enemy," it read. It continued:

> You have to perform a task which will need your courage, your energy, your patience. Remember that the honour of the British Army depends on your individual conduct. It will be your duty not only to set an example of discipline and perfect steadiness under fire but also to maintain the most friendly relations with those whom you are helping in this struggle. The operations in which you are engaged will, for the most part, take place in a friendly country, and you can do your own country no better service than in showing yourself in France and Belgium in the true character of a British soldier.
>
> Be invariably courteous, considerate and kind. Never do anything likely to injure or destroy property, and always look upon looting as a disgraceful act. You are sure to meet a welcome and to be trusted; your conduct must justify that welcome and that trust. Your duty cannot be done unless your health is sound. So keep constantly on your guard against any excesses. In this new experience you may find temptations both in wine and women. You must entirely resist both temptations, and, while treating all women with perfect courtesy, you should avoid any intimacy.

"Do your duty bravely," Kitchener signed off, admonishing the men also to "Fear God" and "Honour the King."

The next evening, the Sixteenth Royal Scots boarded a train to Blendecques, near Haig's headquarters in St. Omer. They arrived the next afternoon and marched for four hours to Wallon Cappel, where they spent the next eight days in billets. On January 21 General Joffre inspected the battalion. Over the next five days, they marched through a succession of French towns, stopping to sleep at Morbecque and Vieux-Berquin. On the morning of January 26, they arrived in Erquinghem-Lys, on the outskirts of Armentières, where they made camp at a place called Fort Rompu alongside the First Battalion of the Worcestershire Regiment and the Second Battalion of the Northamptonshire Regiment, both regular army battalions that had been on the Western Front since November 1914.

It was to be their last day ignorant of war.

Fort Rompu (Broken Fort) still exists on maps of Erquinghem-Lys. Now there's a series of brick buildings and a greenhouse on the spot. It's about a two-hour walk from there through the town of Bois-Grenier to the spot where the Sixteenth Royal Scots first entered the front lines on the evening of January 27.

The British had constructed a maze of lines and support trenches, which they'd named for places back home. McCrae's entered with two New Army battalions that had been in France since August via Shaftesbury Avenue, a long rough communications trench that took them, with tree roots at eye level, through a junction named London Bridge to an area with names that reflected the Scottish and English troops who'd preceded them: Haymarket, Charing Cross Road, Jocks Joy. The water table in this area was extremely high; a photo from the year before shows Col. Philip R. Robertson of the First Battalion, Cameronians, wading through calf-high water in Shaftesbury Avenue looking not exactly amused. October and November had flooded most of the communication trenches, leaving their bottoms nothing but boot-sucking mud.

Just south of a farm called Grande Flamengrie, A and B companies turned right, following the Eleventh Battalion, the Prince of Wales's Own Regiment (West Yorkshire), past Water Farm into a roughly 3,600-foot-long span of trenches a little more than 400 feet from the German lines at their narrowest point. Companies C and D went in the other direction with the Tenth Battalion, Duke of Wellington's Regiment (West Riding), taking up about 2,100 feet of trench that overlooked a slightly wider no-man's-land, with incomplete German trenches about 800 feet away at the closest point. It was Kaiser William's birthday, and as McCrae later remembered, the Germans gave the battalion a "very hot reception" in honor of the day. The enemy artillery were active all night—"our baptism of fire during the night was exceptionally severe," Sir George McCrae wrote—and a soldier named Charles Goodall was wounded during the relief operation.

Because of the high-water table, the trenches couldn't be too deep—instead, they were built like sandcastles, with high earth breastworks, brushwood revetting to keep them from collapsing, and sandbags on top. The wooden frames that held the brushwood also served as hangers for the "pattern webbing" the soldiers wore in full marching order or combat operations—a set of straps that held ammunition, a bayonet, a small haversack, and an entrenching tool. As complex as it sounds, the webbing slipped on easily, allowing the men to quickly turn from quotidian maintenance duties to fighting.

And there was plenty of maintenance to be done. "It was the procedure for the wiring parties, who crawled over the parapet under cover of darkness to have a sprinkling of volunteers from the incoming lot, the leadership to be in the hands of the older soldiers of the regiment giving instruction," Donald Gunn of McCrae's wrote while describing trench life to the *Edinburgh Evening News*. "The cheerfulness and high spirits of our instructors during the first four nights in the front lines probably laid the foundation for the coolness" with which the Sixteenth approached later assignments.[17]

Sang-froid was a necessity in the Bois-Grenier trenches. "The trenches are in a bad state, and the parapets fall in without anyone touching them," Pvt. Reuben Smith of the Dukes wrote in a letter to a friend back home in Yorkshire. "It is awful going into them for water; we have to keep the pumps going all the time." There was "mud and water everywhere," Smith's fellow Duke Lance Corp. J. B. Priestley, who went on to become a famous novelist and playwright after the war, wrote. "A great part of the country around here is under water, for it is always raining here." Priestley grew up near Bradford, which he said he always considered "a bad place for rain, but it is a Sahara Desert compared with this miserable country."[18]

A 1914 British infantry manual specified that trenches should be traversed, or winding, so that a bomb that fell in one section would wreak limited havoc. The Bois-Grenier trenches were duly crenellated, and looked like a square-toothed saw blade when viewed from above, but from there they varied widely from specs. The "firestep" a foot above the trench floor behind the parapet was a place for men to shoot from and also sit when they weren't engaged; at Bois-Grenier it was a muddy ridge reinforced with corrugated metal where possible. Dugouts on trench wall to the soldiers' backs (the "parados") were propped up by wood beams and covered with corrugated metal as well; they collapsed all the time in the rain.

The floor of the trench was an oily, muddy glop mitigated only slightly by narrow "duckboards" in some parts of the trench and bricks in others. The trench "was full of water," Private Rowse of the Grimsby Chums remembered. "You were paddling about in this soggy stuff all the time." The duckboards were constructed of parallel planks joined by battens in some stretches; in others you were lucky to get a board to walk on at all.

Soldiers got a tot of rum at stand-to every morning, along with clean socks and whale oil to run on their feet. The socks and oil were meant to prevent trench foot, a condition like frostbite that rendered soldiers' feet spongy and numb. As the war proceeded, the British military began to consider trench foot a self-inflicted wound and punished those who contracted it.

The Dukes and the West Yorks were there to help McCrae's acclimate to life on the front, not babysitters exactly, even if Australian and New Zealand troops called the trenches near Bois-Grenier "the Nursery." Here they'd learn to adapt to the sight and sounds of artillery shells crossing overhead. They'd learn to clean their rifles before inspection each morning, and went on countless working parties digging and repairing trenches and barbed wire.

Most work went on at night to shield the troops from enemy across the pockmarked and denuded no-man's-land that separated their lines. Stand-to occurred in the minutes before dawn—all activity quietly stopped, all men returned from patrols and working parties to the trench, and the sentries went on alert. You'd stand quietly with bayonets fixed, a bullet in the breech of your rifle, and enough ammunition for any eventuality.

On the battalion's second night in the trenches, Robert Russell of the Sixteenth Royal Scots was killed by a high-explosive shell that hit the dugout where he was sleeping. The following days were "dull," according to the battalion's diary. "Trench warfare is a very stale business," Gunn wrote, "and after a day of gazing through periscopes it lends quite a deal of interest to the game to have the opportunity of climbing the parapet and going in search of adventure."[19] On January 30 the Dukes attempted a raid on the German trenches but weren't successful. Trench raids developed after the British grew concerned about a live-and-let-live spirit developing among the troops on either side of no-man's-land. They were very unpopular with the troops; Haig called them "winter sports."

They usually involved four men who'd "volunteered." A rifleman in the front, two grenade throwers (one primary and one backup), and another rifleman in the rear. Appropriate to the medieval siege conditions the troops found themselves in, they carried clubs and spiked sticks, gruesome weapons for hand-to-hand combat just in case. Usually they'd crawl under the British wire and approach the German trenches under cover of night. There they'd quietly cut wire or, if they were really lucky, go to a spot where a previous patrol had surreptitiously cut some, and jump into a front-line trench.

There, the lead soldier would "dispose of whoever was holding it by bayonet, if possible, without making any noise or clubbing over the head with the butt," Sidney Amatt of the London Regiment remembered.

> Then you'd drop into the trench once you'd established yourself and wend way round each bay. First of all a rifleman would go, leading, and then he'd stop at the next bay which was normally a part which was unoccupied. And the bomb thrower would then throw a grenade towards the next bay of their line, or where he thought it would be, judging from the distance of the other one. Just after it exploded, the man who were leading—the rifleman—

he'd dash round into the trench where the bomb had just gone off and dispose of any occupants that were left behind. And so we'd go on until we'd cleared the whole trench.[20]

The raids did have some advantages. They were a decent way of collecting intelligence and of acclimating the men to traversing no-man's-land. But they also infuriated the Germans, who were likely to respond with bullets and bombs the next day.

McCrae's last day in the trenches was January 31, a misty day that passed without event. During the afternoon they prepared to be relieved by the Eighth Yorkshires, bringing their effects and stores out through Shaftesbury Avenue to Bois-Grenier.

Civilians had more or less abandoned the little village, which German artillery fire had largely wrecked. The church in its center had no roof and "only about a quarter of its steeple left," Priestley wrote. On the corner nearby was an estaminet, a bar and restaurant for the troops named A la Tranquillité—the peaceful spot.

Estaminets served wine, beer, and egg-and-chips suppers. Some offered companionship, a service largely tolerated by the British, though venereal disease became a matter of discipline later in the war, as treatment of it could sap man power. Prostitution was regulated in France, and bigger towns would have separate facilities for officers and enlisted men, marked by blue and red lights respectively. No such comforts were available in Bois-Grenier.

McCrae's four companies simply rendezvoused at Fort Rompu and spent much of February in billets, marching from Fort Rompu to Vieux-Berquin, from Vieux-Berquin to Morbecque, where Kitchener himself inspected the troops on the eleventh. On the nineteenth they returned to Rompu and the next day relieved the Twelfth Battalion, Durham Light Infantry, in the trenches. A, B, and D companies held the firing line trenches to the right of Grande Flamengrie Farm, while C Company, which held the Hearts men and many of their supporters, took posts in support trenches behind the front, posts called Emma, Stanhope, Hudson Bay, and White City.

It began to snow. In retaliation for shots from British snipers, the Germans fired fifteen "whizz bang" bombs at the McCrae's men. Whizz bangs were light shells nicknamed for the noise they made just before and after explosion; troops in their way had little other warning. "It is said to be the only shell one can't get away from," the Canadian soldier Lorenzo N. Smith wrote in a guide to the *Lingo of No Man's Land*. "It travels so fast it beats its own sound."

Other threats had different names. "Woolly bears" emitted thick white smoke when they burst, an "eye-witness" wrote in a Press Office dispatch published by multiple British newspapers on January 14, 1915. Trench mortars were "German undertakers"; the large black heavy howitzer shells known to the French as *marmites* were "Jack Johnsons" to the British, in honor of the American boxer.

It snowed all day on the twenty-second, and that night the Sixteenth's A Company sent a patrol that made it to within fifty feet of the German lines before being discovered; Pvt. Frank Taylor was wounded by a German bullet, a fact Gunn left out of his dispatch to the *Evening News*. Gunn did describe the night patrols and wiring parties as welcome breaks from the tedium of trench warfare; he says one volunteer told him, "When I got out on a wiring party I get some real excitement, better than in a cup tie; and when I get back I'm off for the night, or that, in addition to having some adventure, I also get a good night's rest while the others are doing their monotonous duty on the firestep."[21]

February 24 dawned snowy, frosty, and boring, but the evening was a lot more exciting. At 10:55 AM the battalion received a signal from brigade that a gas attack was coming. A signal banged out on an empty shell case hanging from a trench wall alerted the men. "The company officer was immediately notified, and in a very few minutes every man, clad in his smoke helmet was on the parapet awaiting the attack," Gunn wrote. The artillery, previously quiet, began to pound the other line for an hour, damaging the Germans' parapet. The men wondered if the Germans were firing back—"His or ours?" was a common phrase on the front—but after some time, Gunn wrote, they got a sign the British guns were dominant: "Not a German was to be seen, but their casualty horns calling out a painful wail for stretcher-bearers were distinctly heard, and it was in this way that the men in our front lines knew that all the 'strafing' had come from our side."[22]

The stand-down order came at 12:15 AM. "It turned out later that what gas there was had been sent over some considerable distance further up the line," Gunn wrote. "The Edinburgh men behaved splendidly, and no body of battle scarred veterans could have been more cool under what to newcomers were, indeed, trying conditions. Some of the more adventurous spirits did not like the idea of waiting for the enemy. They wanted to meet them halfway with the bayonet, and a few had to be dragged off the parapet and told to be patient with as much politeness as such a situation would require."[23] This rosy picture is not mentioned in the official diary, but Gunn's account is typical of newspaper accounts at the time, most of which presented success as imminent, the British soldiers as cheery and indomitable, and life in the trenches as a grand adventure with uncomfortable conditions but plenty to laugh about.

When the Sixteenth Royal Scots reentered in the trenches in March, heavy shelling killed Raith Rovers player Jimmy Todd. He was twenty.

Sunday, April 2, was a beautiful spring day in Edinburgh. The night, too, was calm and clear. At 7:00 PM, the Edinburgh City Police received a phone call from military officials by way of the post office that shattered the tranquility—prepare for a possible air raid. At 9:05 PM the police received a further order to take action. Traffic was stopped, lights were lowered all over town, and notification was sent to the Red Cross and the fire station.

Zeppelin *L14*, commanded by Kapitänleutnant der Reserve Alois Böcker, crossed the Firth of Forth around 11:25 PM and turned toward Leith, which it reached ten minutes before midnight. Its first bomb missed the Edinburgh Dock and landed in the water, breaking skylights on two Danish ships docked nearby. Another zeppelin, the *L22* commanded by Kapitänleutnant Martin Dietrich, passed above the *L14*, and circled to the south of town.

Böcker's bombs rained terror on the town, blowing out windows, destroying houses, and wounding and killing people. Bombs fell on Lauriston Place, near Heriot's, on the Meadows, in the Marchmont neighborhood, the Grassmarket, and on the grounds of the Royal Infirmary, among other targets. One bomb fell in front of a tenement building on Marshall Street, killing six people, including a five-year-old boy, and injuring seven others. Another fell on a tenement building in the shadow of Arthur's Seat, killing four-year-old Cora Edmond Bell. Innes & Grieve's whisky warehouse in Leith was completely destroyed, causing £44,000 in losses. Dietrich only managed to drop three, breaking some windows south of town. Home was safer than the front, but the war was no abstraction.

Near the end of March, the Sixteenth Royal Scots moved to trenches a little south in front of the commune of Fleurbaix. After a short break at the beginning of April, they returned to the trenches, and Sir George set up battalion headquarters at a farm called Foray House. "The farmhouse was fairly well hidden and, although shelled frequently, had suffered but little damage," McCrae later wrote. On the morning of April 11, the commander of the Australian troops who were due to replace them came to inspect the digs and found them quite comfortable. At lunchtime, as they waited for Australian troops to relieve them, the German gunners finally found the building.

"For forty minutes over 90 shells of varying calibre were concentrated right on the farm buildings," McCrae wrote. "The third shot found its target right in the thatched roof of the farmhouse and set fire to the building. The whole place was razed to within about two feet of the ground." McCrae and several other officers took shelter in a dugout on the farm's rear wall. A 4.2 shell landed on the fluted semicircular piece of iron covering the dugout, chipping its end. A bigger shell would have sent everyone inside "to kingdom come," Sir George marveled, but "fortunately for them the dug-out most miraculously escaped this fate."

Things got worse—two orderlies who had been sleeping in the room next to the dugout had taken cover, leaving their packs, fully loaded with ammunition, in the room. The fire from the roof set off the ammunition, which "went pop, pop, against the dug-out wall," Sir George wrote. "The tube-built structure was, however, proof against rifle fire so ingeniously discharged." Then the iron walls heated up—"It looked as if the occupants, confined in a very small space, would be roasted alive," McCrae said. They ran to safety, amazingly escaping with no casualties, though Sir George noted three men "got rather bad shell shock."[24]

The exact words the Australian commanding officer used when he learned about the loss of the farm, a division history notes, were "better left unrecorded."[25]

Over the next few days, McCrae's marched to Houlle, near St. Omer, to begin training for an assault on German lines. The Fourth Army left nothing to chance, placing each division on terrain similar to that between them and their objectives, making models of German trenches marked with tape. The battalion's companies practiced crossing the simulated no-man's-land again and again in waves. Men waving flags represented the artillery "lifts" that would precede them as they moved over the terrain.

Overhead, the pilots practiced "Contact Patrol," a method for letting headquarters know where infantry were during an attack. The soldiers were instructed to light flares at various positions; an aerial observer would note them on a map and write their coordinates on a piece of paper that he'd then place in a weighted bag and drop onto a white cloth outside headquarters. As headquarters moved forward, the white cloths would as well, theoretically keeping command mobile as the infantry progressed. The British even invented a ground sheet covered by a venetian blind that could signal pilots in the air using Morse code; the airplanes had a horn to signal in reply.

Information gleaned by airmen through patrols and photography also showed where ground troops could expect to find machine guns and other hazards. British planners believed barbed wire wouldn't be much of a problem for the Tommies; the thundering artillery bombardment would reduce all such obstacles to mere annoyances. The soldiers would walk slowly across no-man's-land and probably keep on walking all the way to Berlin.

8

I THINK WE CAN DO BETTER THAN THIS

The Christmas Day 1915 diary entry by Pvt. Robert Keating of the Fifteenth Battalion, Royal Welch Fusiliers, pointed to yet another challenge facing Gen. Sir Douglas Haig as he assumed command of the Western Front.

Keating's battalion had arrived in France at the beginning of the month and was passing the holiday in trenches near Laventie, south of Armentières. After breakfast on Christmas morning, Keating writes, they shouted "greetings to the Germans over the way." Following encouragement, some Scottish soldiers in their trench ran across no-man's-land and began to chat with the men they'd been trying their best to kill the day before. Keating and the Welsh followed, ignoring the pleas of an officer to return.

The Germans "crowded round us & chatted about old England— one fellow we were talking to was born in Northampton & was longing for the day when he could return," Keating wrote. "They said the war would end in a few months in our favour & that they were absolutely fed up with everything generally." The war cut short this momentary détente. "Just as we were exchanging souvenirs the blooming artillery started and you should have seen us run," he wrote, continuing:

Heaps of fellows got caught in the barb wire, but really there was no danger to us as the shells were dropping on the German trenches. The reason why we rushed back was because our artillery firing on the Germans might entice their snipers to fire on us. However this was not so. Before leaving the Germans one of their officers told one of ours that they would not fire another shot for two days if we did the same, and believe me or believe me not on our part of the line not a single shot was fired until we were relieved by the Irish Guards on Sunday Evening.

Later that evening, the Scots managed to liberate a much larger rum ration than usual, and after Keating retired to his dugout, his mates dragged him out to the top of the parapet, where they had a fire going in a brazier and were cheering on the Germans, who were singing carols. Once they stopped, the British soldiers returned choir, singing "Land of Hope and Glory" and "Men of Harlech" across the killing fields.[1]

The unofficial cease-fire wasn't as extensive as the famous "Christmas truce" the year before, when soldiers on both sides were said to have played football against one another, but to the British command any such fraternization was a sign of how the war was dragging on. If the men didn't hate each other, there was little chance they'd be able to break the stalemate. Haig had to turn this festering situation back into a war.

He hadn't attended the meeting earlier in December in Chantilly, where Britain and its allies decided that the war had to be won in the west, abandoning the hope of a decisive victory in Turkey. Germany nevertheless had to be worn out on all sides—the Russians and Italians attacking in their theaters, and the French and British on the Western Front. The blockade of Germany's ports led by the British Navy would choke supplies. Eventually, Germany's ability to resupply the lines with men, matériel, or food would falter, and peace would follow.

But the Allies weren't equally positioned. The Russian forces had lots of men but were badly undersupplied. And after a year and a half of war, the French were facing a shortage of men; Haig wrote in his diary in January that they were "not likely to stand another winter's war." He set out a three-point plan for ending the war: trench raids through the spring, a three-week "wearing out fight" to sap the Germans' reserves, then "decisive attacks at several points, object to break through."

The weakness of the French was not lost on the Germans. Over Christmas Erich von Falkenhayn, the chief of the German general staff, wrote a memo saying that the French could be knocked out of the war with a grinding attack to drain what blood and treasure it had left.

Germany attacked the French city of Verdun on February 21. It's difficult to overstate the importance of Verdun in the French psyche. The Celtic tribesmen who founded it named it Virodunum, or "strong fort." It had been a flash point in German-French relations ever since. In 1792 the Prussians captured it for about a month, and withstood a long siege during the Franco-Prussian War of 1870. The French loss of Alsace and Lorraine in that war rendered Verdun a crucial brake to any German plan to take Paris, and in the years before World War I, France spent a lot of money turning Verdun into a series of twenty-eight hardened forts.

Falkenhayn would have been foolish to try to take Verdun. But he knew France would use everything it had to defend this symbol of its defiance. In a war still being fought by people mired in nineteenth-century ways of thinking, it was an audacious, thoroughly twentieth-century plan. Falkenhayn didn't want to punch a hole and send in the cavalry. He said he wanted to *bleed France white*.

After the shell scandal, Whitehall wanted to hold any offensive on the Western Front until Haig had the men, and especially the shells, that he needed. Britain had already begun shifting to a war economy, with new munitions factories being built rapidly and a law that gave the government almost unchecked power to keep them humming.

To help Joffre, Haig moved his troops into the lines held by the French Tenth Army and created the Fourth Army to prosecute the coming "Big Push." He put Sir Henry Rawlinson in charge. The war correspondent Philip Gibbs described Rawlinson as follows:

The army commander seemed to me to have a roguish eye. He seemed to be thinking to himself, "This war is a rare old joke!" He spoke habitually of the enemy as "the old Hun" or "old Fritz," in an affectionate, contemptuous way, as a fellow who was trying his best but getting the worst of it every time. Before the battles of the Somme I had a talk with him among his maps, and found that I had been to many places in his line which he did not seem to know. He could not find there very quickly on his large-sized maps, or pretended not to, though I concluded that this was "camouflage," in case I might tell "old Fritz" that such places existed. Like most of our generals, he had amazing, overweening optimism. He had always got the enemy "nearly beat," and he arranged attacks during the Somme fighting with the jovial sense of striking another blow which would lead this time to stupendous results.[2]

Rawlinson was beginning to understand something it would take Haig many months and thousands of lives to appreciate: the tactics they'd been using so far weren't moving the ball. Rawlinson's experience at Neuve-Chapelle and Loos had convinced him that what he called "bite and hold" infantry tactics—limited, quickly fortified advances—were more likely to succeed than grand operations. He and Haig would spend the next months trying to synthesize their incompatible beliefs into a plan.

Haig felt he had only himself and his men to rely on; he didn't consider the other nations' fighting up to the task. "The Italians seem a wretched people, useless as fighting men, but greedy for money," he wrote in his diary on March 12. The Belgian commander Félix Wielemans was "a nice kindly old man, but quite stupid and, I should say, also very lazy." The French were a mess: "My difficulties are to know who is the real Commander in Chief of the French Army. There seem to be so many advisers behind Joffre, and they frequently change," he wrote on March 8. Later that month: "The truth is that there are not many officers in the French Staff with gentlemanly ideas. They are out to get as much from the British as they possibly can."

But Haig also knew his forces were not yet what he needed. "I have not got an Army in France really, but a collection of divisions untrained for the Field," he wrote at the end of March. "The actual fighting Army will be evolved from them." And he was also keenly interested in the development of new armored weapons informally referred to as "tanks." They would be ready by the end of July. "Too late," Haig said in reply.

In early April Rawlinson submitted a plan for an offensive based on bite and hold. "I think we can do better than this," Haig replied. He wanted to surprise the Germans, then turn the war mobile again, with mounted troops exploiting the breakthroughs they were sure to make.

On Tuesday, May 2, Joffre told Haig the offensive could start no later than July 1. In the middle of that month he set his objectives for its first day: the eleven divisions on the Somme would advance about half a mile between Serre and Montauban and take the Germans' second defensive line. Three cavalry divisions would then move miles deeper, sowing chaos and pushing the Germans farther back.

Artillery would be crucial to this plan. The guns the British had were required to cover a lot of enemy ground, especially after Haig decided to set the objectives so deep. They would first pound the German lines and cut the barbed wire so the infantry could penetrate the German positions with ease.

As the French saw it, time was running out. They were losing men at a horrific rate in the abattoir of Verdun—the number would soon reach two hundred thousand, General des Vallières, Joffre's man at general headquarters, told Haig on May 24. "Joffre," Haig wrote in his diary, "was of the opinion that the offensive cannot be delayed beyond the beginning of July."

Haig and Wully Robertson, now the head of the British Imperial General Staff, weren't so sure they could meet that date. They would be so much stronger if they waited till mid-August. And yet their ally needed them. "I came to the conclusion that we must march to the support of the French," Haig wrote after meeting Robertson on May 25.

Haig met with Joffre on May 26; speaking of the losses at Verdun, Haig recounted Joffre's opinion that "if this went on, the French

Army would be ruined. He, therefore, was of the opinion that the 1st July was the latest date for the combined offensive of the British and French." Haig gave him several dates ranging from July to August 15 at which he'd know how ready his army was. "The moment I mentioned August 15th, Joffre at once got very excited and shouted that 'The French Army would cease to exist if we did nothing till then,'" Haig wrote in his diary.

He continued, "The rest of us looked on at this outburst of excitement, and then I pointed out that, in spite of the 15th August being the most favourable date for the British Army to take action, yet, in view of what he had said regarding the unfortunate condition of the French Army, I was prepared to commence operations on the 1st July or thereabouts."

The meeting was a "great success," Haig wrote. The French "are, indeed, difficult Allies to deal with! But there is no doubt that the nearest way to the hearts of many of them, including that of the 'Generalissmo', is down their throats, and some 1840 brandy had a surprisingly soothing effect."

Thanks to aerial observation, the British knew the shape of defenses on the other side of no-man's-land but little else. Over the months of stalemate, while the British and French plotted a breakthrough, the Germans had hardened their positions, digging in even further. Dugouts were deepened, reinforced with concrete to withstand shells, and equipped with stoves. Barbed wire was built up to the thickness—and height in some places—of hedges.

The web of trenches became a city unto itself. There were bakeries. Charcoal-makers. One Bavarian corp's meat operation was more active than the slaughterhouses in two similarly sized towns at home. Front-line butcheries produced so much food they were able to ship surplus back to Germany.[3]

By early 1916 the Germans were aware the British were planning an attack and made further preparations north of the French lines. They also organized their own trench raids to rattle the enemy and take prisoners for interrogation. By June both sides were careful to send out patrols with unit markings stripped from their uniforms. The Germans installed machine-gun nests and concrete observation posts with iron roofs, camouflaged with paint and landscaped with fast-growing ivy.

Verdun was an expensive offensive for the Germans as well, and in early June Russian general Aleksei Brusilov launched an offensive that further sapped reserve troops from the lines in France. If the British could get through the lines, Haig's plan had a chance. The troops stationed in front of the British, however, were prepared to significantly dampen his optimism.

If you visit the Somme today and stand facing the German positions, the tactical challenges the British faced are easy to see. The Germans occupied the high ground all the way from Serre, near the river Ancre, past Thiepval, across the pencil-straight Roman road that still runs between Albert and Bapaume, and south to Fricourt, Mametz, and Montauban. The British held lower ground along much of those lines, with pronounced depressions in several places between them and the enemy.

Two miles northeast of Albert, the tiny commune of La Boisselle lies near that Roman road, jutting out on limestone into the valley created by the Ancre, which flows into the Somme thirteen miles to the southwest. There, on September 28, 1914, the French finally stopped the German advance in a fierce battle.

Both sides dug in near a farm the French called L'Ilot (meaning "small "island") and the Germans less poetically but accurately called Granathof ("shelled farm"). The French got the farm's sturdy vaulted cellars and put them to great use as shelters the Germans couldn't pound to dust with their artillery. Unable to establish superiority above ground, the armies tried to break the stalemate below the earth.

Over the next four months, miners from both sides Swiss-cheesed the land underneath their lines with tunnels and mines that turned the no-man's-land between them into a series of almost impassable craters. One German civil engineer, inspired by the way the French were protected by Granathof's cellars, suggested the Germans build hardened dugouts of their own in the cellars of buildings in ruined La Boisselle. The design was soon adopted all along the Somme front.

When the French turned over the position to the British in July 1915, they'd paid for the real estate with thousands of gallons of blood; the Black Watch soldiers who relieved them assured their counterparts they would honor that sacrifice and hold the line. The Scots chose a name that sounded a bit like L'Ilot for the narrow no-man's-land between their trenches and the German fortifications thirty-five yards away in La Boisselle. They called it the Glory Hole.

To the north of La Boisselle, the distance between the trenches widened to about eight hundred yards across a depression the British called Mash Valley. They called another depression to the south Sausage Valley. There, no-man's-land was about four hundred yards across.

The Germans occupied the brow of land on the other side of the valley and constructed a bewildering series of trenches on the ridge overlooking the British lines, which sat on the lower slopes of two hills named Usna to the north and Tara to the south. Any British soldier trying to cross no-man's-land south of La Boisselle would have to descend into Sausage Valley toward two "redoubts," or fortified and heavily armed salients. Schwabenhöhe was a carbuncle on La Boisselle's south side. Not far south was Heligoland, a salient fortified by machine guns and fed replacement troops via five lines of German positions. Two trenches connected Heligoland to the rest of the system; the British named them Kipper and Bloater.

The La Boisselle section of the front continued south toward the commune of Fricourt. If you drew a line between La Boisselle and that hamlet, then two legs of a triangle about two miles long from that base, the tiny hamlet of Contalmaison would be at its apex.

The approach to Contalmaison from the south today, with Sausage Valley visible on the left.

Photograph by Andrew Beaujon

Historians differ on how much Haig expected to achieve, and whether he expected a breakthrough that would allow him to send cavalry troops through to start a pursuit of Germans like Napoleon did at the Battle of Jena–Auerstedt in 1806. His January plan specifically said breaking through would be the object of the year's attacks. But the word *breakthrough* is missing from two key pieces of correspondence in June with Rawlinson.

Roughly speaking, there are two schools of thought with regard to Haig's competence. First, the "Lions led by Donkeys" school, which takes its name from a book titled *The Donkeys* by the historian Alan Clark about him and other generals. Then there's the revisionist school, which holds that Haig did the best he could with a barely trained army and that the British, faced with war on a scale that didn't exist two years before, learned much from the Somme, lessons they used to hasten Germany's collapse in 1918.

That school says Haig didn't really expect a breakthrough at the Somme but wisely made contingency plans in case one occurred. By grinding down the Germans, the Somme and later offensives loosened the lid on an eventual victory. The context of his time is important here: Haig was a member of the upper classes who had been brought up with the conviction he'd been bred to lead, and imbued with a religious faith that led him to believe success was always just around the corner.

On Wednesday, May 31, Haig traveled to Dury, just south of Amiens, to meet with French generals Joffre and Castelnau at General Ferdinand Foch's headquarters. The party then traveled to Salieux, about two miles to the west, to meet with French president Raymond Poincaré, prime minister Aristide Briand, and the minister of war Gen. Pierre Roques in the presidential railway carriage.

The French situation was grave. Poincaré had just returned from Verdun, where generals Philippe Pétain and Robert Nivelle told him Verdun would soon be taken. They desperately needed the British to relieve some of the pressure. Haig assured him he had his government's permission to make arrangements to do so.

"The only question was, when is the most favourable date for attacking," Haig wrote in his diary. "General Joffre, who alone knew the situation fully (at Verdun and in Russia, Italy, etc.) had asked me to be ready by the beginning of July. I had arranged to comply with his request."

On June 6, Haig made his way home to meet with the War Council and shore up arrangements for the offensive. At Dover, a military landing officer showed him a telegram containing startling news—Kitchener had drowned the day before. He had been aboard the British cruiser HMS *Hampshire* when it struck a German mine in the North Sea. He was on his way to the Russian port of Arkhangelsk to hold secret talks with Russia, whose support for the war was wavering after sustaining unimaginable casualties.

Kitchener had boarded the ship at Scapa Flow in the Orkney Islands. The ship's captain, Herbert Savill, took an unusual route to the west of the islands, perhaps because of a storm or reports of U-boat activity (conspiracy theories abound). The Hampshire hit a mine at 7:40 PM and sank so quickly the seamen aboard had no time to kick off their boots to help them swim to safety. Of the more than seven hundred people aboard only twelve survived.

Kitchener's death was a national tragedy. Haig's response was some-what restrained: "Ship struck a mine and sank. Sea very rough," he wrote in his diary. That appears to be the extent of his private mourning.

The next day, after meeting with the War Council at Downing Street, Haig met up with his wife, Doris, and their children for lunch. They repaired to the Alhambra Theatre on Leicester Square to see an act called the Bing Bong Brothers. ("We all enjoyed ourselves," he wrote.) He met with Prime Minister Asquith and Colonial Secretary Andrew Bonar Law, then left for a meeting with King George, who argued that the cavalry was costing Britain too much and should be reduced. Haig told the king doing so "would be unwise, because in order to shorten the war and reap the fruits of any success, we must make use of the mobility of the Cavalry."

Two weeks later Haig was back in France. Joffre came to see him to fix a final date for the beginning of the offensive. Haig was annoyed—Joffre now wanted the attack to start on July 1. Haig had made great efforts to meet Joffre's demands for an earlier offensive and had set a date of June 25. If they delayed past that point, he feared, the Germans might notice their lines were thin and attack elsewhere. They finally agreed on June 29, with Rawlinson and Foch having agency to delay it due to weather.

Haig had twenty-six divisions. The French had fourteen. The tanks weren't yet ready, but he had cavalry units in reserve to exploit successes. An intelligence report he'd received on June 16 said the Germans had thirty-two battalions, with sixty-five more that could be used as rein-forcements. (Among those was the Sixteenth Bavarian Reserve Infantry

Regiment, stationed at Fromelles; its runner was a strange young Austrian named Adolf Hitler.)

Haig would have nearly 1,800 guns to prepare the attack. The Fourth Army alone had about 1,500 guns along its fourteen-mile front and three million shells. It planned to fire about two hundred thousand each day preceding the attack. The shells weren't ideal—most of them were ill suited to destroying defenses or cutting wire, but the theory was that firing so much poundage at the enemy lines would accomplish those goals anyway.

On June 15 a set of meticulously prepared secret orders were issued. "In conjunction with the rest of the Fourth Army an attack on the German positions is to be made by III Corps," they began. The plans for infantrymen were simple, general headquarters being loath to burden an army made up of recent recruits with too much to think about.

Maj. Gen. Edward Ingouville-Williams commanded the Thirty-Fourth Division, which was made up of three brigades, which were in turn made up of battalions. Four battalions of the "Tyneside Irish"—men of Irish extraction from the Newcastle area—made up the 103rd Brigade, commanded by Brig. Gen. N. J. G. Cameron. The 102nd Brigade comprised four battalions of "Tyneside Scottish" and was commanded by Brig. Gen. Trevor Ternan. And then there was the 101st Brigade, which included the Tenth Battalion, Lincolnshire Regiment (the Grimsby Chums); the Eleventh Battalion, Suffolk Regiment; and the Fifteenth and Sixteenth battalions of the Royal Scots. Its commander was Brigadier-General Robert Gore.

The Thirty-Fourth Division's orders were to capture everything up to the eastern outskirts of Contalmaison. On the right of La Boisselle, the Grimsby Chums and the Fifteenth Royal Scots would take the first reserve line. The Eleventh Suffolks and McCrae's would take the intermediate line. A party of four eight-man bombing squads led by lieutenants Rotherford and Connolly of the Tyneside battalions would take La Boisselle at about the same time. After their success, the 103rd Division would push through Contalmaison and occupy a line that would put the army in position for the next assault on Pozières.

The British had grand plans for the especially fortified parts of the line the Thirty-Fourth Division would assault. Two large underground mines would knock out the enemy trenches and machine guns on either side of La Boisselle. The first, known as the "Y-Sap" mine, would destroy a machine gun nest on the north side of the village, across Mash Valley. The second, known as Lochnagar, would destroy Schwabenhöhe. It was a monster.

Lochnagar was named for the trench it started from. The Royal Engineers' 185th Tunnelling Company began it in late 1915, plunging a diagonal shaft ninety-five feet under no-man's-land. The 179th Tunnelling Company took over the project in March 1916. About fifty feet down that first shaft, they began driving a straight gallery about five hundred feet in front of the British line. About one hundred feet from the German trenches, it branched into a Y with a large chamber at the end of each tine. It was meant to destroy the front-line trench, take out the machine guns on the Schwabenhöhe, and kill troops who had been driven underground by the artillery bombardment.

It was slow work, conducted silently by miners who'd learned their crafts carving tunnels in cities and in mines all over Britain. For the Y branch and the last thirty-four feet of gallery leading up to the split, they used bayonets to pry out the fractured chalk, and when they made good progress in a day they'd move forward eighteen inches. They worked in series, their boots off and standing on a carpet of sandbags, the man in front loosening the friable stone, a man underneath catching the spoil and passing it back through a line of men who put it in sandbags and handed it back till they got to the tunnel's entrance.

At times, using naked ears, geophones, or even biscuit tins filled with water, they could hear the Germans working on a defensive mine system below them. The miners knew that if they were detected the enemy would fire a torpedo called a camouflet through the walls, sending them to a lonely death far below no-man's-land.

Had Haig been able to wait until August, the Lochnagar miners might have gotten all the way to the German lines. But they ran out of time to make the chambers big enough for the huge amount of explosives they believed was required for the job. So they stuffed as much as they could into the chambers and packed the overflow into the galleries leading up to them. They used ammonal, a cheap explosive that was more powerful and readily available than black powder—thirty-six thousand pounds of it in the right chamber, twenty-four thousand pounds in the left. Outside the junction of the Y, they tamped it solid for 350 feet.

On the other side of La Boisselle, time was running out in another way. Right before they finished digging, the Y-Sap miners heard Germans "sinking down on top of us," a later company report recorded. The Germans, it seemed, had some idea what was going on under the earth.

On the date of the big push, the mines were to blow two minutes before zero hour. They'd knock out the machine guns, destroy the Germans' underground system and trenches, kill any troops nearby, and form a defensible "lip" around the resulting crater.

Heligoland wouldn't be destroyed by a mine, so the 101st Division would strafe it with two Stokes mortars, a simple but effective weapon that was basically a tube attached to a plate, with legs at its front. Its operator would aim it and drop in a bomb with a propellant in the back that would explode when it hit the plate, sending it hurtling toward the target. Lt. Leslie Kitton of the Sixteenth Royal Scots had trained in using the Stokes. He and a small detachment would take up a newly dug position outside Heligoland the night before the attack by Lieutenant Parkinson and the "Pioneer" troops of the Eighteenth Northumberland Fusiliers, another Tyneside battalion. Kitton's rockets would hammer any Germans who managed to free themselves from the bombed dugouts and try to grab hold of machine guns.

Artillery would pound the German lines for five days before the assault, destroying their trenches and cutting their defensive wire with shrapnel. There would be no shell shortage this time: the artillery received 1.5 million shells, more than ever before.

At the moment of infantry attack, the heavy artillery would lift to further objectives while the field artillery would "gradually rake back to the next line" at a speed to be "calculated so that the shrapnel barrage moves back faster than the infantry can advance."[4]

Troops were to move purposefully, "to make direct over ground for the objective allotted, irrespective of the progress made by the troops on their flanks." They would move in waves.

Since the attack was taking place in summer, they wouldn't take their heavy greatcoats or large packs—those would be left behind at the Hospice Albert. They'd take their rifles, of course, and Thirty-Fourth Division orders called for every infantryman to carry two bandoliers with 220 rounds of small arms ammunition, two Mills grenades, rations to last him all day and an iron ration in case he got stuck without food later, a waterproof cape, two smoke helmets, and goggles. They'd each have a pick or a shovel stuck behind their haversacks, and men of all ranks were to wear a large bright-yellow triangle made of cloth, with sixteen-inch sides, over the small haversacks on their backs so observers could track their progress. Wire cutters were to be given to as many men as possible.

Hand grenades were in short supply. "They must not be thrown indiscriminately," the orders read. Advancing troops were to collect tools and ammunition from any wounded comrades and carry them forward; under no circumstances were they to leave the assault to assist the wounded. Carrying parties in the rear would help them as soon as possible.

The entire load came in at about sixty-six pounds, significant and uncomfortable, but still less than the weight many soldiers carry today. Fortunately, they weren't expected to run but to walk in waves toward the devastated German lines and the trashed wire that once protected them.

The day the orders were issued, the 101st Brigade moved back into the front line. Brigadier General Ternan of the 102nd Brigade moved his headquarters to Villa Rochers, a "palatial billet" that had "somehow escaped notice," a Thirty-Fourth Division history notes with admiration.[5] Ternan's men, and those of the 103rd Brigade were stuck doing the backbreaking work necessary to prepare for a big assault— digging assembly trenches, stocking "dumps" with equipment, water, ammunition, and everything else one might need to successfully break through enemy lines.

By June 24 the dumps were complete, as were a series of deep dugouts on the far side of the Usna and Tara hills. Each dugout was about twenty feet deep and connected by underground passages. Supplies moved up to the front by rail and cart, but men were usually the last mile of track, carrying matériel to collection points slowly through crowded trenches.

The Thirty-Fourth Division command left Albert on June 24, anticipating retaliation from German artillery once the attack began. Some comedian put a sign up in Albert saying "To Bapaume." Headquarters issued large-scale maps to battalion commanders showing the German trenches, but not before letting them agree on new names for the trenches they'd soon be taking over. A member of the 101st Brigade named one strong point behind the line Scots Redoubt after his homeland.

At dawn on June 24, troops in the German 119th Reserve Infantry Regiment were preparing to switch over to daytime duties. It looked like a pleasant day. The skies were blue as the sun began to edge over the horizon. The troops all had their morning coffee, and sentries who'd been on duty all night keeping an eye on the sector between the village of Beaumont Hamel and the river Ancre were preparing to lie down for a well-deserved rest.

And then the skies began to rain metal. At 5:00 AM, "a storm of artillery broke with a crash along the entire line," Landwehr Leutnant M. Gerster of RIR 119 remembered. "As far as the eye could see clouds of shrapnel filled the sky, like dust blown on the wind."

There was no respite all morning. "All around there was howling, snarling and hissing," Gerster remembered. He continued:

> With a sharp ringing sound, the death-dealing shells burst, spewing their leaden fragments against our line. The balls fell like hail on the roofs of the half-destroyed villages, whistled through the branches of the still-green trees and beat down hard on the parched ground, whipping up small clouds of smoke and dust from the earth. Large calibre shells droned through the air like giant bumblebees, crashing, smashing and boring down into the earth.

All along the line, troops took refuge in their reinforced dugouts. "Nobody could take a step along the trenches," Gerster remembered. "All work, all movement became impossible."[6]

The air filled with dust kicked up by heavy shells crashing into the trenches and the ruined villages, where the Germans had also reinforced basements and other hiding places. Rain that afternoon grounded the dust as loose mud, making it especially difficult for troops behind the lines to send food or supplies to those who were pinned down. When they tried, British aviators spotted them and called for renewed bombardment. The efforts had to be abandoned.

The bombardment went on for days. The Germans called it *Trommelfeuer*, or "drumfire," because the explosions sounded like someone beating the heck out of a snare. "Shells were rushing through the air like droves of giant birds with beating wings and with strange wailings," Gibbs wrote. "The German lines were in eruption. Their earthworks were being tossed up, and fountains of earth sprang up between columns of smoke, black columns and white, which stood rigid for a few seconds and then sank into the banks of fog. Flames gushed up red and angry, rending those banks of mist with strokes of lightning. In their light I saw trees falling, branches tossed like twigs, black things hurtling through space."[7]

The sound was appalling. "The guns thundered and roared endlessly. All day long it went on, with only brief pauses," Reserve Leutnant Wilhelm Geiger of the 111th Reserve Infantry Regiment remembered.[8] Troops in dugouts had little to do but watch their effects swing on hooks, as long as the light from their tallow lights hadn't been put out by the pressure, as explosions shook the earth around them. With fresh food scarce, many subsisted on "iron rations"—biscuits, preserved meat or bacon, preserved vegetables, and coffee.

They all knew the bombardment was a prelude to an attack. They just weren't sure when it would come. Intelligence from several captured British soldiers and one deserter suggested the attack would begin on June 29. The unshaven and hungry troops, furious after the bombardment, ached to fight. They were exhausted from the high state of alert at all times. "All longed for an end to it one way or the other," Gerster recalled. "All were seized by a deep bitterness at the inhuman machine of destruction which hammered endlessly. A searing rage against the enemy burned in their minds."[9]

Mist and rain delayed the original British attack, pushing it from June 29 to July 1. Two more days of bombing were tacked on to the original five-day plan.

The front-line trenches were smashed, with bits of wood, metal, and smashed ordnance everywhere. Stairways down the dugouts were half-buried with dust. "There was just one single heart-felt prayer on our lips: 'Oh God, free us from this ordeal; give us release through battle, grant us victory; Lord God! Just let them come!' and this determination increased with the fall of each shell," remembered Unteroffizier Friedrich Hinkel of the Ninety-Ninth Reserve Infantry Regiment's Seventh Company. "You made a good job of it, you British! Seven days and nights you rapped and hammered on our door! Now your reception was going to match your turbulent longing to enter!"[10]

Notices posted in German dugouts from 1915 instructed soldiers to "race to the parapet when the enemy attacks." The Germans were stretched, tired, hungry, and angry. But if they could get to their positions before the British made it across no-man's-land, they believed they could hold their lines. They would not greet them with carols this time.

9

OVER THE TOP

Late on the night of June 29, 2nd Lt. Thomas Millar of McCrae's led a party including another officer, two sergeants, and fifty other ranks from his battalion quietly across no-man's-land to see how well the artillery had cut the wire protecting German trenches. The ground was wet after the heavy rains that had delayed the big attack, and men in some of the British trenches were knee-deep in mud and water. It was imperative that they knew more about the ground they'd be crossing en masse when the whistles blew.

Millar and his men blackened their faces with burned cork and left behind all identifying information—identity discs, badges, pay books—in case of capture. At first it was a caper. They crept silently across the field toward the white chalk scars of the German lines. But what they discovered on the other side was terrifying: three-foot long crossed iron stakes bound with thick wire, followed by a second, heavier row of "knife rests"—sturdy rectangular frames wrapped with more wire—and yet another row of wire beyond them. The shells had done little to destroy the barriers. Soldiers would never get through these obstacles en masse.

The party began cutting the wire to examine how tough it was, but then they heard a terrifying sound: the pop and fizz of Very lights, red and white pistol-fired flares. Weren't the German sentries supposed to be underground? The night sky lit up around them, freezing them like burglars in front of a safe. The sounds that followed were a hierarchy of increasing awfulness: steps, shouts, clicks, then the rapid hammering of metal on metal as a machine gun opened up.

Millar's men began to fall into the wire. He shouted for the party to withdraw. Four men's bodies dangled on the wire as the light from the flares faded, denied even the dignity of falling to the ground. Three others were wounded; they carried away one man who'd been shot through both legs. They scurried back to their wet trenches as the Germans shot into darkness behind them.

In a report afterward Millar wrote that the wire "showed very little signs of shelling and was not destroyed to any considerable degree whatever. It formed a very effective obstacle."[1]

British troops sleep in trenches near Contalmaison in 1916. Sleep was one of the few respites in trench life, which was hard and dull and often interrupted by unimaginable terror. Troops would dig dugouts and cubbyholes, stack sandbags on the sides, and cover them with whatever they had lying around.

Photograph by Lt. John Warwick Brooke, Collection of the Imperial War Museum

Closer to La Boisselle, the Tyneside Scots had led concurrent raiding parties that also showed the German lines to be "much stronger and more difficult to get through than had been anticipated," as a report said. They, too, found themselves lit up by Very lights and under rifle and grenade fire, and though they reported the wire in the sector they examined was passable, they said the German trench was firmly held.

Both reports contradicted official optimism about the coming assault. Neither occasioned any change in plans.

Unfettered optimism blared from Haig's diary entry for June 30. "With God's help, I feel hopeful," he wrote. "The men are in splendid spirits." He continued:

> Several have said that they have never before been so instructed and informed of the nature of the operation before them. The wire has never been so well cut, nor the Artillery preparation so thorough. I have seen personally all the Corps Commanders and one and all are full of confidence.

In the forward trenches, the front-line troops dozed on the fire steps and in dugouts if they were lucky; activity was all around them as the army made final preparations for the morning's assault. The ground had finally dried from the previous days' heavy rains. The heavy artillery continued its percussive assault, though at a more relaxed tempo than in daylight. "Pioneer" troops from the Eighteenth Northumberland Fusiliers dug ditches forward into no-man's-land, creating narrow, shallower "jumping out" positions. They dug another tunnel a few hundred yards out, creating a position from which Kitton could fire his Stokes mortars at Heligoland. If the Germans heard any of this activity they didn't react.

Most likely, there was no reason for them to waste their time firing on a few men with shovels. The Germans had tunnels under no-man's-land, as well as "Moritz" listening devices, which used copper plates buried in the ground to pick up vibrations from British field telephones. Late at night on June 30, a Moritz intercepted a message from headquarters wishing the troops luck the next day; the intelligence was dutifully conveyed to headquarters and relayed to frontline regiments.

They already had warnings that had traveled over ground. On June 23 Pvt. Victor Wheat of the Fifth Battalion North Staffordshire Regiment, which was due to attack north of McRae's at Gommecourt, was wounded and captured while part of a wire party; under interrogation gave up the aims of the attack, although with the wrong start date. Other prisoners and a deserter named Pvt. Josef Lipmann of the Second Battalion Royal Fusiliers gave similar information.

The Germans didn't know exactly when the attack would begin, but they did know that the British wouldn't send their men running into an artillery barrage. Their best, most actionable intelligence about the attack would be the moment the shells stopped pounding their front lines.

———————

McCrae's battalion spent the night of June 30 in Bécourt Wood, a small woodland about half a mile behind the front line. The copse surrounded a château where, at 2:00 AM, the battalion's officers met to go over arrangements for the attack, which was scheduled to begin five and a half hours later.

At 2:30 the battalion's cooks served breakfast to the men. Most men in the British lines got tea and biscuits early on July 1, 1916, but thanks to some creative acquisition in Albert, McCrae's men got bacon and eggs. Few slept that night. Men who hadn't done so already filled out the wills in their army pay books. Harry Wattie had already left everything to his mother, the historian Jack Alexander writes, while Duncan Currie, perhaps flush with the invincibility of youth, neglected to make any such arrangements.

Back home it was shaping up to be a normal Saturday. The *Edinburgh Evening News* was preoccupied with the treason conviction the day before of the Irish separatist Sir Roger Casement, charged with attempting to obtain German aid for a rebellion against British rule. Naval recruiting was going well in Edinburgh after the Battle of Jutland at the beginning of June, and the police courts were unusually quiet thanks to the war. Arrests for drunkenness, disorderly conduct, and theft were all down considerably over the year before. Nevertheless, the city still held scoundrels. A soldier who worked as an officer's servant at the Drummond Place billets appeared in the courts, charged with scamming a laundress into endorsing a check from a dead soldier that he was then accused of cashing.

In football the sorry state of most Scottish clubs' finances stood in stark contrast to those of Celtic and Rangers, which announced they would pay nice dividends to shareholders—20 percent and 10 percent, respectively. Hearts weren't in any such position. The club's revenue had plummeted for want of men to play and watch football, but expenses had fallen as well, and it ended the previous season with a profit of £212. Compared with the finances of the Glasgow clubs, the *Evening News* wrote, Hearts' balance sheet was "a most instructive document."

There was boxing news from New York, where on Thursday Jack Dillon had battered Frank Moran at the Brooklyn Dodgers' former home field of Washington Park in Park Slope. All Edinburgh's theaters and cinemas had a busy weekend planned. The Princes Cinema planned multiple showings the next week of *An American's Home*, a dark prediction of a United States invaded by enemies after pacifists stopped it from preparing from war.

The *Evening News* also carried a report from Sir Douglas Haig on June 30. Amid heavy bombardment of the German positions, the British had sent raiding parties across no-man's-land, all of which were successful, "inflicting heavy casualties on the Germans" as well as capturing prisoners and matériel. In addition to the bombardment, Haig wrote, British discharge of smoke and gas had forced the Germans to disclose the locations of their batteries.

The Grimsby Chums had spent the last couple days in the front line, having relieved the Fifteenth Royal Scots on June 28. Private William Rowse wasn't with his battalion-mates—he was on orderly duty, making trips to the great cookers behind the lines to fetch meals and bring them to the lads up front. Then he'd take the empty containers back to the water tanks next to the artillery emplacements, where they'd be washed out and made ready for the next meal.

Rowse had had close shaves already—on the Chums' first days on the line near Bois-Grenier, he spent nights in a working party that dug and repaired trenches. They were digging a new communication trench in an apple orchard, and Rowse rested his rifle against a tree while he worked. Suddenly the rifle fell flat; when Rowse went to pick it up he saw an enemy bullet had hit the woodwork on his rifle, ruining it.

But that day as he humped empty containers to the water tanks, a large gun nearby overheated and blew up with a shell in its cannon tube. Rowse was injured and removed to a hospital. It seemed like bad luck at the time.

Across no-man's-land, a German machine gunner named Christian Fischer stood at the entrance to his dugout at 4:30 AM on July 1, waiting for the shellfire to lift so he could kill the men who'd forced them underground for days. The soldiers "waited anxiously for the enemy attack," he remembered. "We wanted to get back at the Englishmen."[2]

Half an hour later McCrae's men left Bécourt Wood for their assembly positions. In C Company, most of the Hearts lads were with one another—Wattie and Paddy Crossan were with Jimmy Hazeldean, whom McCartney had signed from Portobello Thistle Juniors two months after Paddy and the others had left town for training. He played only five games before following them into McCrae's. Currie, Ernie Ellis, and Alfie Briggs were nearby. Annan Ness was at headquarters with McCrae, as was Jimmy Boyd, who had been deputized as a runner during the battle. Boyd was a former "Cow Puncher" from Mossend who had signed with Hearts a few months before the Usher Hall meeting and, unlike his brother Archie, never had enough time in the club's system to make the first team.

The battalion marched through communications trenches with names that sounded like home—Dundee Avenue, Carnoustie Street, Monymusk, Arbroath, Bonnymuir. All were stuffed with men making last-minute preparations for the assault. Their neighboring battalions in the assault were making their ways up, too. The Eleventh Suffolks were having trouble getting into their jumping-off trenches in Dundee Avenue, a trench called New Cut B, and Monikie Street. The right of the 102nd Brigade, occupied by the Tyneside Scottish, had pushed too far down into the crowded ditch.

They pushed forward, past the first-aid posts set up at various junctions—Arbroath and Monymusk streets, Mercer and Monifieth, Kirkcaldy and Methuen. Those would treat minor wounds. The severely wounded would be moved to advanced stations at Bécourt Château and elsewhere; from those points motorized ambulances would take more serious cases back to field hospitals. In addition to the troops moving up, the trenches were throbbing with men carrying stores and ammunition forward; behind them they could hear carts, vehicles, and railway cars banging and crunching the ground as they moved supplies into position.

McCrae's Battalion and the Fifteenth Royal Scots would leave from a kink in the line, an almost M-shaped salient, or maybe a cresting wave, when viewed from above. A Company would go first, led by Capt. Peter Ross. C, led by Capt. Lionel Coles, would go next, followed by D, led by Capt. Andrew Whyte. B Company, led by Capt. Napier "Nap" Armit would follow the other groups, carrying spare equipment and stretchers.

At 6:16 AM the Sixteenth Royal Scots reported they were in position. The sun was pushing away the night's cloak that had sheltered them as they moved forward, and the larks were singing. There was nothing to do now but wait. Coles moved up and down the line, shaking hands with the men.[3] He'd taken off his officer's tunic and would be almost indistinguishable from the men as they went over—a wise precaution that might deprive a German gunner from a desirable target. Many of the men smoked cigarettes. Coles smoked a pipe. The temperatures were warming up. The weather report called for a hot day.

A view of Contalmaison in 1916, painted by J. B. Morrall. Most of the village, including Contalmaison Chateau, had been destroyed by artillery fire, and only part of the church remained.

Collection of the Imperial War Museum

British pilots noticed early on during the war that any summer day that looks perfect on the ground at the Somme looks very different from the air. On the morning of July 1, 1916, a haze covered the rolling fields north of the river Somme, and you could only see it from above. It looked like "a second horizon, veiling the earthy one beneath," Lt. Cecil Lewis of the Royal Flying Corps' Third Squadron wrote after the war.[4]

Inside that second horizon, Sir George McCrae was upset. Brigadier General Gore had ordered the commanders of each battalion to stay put when their men advanced. McCrae had promised during recruiting meetings back in Edinburgh that he would put no one into danger that he wouldn't face himself, and he was gutted to watch his men walk ahead of him to their assembly points. But Gore's order would later prove vital to preserving the brigade's command structure.

There were already enough things Gore didn't like about the plan for that day's assault. The curve of the front lines put the Fifteenth Royal Scots ahead of the Grimsby Chums, who would leave to their left. The orders even called for the Fifteenth Battalion to leave a minute or so early, so they'd be two hundred yards from the German front line at zero hour. If the great artillery bombardment hadn't taken out the guns of La Boisselle or Sausage Redoubt, the Chums would be walking into a massacre.

Some of the troops at the front were able to look at the field that awaited them. In the trenches in front of La Boisselle, men looking through periscopes could see the German barbed wire was not cut. The terrain between the lines was particularly bad—the ground looked like hardened oatmeal, with tall grass growing wild amid the shell holes of various sizes and depths that arrayed down the hill into Sausage Valley.

Across the valley, past a complex web of German trenches and up a sunken road was what was left of Contalmaison. Behind the wire, they could see the piles of white chalk outlining the German trenches, as well as the blackened and chopped skeletons of trees. The trunks stood in neat rows, planted the French way.

Lewis looked down on them from his bizarre-looking Morane-Saulnier "parasol." The French-made machine had but one daring wing above the pilot's head stabilized by a great mast with wires that fanned out from it like children dancing around a maypole. A pilot couldn't see much above him, but the lack of a bottom wing made the Parasol ideal for observation. Lewis's orders on July 1 were to fly a two-and-a-half-hour shift over the battlefield, steering clear of La Boisselle just before zero hour.

Through the haze, Lewis could see the devastation already wrought by the seven-day bombing. "Square miles of country were ripped and blasted to a pock-marked desolation," he wrote two decades later.[5]

At 6:25 AM the British artillery began throwing everything it had at the German line. "Even in the air, at four thousand feet, above the roar of the engine, the drumming of firing and bursting shells throbbed in our ears," Lewis recalled.

Inside the dugouts, the German soldiers endured the same waves of pressure. They made the flames of their candles dance.

At 7:05 the heavy ammunition lifted, moving to targets farther away. Now only the lighter field artillery kept its fire on the German trenches. Gerster, Fischer, and the thousands of German troops who'd been held prisoner by the shells of June wouldn't have to wait much longer to get revenge. Some made it out of the dugouts and took up positions at machine guns.

The Scots wanted to advance with bagpipers in front of them. The legend of the piper had been a part of Scottish military history for hundreds of years. As a rule, those legends occasioned mixed results for the individual musicians, who gained the greatest fame for playing as they lay dying.

George Findlater of the Gordon Highlanders was celebrated for playing after being shot in the 1897 battle of Dargai Heights. Daniel Laidlaw of the Seventh Battalion, King's Own Scottish Borderers, was awarded the Victoria Cross for piping his unit over the top at Hill 70 at the Battle of Loos with "Blue Bonnets over the Border."

Of the two hundred or so pipers at Loos, some fifty were killed or wounded. Laidlaw lived and became an iconic figure of Scots' bravery in the face of unbearable odds. The image resonated with the enemy as well; one German military medal depicted a skeleton playing bagpipes as a harbinger of death.

The Tyneside Scots and Tyneside Irish all planned to advance with pipers at the front. The Fifteenth Royal Scots would be piped over the top by David Anderson, a twenty-six-year-old Edinburgh police officer. "I did not like to think of the boys going into action without the pipes," he said later. Willie Duguid was the Sixteenth's piper, and he petitioned Sir George for the right to perform the same function for his battalion. Sir George, perhaps not as mesmerized by legends as other commanders, refused.[6] Pipers served a more important function in the war: they often led the stretcher brigades that would carry wounded men back to the lines.

Up and down the lines the calls came. "Twenty minutes to go!" "Ten minutes to go!" "Five minutes to go!"

Almost two miles south, twenty-one-year-old Capt. Wilfred Nevill prepared two footballs for his men in the Eighth East Surreys to follow across no-man's-land toward Montauban. On one he'd written "The Great European Cup-Tie Final. East Surreys V Bavarians, Kick Off at Zero!"[7] He planned to kick them over and have his men follow the ball across no-man's-land, toeing it forward as they advanced.

The din from the hurricane bombardment was astounding. It would probably be impossible for anyone to hear bagpipes over it. Back in the jumping-off trenches, men were packed so close they had to ask one another for help if they needed anything from their haversacks. Some men prayed. Others wiped their brows as the rising temperatures heated the helmets Tommies jokingly called "tin hats."

The order came to fix bayonets. Ordinarily, this action made a metallic clink so loud that troops put their tunics around the knives to deaden it; there was no need to do so now.

McCrae's men had three rushes ahead of them: a little more than a thousand feet to the first trench, then another 4,600 to Peake Wood, then the last half mile into Contalmaison. All in all a little more than a mile and a half—about a quarter of the distance the Hearts lads would cover during ninety minutes on a typical Saturday at Tynecastle.

"Three minutes to go!"

The Grimsby Chums were arranged in a front of three companies to the left of the Fifteenth Royal Scots. C Company was on the far left, B in the center, and A right next to the Edinburgh troops. Their objective was the Bloater trench between La Boisselle and Heligoland. The

Fifteenth were to go to the right side of Heligoland, toward a trench named Kipper. They were to jump out a little early before the Chums, who didn't know why they were being held back. At two minutes before zero hour, they got their answer about a hundred yards in front of them.

At 7:28 AM a coal-mine manager from Kilmarnock named James Young took hold of the T-shaped plunger in the wooden box connected to wires in the Lochnagar tunnel and pressed it down. The action turned a small generator inside the box that sent a high-voltage charge through the wire connected to it by two metal terminals. The charge triggered twelve detonators along the line, each with a guncotton primer attached. The thirty tons of ammonal packed in the Lochnagar tunnel exploded.

The noise could be heard in London.

Eight thousand feet above them, Lewis watched the explosions of Lochnagar and Y-Sap from over Thiepval. He described it:

> At Boisselle the earth heaved and flashed, a tremendous and magnificent column rose up into the sky. There was an ear-splitting roar, drowning all the guns, flinging the machine sideways in the repercussing air. The earthy column rose, higher and higher to almost four thousand feet. There it hung, or seemed to hang, for a moment in the air, like the silhouette of some great cypress tree, then fell away in a widening cone of dust and debris. A moment later came the second mine. Again the roar, the upflung machine, the strange gaunt silhouette invading the sky. Then the dust cleared and we saw the two white eyes of the craters.[8]

In the Grimsby Chums' lines, soldiers described hearing a "terrific roar." Stones, dirt, and chalk showered the McCrae's men. Across no-man's-land the explosion ravaged Schwabenhöhe, where most of the 110th Reserve Infantry Regiment's Fifth Division simply ceased to exist. As the smoke cleared and dirt completed its round trip through the sky above La Boisselle, the Chums could see a crater ninety yards across and twenty-three yards deep. As the engineers had hoped, the explosion created a fifteen-foot-high "lip" at the crater's edge, which the Chums were meant to hold after they cleared their first objective. What they couldn't see was whether the crater had swallowed all of Schwabenhöhe; what they couldn't know is whether the explosions had knocked out the machine guns on its flank.

The Royal Engineers had foreseen the difficulty the Chums might have with machine gun fire. Just after the mine explosion, 2nd Lt. Otto Behrendt, the son of a Prussian immigrant to Lincolnshire, instructed his men along the Pitlochrie Street trench to throw four "P bombs," canisters that emitted a thick cloud of smoke. The wind was blowing faintly, and Behrendt was wary of creating a cloud so thick that the attacking troops wouldn't be able to see through it.

Almost immediately German machine gunfire began to hit the edges of the trench where Behrendt, his men, and twelve members of the Eighteenth Northumberland Fusiliers who'd carried the smoke bombs into position sheltered. High-explosive and shrapnel shells from German artillery positions farther back followed. The cloud drifted left as Behrendt hoped, but the enemy's prompt defense was, to say the least, not a good sign.

At 7:30 AM the artillery lifted, and whistles blew in trenches from Serre to Montauban. The Fifteenth Royal Scots' first two waves were already across the first German trench. Its second two divisions climbed ladders that had been fixed at the top and bottom by planks to prevent them from falling, with four-inch pegs hammered into the parapet to help them hoist themselves "over the top" and into no-man's-land. David Anderson jumped in front of them and began playing "Dumbarton's Drums," the quick march of the Royal Scots. They began to stride forward purposely. To their left, the Grimsby Chums were hoisting themselves up and debouching through holes in the wire cut the night before, trying to keep their eyes forward and not gawk at the smoldering gigantic crater next to them, with its billowing smoke cloud moving lazily toward La Boisselle.

Across no-man's-land, the Germans, too, clambered out of their dugouts. Some of the staircases had been buried by shell explosions, so soldiers had to scrabble blinking up a slope into the intense morning sunshine. They found their front lines almost ruined, Landwehr Leutnant M. Gerster remembered. "The actual front line trench no longer existed, instead crater overlapped crater where it had once been," he wrote. Everywhere they looked they saw the shell's grim signatures: "Where earlier protected sentry positions and shell proof observation posts had stood, rubble heaps, railway lines and concrete blocks were all that was left. How little human hands could do against the work of the machinery of destruction!"[9]

But the Germans had one advantage over the British troops bearing down on them. They had a shorter distance to go. They raced to the parapets and the unmolested machine gun positions, setting up more machine guns on the chalky ridges at the front of what was left of their front line trenches. The gunners loaded and sighted their weapons. In many places, the British were well within view as they crossed the valley below.

The sun was in British soldiers' eyes as they approached their first objective. In front of them, chalk from the Lochnagar explosion had given no-man's-land a coating of chalk dust that looked almost like snow. Smoke and dust and summer mist filled the air at first. Then the sickening, clattering sound of machine guns joined them. Ahead of the British soldiers in many places was wire uncut by shells.

Pipers led troops on both sides of La Boisselle. The Tyneside Scottish had recruited an astonishing twenty pipers when they'd formed in Newcastle, England, signing up displaced Scots and men of Scots descent with the motto "Harder Than Hammers" and leaflets evoking "the pipes a calling." Pipe Major John Wilson led the Twentieth Battalion's charge across Mash Valley, "playing as though he would burst the bag," an observer later wrote. "How he escaped death I can't understand for the ground was literally ploughed up by the hail of bullets," he continued. "But he seemed to bear a charmed life and the last glimpse I had of him, as we too dashed out, showed him still marching erect, playing furiously, and quite regardless of the flying bullets and the men dropping all around him."[10]

Wilson's battalion mate and uncle Garnet "Aggy" Fyfe was not as lucky: "He was riddled with bullets, writhing and screaming," Private J. Elliot of the Twentieth remembered. "Another lad was just kneeling, his head thrown right back. Bullets were just slapping into him knocking great bloody chunks off his body."[11]

To their right, the Twenty-First Battalion jumped out of the trenches with their pipers skirling. "It was like all hell let loose," piper George Griffiths remembered.[12] He got caught on barbed wire and had to drop his pipes and take up a rifle. When he got to the German trenches, he jumped down and saw his fellow piper Willie Scott lying dead inside. He was still holding his pipes.

David Anderson marched across the first and second German lines. Between the third and fourth lines he was hit on his right side. He sat down and found he could no longer play. "I remember that when I found I could not blow the pipes any longer I waved them above my head and shouted to the boys to 'Come on,'" he said later.[13]

The more legendary accounts of Anderson's march across no-man's-land came from his fellow soldiers, who said he threw down his pipes, grabbed a German rifle, and began fighting. Others said he was sitting on the edge of a German trench piping "as if going on Church parade to St. Giles.'" Another has the Germans surrendering to him, terrified of his bagpipes.[14]

What's for certain is that he lost his pipes on the battlefield, which years later he said was his only regret about July 1. "They were grand pipes."[15]

The machine guns started rattling almost the moment the second waves of the Fifteenth Royal Scots and the first waves of the Grimsby Chums left their trenches. The Germans at La Boisselle and Heligoland sprayed them with "the most intense Enfilade machine gun fire," the Chums' war diary reads. Some survivors swore the enemy aimed at their knees—in order to hit them again as they fell.

The diary tells the story quickly: "Advancing with the utmost steadiness & courage, not to be surpassed by any troops in the world, yet the distance they were away from the German Trench (800 yards) & the intensity of the machine gun fire did not allow of the possibility of reaching & penetrating the enemy's line."[16]

Five minutes later, the Eleventh Suffolks were due to enter the same meat grinder behind the Chums. To their right would be the Sixteenth Royal Scots.

At 7:35, the whistles blew for McCrae's men. Pvt. Harry Downie of A Company was one of the first over. Downie, a Gorgie lad, was a boxer like his father, also named Harry Downie. Young Harry was killed almost immediately; one bullet struck a metal mirror in his left breast pocket, leaving an indentation on the fourteen photographs he carried there. The top one was a picture of him with his mother.[17]

Machine guns fired from the Bloater trench in front of the Suffolks. "Silently our machine guns and the infantrymen waited until our opponents came closer," Oberleutnant Kienitz of the 110th Reserve Infantry Regiment's machine-gun company remembered. "Then, when they were only a few metres from the trenches, the serried ranks of the enemy were sprayed with a hurricane of defensive fire from the machine guns and the aimed fire of the individual riflemen."[18]

C Company followed A. Coles walked his men down the hill smoking a pipe. "Ye dirty bastards," one man shouted. "I'm comin' for ye!"[19]

The Suffolks absorbed the same enfilade fire that devastated the Grimsby Chums. "In spite of the fact that wave after wave were mown down by machine gun fire, all pushed on without hesitation though very few reached the German lines," their war diary reads. A battalion historian wrote that "men were spun round and dropping everywhere."[20]

"As effective units," a Thirty-Fourth Division history reads, "those two battalions had ceased to exist by eight a.m."[21] There were at least 30 machine guns trained on them.

North of La Boisselle, the Twenty-First Tyneside Scottish was taking similarly intense fire. Pvt. Thomas Easton remembered seeing British dead hanging on the supposedly cut wire, where "their bodies formed a bridge for others to pass over and into the German front line."[22]

The Hearts lads and most of C Company made it across no-man's-land and across Kipper trench. The second trench was protected by two layers of wire; a trench called Wood Alley led perpendicularly off it toward Scots Redoubt. At the entrance to the trench, Raith Rovers' Jimmy Scott was shot in the stomach and Alfie Briggs was shot in five places.[23]

Not long afterward, Peter Ross, the only officer standing in A Company, rushed a machine gun and was shot in the neck and stomach. Ross was a brilliant mathematician and knew his odds—in unimaginable pain, he begged, then ordered two of his men to kill him.[24] B Company had by this point gone over the top, and Captain Armit was able to establish a command in front of the Wood Alley entrance.

Coles and C Company pushed on. Some members of the Fifteenth Royal Scots were up by Round Wood, trying to join with members of the Twenty-First Division, which had attacked to their right. At 8:45 AM Coles sent a note to battalion headquarters saying he'd made it all the way to Peake Wood, within sight of Contalmaison. The note said his units were weakened, but that they were reorganizing. In fact, C Company had picked up men from a number of battalions, forced by machine-gun fire to the right of their planned attack. Coles was undaunted. He made plans to attack the village.

Some relatively organized parties of the Grimsby Chums still existed at 9:00 AM. Second Lt. John Turnbull led one of them, and at that hour found himself on the left side of the Lochnagar crater. "Very puzzled with the rotten crater, which was in the wrong place," he remembered.[25] The crater "was still hot as an oven after just being blown up," his fellow officer A. Dickinson recalled decades later.[26] German machine guns from La Boisselle were tearing up the lip of the crater, where members of the battalion sheltered; men who got hit rolled down into its smoldering maw.

Turnbull moved along the lip, trying to find a route to La Boisselle, when he was hit in the back. Dazed, he crawled back into the crater, where an officer from the Tyneside Irish gave him a drink of whisky. There were three other officers stuck behind the parapet created by the explosion; Turnbull described it as being of "uncertain thickness and very crumbly. There was a certain amount of cover for all but very shallow."[27]

Turnbull received word that some of the Lincolns were in a sunken road. There was in fact just such a mongrel party led by Captain Andrew Whyte and 2nd Lt. Robert Pringle of the Sixteenth Royal Scots' D Company in the sunken road near Contalmaison. They'd gone over the top

British troops in a sunken road between La Boisselle and Contalmaison, July 1916.
Photograph by Lt. Ernest "Baby" Brooks, Collection of the Imperial War Museum

after C Company and now, with about thirty men of other ranks with them, somehow made it farther than anyone.

The village was protected by a trench the British called Quadrangle, and machine-gun emplacements they'd named Edinburgh Castle and Leith Fort. Wire protected this trench, too. Whyte and Pringle rushed it, only to be met by machine-gun fire. Both men were injured and captured.

———————

By 10:00 AM, Thirty-Fourth Division's attack existed only on paper as small parties of men held on to small gains in scattered spots around the field. Ingouville-Williams attempted to send the 207th Field Company of the Royal Engineers across no-man's-land, but machine-gun fire kept them pinned down in the British lines.

Coles was by this point in the sunken road near Contalmaison with most of the Hearts men who could still walk: Ernie Ellis, Jimmy Hazeldean, Harry Wattie, Annan Ness, Duncan Currie, and Paddy Crossan. Edward "Teddy" McGuire, a reserve team player who McCartney had recruited around the same time as Hazeldean, was with them. So was Second Lieutenant Millar, who'd led the unhappy raid a few nights before. Some stranded Suffolks had joined the company, which was at half strength—a relatively robust force, the way things were going.

Standing on the same road to Contalmaison today you can see the reconstructed spire of its redbrick church come into view as you pass a copse of trees called Peake Wood, now the site of a small British cemetery. A 1916 painting of the village held by the Imperial War Museum shows the church as a lonely, mostly ruined building at the end of a sunken road with charred half trees planted neatly in three rows along the approach.

Quadrangle trench was about five hundred yards in front of the church. In addition to the machine-gun emplacements, soldiers holding it had about fifteen machine guns ready to fire at anyone bold enough to try to cross. The artillery further back was also ready.

At 10:00 AM Coles gave the order to attack, and the men ran forward, where the guns proceeded to cut them to pieces.

The Germans "poured fire into the oncoming columns, so that the assaulting forces went down like ripe corn before the scythe," Landwehr Leutnant Alfred Frick of 28th Field Artillery Regiment's Sixth Battery Reserve remembered. "In consequence, the enemy casualties were simply enormous."[28]

Ellis fell. Hazeldean was shot in his left thigh. Jack Alexander writes that Ness saw Currie and Wattie drop. A shell, he writes, exploded in front of Crossan, who was running toward Quadrangle with two men from the Eleventh Suffolks. All three men vanished.[29]

───────────

A hundred yards ahead of the crater, Maj. Spencer Acklom of the Twenty-Second Tyneside Scots was stuck in the middle of the third line with about two hundred men. Things weren't exactly going to plan for him, either. A party of four eight-man bombing squads led by lieutenants Robson Wilson Rotherford and Thomas Connolly of the Tyneside battalions was supposed to have taken La Boisselle not long after the assault. But as Rotherford and Connolly advanced on the hamlet, parties of enemy troops began assaulting them from behind. Rotherford lost twenty-two men and was himself wounded but carried on down a communication trench toward La Boisselle. They threw grenades at the Germans, who returned fire with rifle grenades. His party was soon down to two men. One was killed, and the other, Private Johnson, was wounded. Rotherford and Johnson followed their path back and made it to Acklom.

In the crater, Turnbull was frantically sending runners to headquarters asking for help. Four made the outward journey but never returned. He had about a hundred unwounded men and about as many who couldn't walk, and it soon became clear their only real hope was to wait for dark. That was still a long way off. Then, as if things couldn't get worse, the British began shelling them by mistake. Turnbull spied an airplane overhead and desperately signaled it with a mirror, to no effect. A colonel was lying wounded nearby; Turnbull asked him for permission to send up a flare. The pilot saw that and returned; in due course the friendly fire stopped. The Germans began firing at the crater even harder.

Turnbull was fighting sleepiness—a not uncommon reaction to sustained artillery fire. At one point, some of the unwounded men wanted to make a break for their home trenches. He cursed—"I asked them what the **** they thought they were doing and ordered them back, and they all meekly went back, much to my surprise."[30]

Second Lieutenant George Russell of the Sixteenth Royal Scots actually made it over Quadrangle at the time of the charge that erased so many of the Hearts players. He and about thirty men tried to fight their way into Contalmaison. At 10:35 he sent a message asking for help; it was his last communication before the Germans counterattacked.

At 11:00 AM Coles decided to fling himself one last time at Contalmaison. He and his servant John Bird rushed the trench. A machine gun found him. Bird disobeyed orders and stopped to help him. He was shot, too. A half hour later, Coles's note from 8:45 AM made it to headquarters.

––––––––––––

At noon Haig received information that things were going relatively well. "We hold the Montauban-Mametz spur and the villages of those names," he wrote in his diary. "The enemy are still in Fricourt, but we are round his flank on the north and close to Contalmaison." After lunch, Haig motored to Querrieu, where Rawlinson was commanding the Fourth Army from a château.

Dead and wounded men lay between the two lines; machine-gun and rifle fire raked anyone who tried to help them. They needed first aid, but they also needed water. Many were simply baking in the midday sun.

All afternoon the forward troops tried to hold or consolidate their positions while their headquarters helplessly waited for dark. The Royal Engineers and Pioneer troops from the Eighteenth Northumberland

Fusiliers worked to open two "Russian saps," or shallow tunnels, across no-man's-land. One went to the German front line approximately across from the point where the Royal Scots had jumped out earlier, and the other to the crater. The Pioneers began carrying small amounts of food, water, ammunition, and other supplies to the front-line troops. Movement through the narrow passages was slow, held up by stretcher bearers and wounded men moving in either direction.

Ingouville-Williams was aware by late morning that the attack had been a disaster. In the evening he requested troops to staff his trenches in case the Germans counterattacked after dark. Men from a cyclist's company and cavalrymen cooling their heels filed in to garrison the front.

At 5:40 PM McCrae received a message from Captain Armit saying he, along with four men from B Company and 150 men from other units were holding a position at the entrance to Wood Alley, and that the enemy were in trenches nearby.

At 9:00 PM divisional headquarters ordered the commanders of the 101st Brigade's battalion commanders to move forward; only Sir George McCrae was still there to receive the command. He would take with him Maj. T. D. Temple from the Twenty-Seventh Tyneside Irish. It was a "strong combination," according to the divisional history: "The fearless 'amateur,' whose cheerful optimism soon spread through all his command, and the tried regular, who had then just made his twelfth trip 'over the top.'"[31]

Sir George received the order at 9:20 PM. At 9:25 he, Temple, and a passel of others who had made up headquarters set out to join their men. They left in two parties, Sir George's working its way slowly through the newly opened sap across no-man's-land. Heavy artillery fire made the going slow; it was 3:30 AM when he reached the forward positions close to Scots Redoubt.

As July 1 ended, Major Acklom of the Twenty-Second Tyneside Scots had moved back one line and German shells had shrunk his party of 200 men to 160. Men from the Nineteenth Division tried to bring them supplies, but units along the way commandeered the precious goods. Acklom was finally able to establish a telephone link to head-quarters. And Turnbull was still in the crater.

A newspaper photo taken before the Somme campaign shows Lt. Richard Cuthbert Lodge with Capt. Peter Ross. Lodge was quite tall, and Ross was short. "The long and the short of it," the caption reads.

Lodge, 2nd Lt. George Hamilton, and about 150 men had established themselves outside Scots Redoubt when Sir George McCrae arrived to join them. Two hours later, the second headquarters party finally arrived, having endured some unpleasantness with the enemy at Scots Redoubt on their way up to Lodge's position.

Nearby, Nap Armit had about 140 officers and men, mostly from the Sixteenth Royal Scots but also the Grimsby Chums and two battalions of the Tyneside Irish.

At 1:00 PM, two bombing parties set out from the position. Second Lieutenant Hamilton led one going up the Horseshoe line from Wood Alley; Lt. Leonard Robson of the Fifteenth Royal Scots led the other, which was tasked with taking Scots Redoubt and clearing the communications trenches that led to it. Hamilton made it 150 yards up the trench before being stopped by a barricade. Robson, on the other hand, took Scots Redoubt, as well as around fifty prisoners. The battalion took up its post in the strong point, which it continued to hold despite German counterattacks all day and night—their defense was "of a very active nature," a divisional history reads, and there were "constant bombing scraps."[32]

At 9:00 PM, four sections of the 207th Royal Engineers were able to join McCrae and the lads to help consolidate the redoubt. Two hours and forty-five minutes later, the Sixteenth's quartermaster managed to get food and water up to Scots Redoubt, as well as four hundred rifles and much-needed bombs and ammunition. The soldiers holding the strong point got freshly cooked meat and groceries and, for the first time since the attack, ate a full meal.

The next afternoon, Ingouville-Williams had received two companies from the Seventh East Lancashire Regiment, which was assigned to the Nineteenth Division. He set them on Heligoland. They crossed no-man's-land via the Twenty-First Division's trench and cleared the redoubt by 5:30 PM.

All night there was hard, close fighting. Jack Alexander writes that Cpl. John Veitch saw Ness and Lodge with McCrae, who was giving orders and shooting at attackers himself.[33]

Scots Redoubt held. At 6:00 the next morning, the East Lancashires appeared, having cleared the trenches by Heligoland overnight before connecting with the party in Scots Redoubt. They also connected with those taking shelter near the crater.

Rotherford and about a hundred men from Major Acklom's group pushed out to the right of the crater, consolidating the area in front of Heligoland. The Nineteenth Division fought its way through La Boisselle. It was tough work, with grenades doing a lot of grim business. By midday, it was theirs.

Back at Scots Redoubt, the Germans tried one last assault at 3:00 PM on July 3. The Sixteenth drove them back. During the attack, Ingouville-Williams made his way up to Scots Redoubt for a visit. He was overcome with emotion when he saw the men holding the strong point, and a divisional history says he gave "a cheery word to the men, saying over and over again, 'Well done, lads, well done, you've done damned well.'"[34]

At 9:00 PM McCrae got word the Germans were going to try again and ordered the men to stand to, but no attack appeared. At midnight, troops from the Twenty-Third Division began the process of relieving the Thirty-Fourth Division from their forward positions. "The party under Sir George McCrae did not wish to be relieved," the division's war diary notes, saying they were "rather exhausted although their spirit was excellent." Even after three days of sheer hell, the Sixteenth Royal Scots still wanted to fight.

Orders are orders. By 3:00 AM, the relief was complete. The troops marched under cover of darkness to Bécourt Château, where they bivouacked for a few hours before marching six miles to billets in the large army camp at Hénencourt Wood.

That afternoon, they took roll, the company commanders shouting the number of their men, followed by "all present and correct, sir!" Eight hundred and fourteen members of the Sixteenth Battalion of the Royal Scots had assaulted German positions on July 1. Four days later, 178 men remained. Six hundred and thirty-six men were missing, killed, or wounded. Nearly 80 percent of the battalion was gone. "I couldn't bring myself to believe they had gone," Alexander quotes John Veitch. Veitch's company, A, was particularly hard hit. "It nearly had me greeting [Scottish dialect for "weeping"], to think of that fine company, the best in our fine battalion, lying out there in no man's land."[35]

Two evenings earlier, officers from the Thirty-Fourth Division had walked in relative safety in no-man's-land in front of the former German front line. A division historian describes a feeling of optimism: "We were all cheerful, in spite of the poor dead lying thickly around us. The sun shone brightly. Were we not strolling about at our ease within a few yards of what, three days ago, was the Boche's front line? Things were undoubtedly coming our way at last."[36]

July 1, 1916, was the worst day in British military history: 19,240 men died in pursuit of the few hundred yards Haig gained. But even in that context, the Thirty-Fourth Division's losses near La Boisselle were staggering: 2,480 dead, 3,587 wounded, 313 missing. On July 3 there were still wounded in the field who couldn't safely be evacuated in the daylight for fear of sniper fire. That was especially true on the slopes of Tara and Usna, where the dead lay in the rows in which they'd advanced, a hideous knocked-over tableau of where they stood when the machine guns had cut them down.

10

THE CITY OF BEAUTIFUL NONSENSE

For three nights in Grimsby, excited citizens gathered at the Tivoli Cinema to watch their boys in action. An exclusive film of the Tenth Lincolnshire Battalion's training was to be shown alongside a short American film starring Beverly Bayne and Francis X. Bushman. In the Grimsby Chums picture, taken back when their uniforms were still "Kitchener's blue" serge owing to a khaki shortage, the soldiers exercised on English fields. They practiced signals with flags, dug trenches, and rehearsed bayonet attacks wearing padded suits. The wives, mothers, friends, and other relatives watching cheered their lads.

The picture showed from July 3 to July 5. It would be several more days before the news reached town that 80 percent of the battalion had been wiped out on July 1.

To read the newspapers in Grimsby, Edinburgh, or anywhere else in Britain, you'd think the war was going extremely well, and that the opening days of the Battle of the Somme were a glorious romp. *Daily Chronicle* reporter Philip Gibbs's account was picked up by newspapers all over Britain and made it across the ocean to the *New York Times*, which ran it on July 4:

"They went across toppingly," said a wounded boy of the West Yorkshires, who was in the first attack on Fricourt.

"The fellows were glorious," said another young officer who could hardly speak for the pain in his left shoulder, where a piece of shell struck him down in the Mametz Wood.

"Wonderful chaps," said a Lieutenant of the Manchesters. "They went cheering through the machine gun fire as if it were just the splashing of the rain. They beat everything for real pluck."

In such accounts, negative consequences landed mostly on the Germans, also "wonderful men," according to an officer of the Northumberland Fusiliers whom Gibbs quoted. The officer explained that the Germans "work their machines till they are bombed to death."

In Gibbs's telling, machine gun and artillery fire was heavy between La Boisselle and Contalmaison—"'They threw everything at us except half crowns,' said a man of the Royal Scots"—but men from that battalion, as well as nearby men from the Suffolks and a "Lincolnshire lad" told Gibbs they had not only persisted through the onslaught but "advanced at the double and captured batches of men who had no more stomach for a fight."

There were British casualties, of course, but "the proportion of lightly wounded men is high."

The unvarnished truth arrived by different means: British Army Form B 104-81A: Notification of Wound; Army Form B 104-82: Notification of Death; Army Form B 104-83: Notification Soldier posted as missing. Newcastle Libraries owns a remarkable photo of women in West Sleekburn waiting at Hall's Corner for the mail to arrive from Newcastle on July 3. Kids toddle nearby, playing or clinging to their mothers' long skirts, which most wear with aprons on top. The women stand chatting in a loose semicircle, passing the time near a postman in a hat who, in a few minutes, will hand some of them an envelope containing a life-altering slip of paper.

In Edinburgh newspapers, often on the same page as the sunny narratives that portrayed men returning from the battlefield, "grinning as though they had come from a 'jolly' in which they had been bumped a little" were the grim lists of "Scots Who Have Died for Their Country."[1] That feature took up ever more space on the page as July wore on.

Brief articles began to amplify the dissonance between what the public knew and what the official accounts told them. The *Scotsman*, July 13: Mr. John McCartney reports a letter from the front, saying several of the Hearts players were wounded, including Corporal Briggs, Sergeant Currie, and Private Hazeldean. The *Fife Free Press* on Saturday, July 15: "Much anxiety is felt as to the fate of Private James Scott, Royal Scots, the popular Raith Rovers' player, who took part in the great attack." The Dundee *Evening Telegraph and Post*, August 4: "While no official word has been received by relatives of the men, it is learned that Harry Wattie and Ellis, two of the Hearts of Midlothian players, who joined the Royal Scots in November, 1914, have been missing since the beginning of last month."

Newspaper readers in Britain were involuntary consumers of an industry of disinformation that dated back to the beginning of the war, when a Liberal Party politician named Charles Masterman gathered writers and journalists to decide how the government should censor war news as well as how it should make its case to neutral nations like the United States.

The journalists said they wanted little censorship. But for the most part, British newspapers didn't consider themselves to be independent of the war effort—their owners, employees, and readers wanted Britain to crush Germany.

Even the *Manchester Guardian* had changed its stance. On August 4, 1914, the day Britain declared war, the northern paper argued in an editorial that it was "the patriotic duty for all good citizens to oppose to the utmost the participation of this country in the greatest crime of our time." An abrupt, if mournful, about-face led the next day's paper: "Now there is nothing for Englishmen to do but to stand together and help by every means in their power to the attainment of our common object—an early and decisive victory over Germany."

On August 8, 1914, in the name of "securing the public safety," the British government passed the Defence of the Realm Act. It was originally designed to provide consequences "to prevent persons communicating with the enemy or obtaining information for that purpose," but its purpose crept outward as the war got longer. On August 12 the act was broadened to give the military power to seize land and buildings in the name of defense and vastly expanded police search powers. The government added to the act through the fall. In October, for example, it became illegal to own film for moving pictures without a permit.

The act grew even more teeth in November. Now it viewed as its responsibilities the duty "to prevent the spread of false reports or reports likely to cause disaffection to His Majesty or to interfere with the success of His Majesty's forces by land or sea or to prejudice His Majesty's relations with foreign powers."

The government was not shy about using this expanded authority. A reporter named Charles Carter Dyson was charged in police court in Portland, England, under the Defence of the Realm Act on April 8, 1915, with "transmitting news to the press calculated to be of service to the enemy," as an account in the *Edinburgh Evening News* and many other British newspapers read the next day. Dyson reported to several London papers about the sinking of the German submarine *U-29*. Edward Newman, the editor of the local paper *Southern Times*, landed in court for publishing Dyson's report. Newman protested that a London paper had published even more about the *U-29* sinking, and that the censors there had approved it. "An Admiralty witness, pressed by the defense, was unable to give a reason for his opinion that the news was likely to help the enemy," the *New York Times* reported a few days later. Dyson and Newman both lost and had to pay fines.[2]

Such inconsistency and lack of clarity would characterize British information efforts throughout the war, particularly with regard to newspaper reporting.

The first war correspondents were cowboys. An American living in Belgium named Granville Roland Fortescue provided the *Daily Telegraph* with perhaps the biggest scoop of the war: the German invasion of Belgium. Fortescue was a former Rough Rider who'd been wounded at the Battle of San Juan Hill, where he fought alongside his cousin Teddy Roosevelt. "Rolly" knocked around the world after that, landing in Belgium. He was in Brussels on August 2, 1914, trying to find out what was going on when he overheard two Belgians talking about German troops crossing the border near Visé. "This information I telephoned direct to the *Daily Telegraph*," he wrote in a memoir. "By using the telephone I got the news into London before any rival."[3]

Fortescue's reporting was as unwelcome in Brussels as it was to Britain's ruling class, which was still debating how or whether to join the war. Belgium denied it had been invaded, leaving the *Telegraph* in the dicey position of trusting a freelancer on one of the most consequential stories it would ever publish. He was correct, and the *Telegraph* offered him a contract.

Other British papers scrambled to get reporters across the channel. In September, Kitchener, whose hatred of the press cannot be overstated, tried to kick them all out of France, but Philip Gibbs of the *Daily Chronicle* proved particularly entrepreneurial when it came to getting around War Office restrictions.

Gibbs got himself appointed as a Red Cross commissioner, ostensibly so he could report on French field hospitals, which gave him freedom of movement around the country. And he got his copy to the *Chronicle* by using the War Office as an unlikely courier: he ordered one of its couriers to bring envelopes to London marked "The *Daily Chronicle*, Care of the War Office—URGENT."[4] War Office employees in London sent them on to the paper, apparently without any reservations.

Masterman spent the autumn of 1914 setting up his secret propaganda office in London's Wellington House. In 1914 the word *propaganda* hadn't acquired the sinister sheen that glosses it today; it was a Roman Catholic term of art for which *advertising* is a rough equivalent. Masterman adopted it for the task of convincing neutral countries in Scandinavia, Central and South America, and especially North America that they should join the war on the side of the Entente forces. This was by no means an easy task in the United States, which had a sizable German-immigrant population and a newspaper baron, William Randolph Hearst, who was extremely sympathetic to the kaiser.

Wellington House began courting the United States in perhaps the only way it would occur to turn-of-the-century members of the British upper classes: it targeted elites, sending pamphlets to American swells who Masterman hoped could nudge the country into Britain's corner. Britain sent letters every month to Catholic priests in the United States and Canada, and to protestant clergy in the United States, Scandinavia, and Holland.

Masterman had his own shaky relationship with Britain's upper crust. He had been good friends with David Lloyd George until he ran a less-than-successful political campaign and felt Lloyd George hadn't helped him much. He was odd looking, and his wife believed Prime Minister Asquith and his contemporaries viewed him among the "small fry" of the Liberal Party, but he had nevertheless apparently internalized the prejudices of the ruling classes.[5] His office favored establishment outlets like the *Times* and the *Daily Telegraph* over popular press titles with much larger circulation, like the *Daily Mail* and the *Daily Mirror*. The average citizen was far likelier to get news from such outlets, or even from topical songs and comedy at the music hall. But the educated classes looked down on both, especially the cinema, and plans for silver-screen propaganda didn't appear until the war was well underway.

Wellington House was hampered by the military's tortured relationship with the press. Kitchener appointed a man named Ernest Swinton as the only official war correspondent at the outbreak of the war, a position he held for months. Teddy Roosevelt once again intervened in an unexpected manner, writing Foreign Secretary Sir Edward Grey in January to complain about Britain's ban on war correspondents, using an argument that resonated in Whitehall: Germany was making American reporters welcome.

The British Army reluctantly credentialed a press corps, albeit a very small one; six correspondents would anchor coverage of the war in Europe. Gibbs made the cut, as did William Beach Thomas of the *Daily Mail* and *Daily Mirror*, Percival Phillips of the *Daily Express* and *Morning Post*, H. Perry Robinson from the *Times* and the *Daily News*, Basil Clark of the Amalgamated Press, and Herbert Russell from Reuters.

The army granted them all the honorary rank of captain and issued them officers' uniforms with green armbands. Thus attired, they were perfectly situated to present the government's point of view, while always observing grave restrictions on even sanctioned information. "Say what you like, old man," Brig. Gen. John Charteris, who oversaw the press section at general headquarters reportedly told a correspondent who wanted to know the ground rules. "But don't mention any places or people."[6]

The reporters worked from châteaus and traveled the Western Front in chauffeured cars, accompanied at all times by an overseeing officer. After a day of reporting under these strictures, the correspondents all gathered in the evening, decided together what story they'd present to the readers back home, then repaired to their desks to empty their notebooks into the official narrative. A censor then edited each story and prepared it for delivery to general headquarters, which conveyed each report to the War Office back in London. The War Office then delivered the dispatches to newspapers. It was only at this point that the reporters enjoyed what would under any other circumstances be a reporter's fantasy—the newspapers were not allowed to alter or shorten their reports in any way.

Very rarely would the reporters be able to talk with French or, later, Haig, for attribution. Interviews were a new practice imported from the United States, and when generals allowed them, they didn't allow reporters to quote them. "I think I understand fairly well what you gentlemen want," Gibbs remembered Haig saying to the press when he met them in June 1916. "You want to get hold of little stories of heroism, and so forth, and to write them up in a bright way to make good reading for Mary Ann in the kitchen, and the Man in the Street."[7]

Some general headquarters staffers reportedly thought it was hilarious to lie to reporters to see whether they'd believe them, the historian Stephen Badsey writes.[8] One of them was Lt. Col. James Edmonds, who after the war was put in charge of the historical section of the Committee of Imperial Defence. His tasks included overseeing the official *History of the Great War*, almost half of which he wrote himself.

A reporter named Keith Murdoch managed to break unapproved news in 1915. Murdoch was an Australian and landed at Gallipoli in September 1915 to report on antipodean troops fighting there. Distraught at the disastrous campaign, Murdoch decided to smuggle an uncensored account of the fighting to London. But a *Guardian* reporter named H. W. Nevinson ratted him out to authorities, who arrested Murdoch in Marseilles on his way to London and took his notes. When he finally got to England, Murdoch dictated his recollection of the account, written by Ellis Ashmead-Bartlett of the *Daily Telegraph*, in what purported to be a letter to Australian prime minister Andrew Fisher. David Lloyd George hated the Gallipoli campaign and, upon learning of the letter, sent it to Asquith, who had it printed and distributed at the War Office. It leaked, of course, and the *Times* printed a similar account by Ashmead-Bartlett, contributing greatly to the British abandoning their adventures in the east and concentrating on the Western Front instead.[9] Keith Murdoch returned to Australia a few years after the war ended, but his son Rupert went on to have many further adventures in British media.

The army placed even tighter restrictions on photography, which it believed could show the enemy far more than text reports. It didn't allow an official photographer at the Western Front until spring 1916, when it sanctioned Ernest "Baby" Brooks as the first. But as concerned as it was about still photos, the War Office was ambivalent about film—again, likely because its managers from the upper classes looked down on cinema. The only restriction it placed on cameramen was that they weren't allowed to use color film, which was a nascent technology at the time and tended to make colors—red in particular—look especially bright.

Nevertheless, Wellington House began making newsreels to play before features and in mid-1915 charged a cinema committee with making the film *Britain Prepared*, which showed troops training, the manufacture of ammunition, and navy ships plowing majestically through the seas. The film did well in Britain, and Masterman dispatched filmmaker Charles Urban to try to sell it in the United States. There, people in the film business gently told Urban they thought it was "too intellectual" for Americans.[10] What they really thought was that it was boring.

The tepid response to *Britain Prepared* tamped down expectations for *The Battle of the Somme*, which went on to become one of the most popular films in British history. In Edinburgh, cinemas had to stay open from 11:00 AM to 10:30 PM to accommodate the crowds. At least twenty million people bought tickets for the film in its first six weeks.

Geoffrey Malins and J. B. McDowell made *The Battle of the Somme* under technical conditions almost as hazardous as the war they were covering. Motion picture film was extremely flammable, and the Germans sometimes fired on cameras, thinking they were machine guns.

Other technical and practical constraints on camera operators had an enormous effect on how we think about the war today. There were no zoom lenses, and enemy soldiers were unlikely to shoot around a documentarian crazy enough to venture into no-man's-land. So they shot battlefields from behind the front lines, where the frequent gray skies of northern France and imprecise lenses rendered the action ahead of the lines as a blur. Unable to show all the viscera of battle, Malins and McDowell decided to recreate some of the scenes from the safety of the support lines. But much of what viewers saw was real, if incomplete—men marching off bravely toward battle, then limping back wounded. What happened in between was only witnessed by those in the fight.

The War Office Cinema Committee invited American filmmaker D. W. Griffith, fresh off the success of *The Birth of a Nation* and *Intolerance*, to tour the Western Front in May 1917. It was a month after the United States finally decided to enter the war, and Griffith was working on a propaganda film called *Hearts of the World* to steel American resolve. But Griffith was dismayed by how unfilmable he found the real-life conflict. "Every one is hidden away in ditches," he said. He continued:

> As you look out across No Man's Land, there is literally nothing that meets the eye but an aching desolation of nothingness—of torn trees, ruined barbed wire fence, and shell holes.
>
> At first you are horribly disappointed. There is nothing but filth and dirt and the most sickening smells. The soldiers are standing sometimes up to their hips in ice cold mud. The dash and thrill of wars in other days is no longer there.
>
> It is too colossal to be dramatic. No one can describe it. You might as well try to describe the ocean or the Milky Way. The war correspondents of today are staggered into silence. A very great writer could describe Waterloo. Many fine writers witnessed the charge of Pickett's army at Gettysburg and left wonderful descriptions. But who could describe the advance of Haig. No one saw it. No one saw a thousandth part of it.[11]

Hearts of the World instead told the story of the war in miniature, pitting Robert Harron as an American boy in France who fights to save a girl, played by Lillian Gish, from German perfidy, including an officer who attempts to rape her.

From the outset of the war the British press, particularly bottom-feeding publications such as *John Bull*, portrayed Germans as murderous half beasts. The Germans proved terrible at countering this crude propaganda, and they weren't any better at making their case when their war actions spurred particular outrage, even if they were arguably justified. From a German point of view, for example, the *Lusitania* was probably carrying munitions, making it a legitimate target. In 1982 Britain's Ministry of Defence warned divers exploring the wreck that "there is a large amount of ammunition in the wreck."[12] Whether that's an acknowledgment of the thousands of cases of small arms ammunition the government had previously acknowledged or an admission of more deadly cargo is a matter of hot debate even now.

Britain had another huge advantage over the Germans. At the start of the war it cut German transatlantic cables, giving it a near monopoly on information exported to America. Sir Gilbert Parker ran Wellington House's US efforts, and after the *Lusitania* sinking arranged for a bogus German medal to be sold that appeared to commemorate the disaster as a great source of pride. Thousands of copies of the medal were sold in the United States.

The British lies about Germany were often outrageous. One particularly grim libel was the "Corpse Factory" affair. It began as a hoax foisted by Charteris on a Chinese newspaper, with the hope the fake news would travel back to Europe. It did. The *Times* and the *Daily Mail* carried the story of a *Kadaververwertungsanstalt*, a factory to which the Germans transported their war dead to be turned into candles.

But the less obvious lies were just as corrosive. The government's propaganda operation reorganized several times as the war went on, but its belief that the public would not question official accounts never wavered. Harold Harmsworth became Lord Rothermere after he founded the *Daily Mail* with his brother Alfred, who became Lord Northcliffe. Both showed an unnatural talent for entertaining as well as informing their audiences, and Northcliffe and his fellow outsider Lord Beaverbrook, a Canadian who owned the *Daily Express*, worked their way into the British propaganda machine.

"We're telling lies, we daren't tell the public the truth, that we're losing more officers than the Germans, and that it's impossible to get through on the Western Front," Rothermere told attendees at a dinner party in November 1917. Among them was Masterman, who told his wife, and it is from her diary that we have the account of his quotes. "You've seen the correspondents shepherded by Charteris," he continued before delivering a blistering indictment of the entire British information economy. "They don't know the truth, they don't speak the truth, and we know that they don't."[13]

As successful as Beaverbrook, Rothermere, and Northcliffe were with their print properties, Beaverbrook realized as the war went on that propaganda got far more bang for its buck at the cinema. In 1916 more than twenty million tickets to the movies were sold each week; Britain's population was forty-three million. Beaverbrook eased the propaganda operation's emphasis toward visual media and oversaw a newsreel issued twice per week, *The War Office Official Topical Budget*. By 1918 he'd decided that the public had become "jaded" by unrelenting coverage of the mud and blood in France and Belgium, and he dispatched a cameraman to join Gen. Edmund Allenby in his campaign in Palestine.

Allenby was in the Middle East for similar reasons as Beaverbrook's cameraman. Despite the happy tales of battlefield success it was seeding in the press, the British government was alarmed by the lack of progress on the Western Front. Allenby lost his command on the Western Front after warning Haig that replacement troops were not trained adequately to do anything at the Battle of Arras but die. Lloyd George soon sent him to Cairo in the hope that he would deliver a victory to the increasingly war-weary public. "Jerusalem by Christmas," Lloyd George said in his instructions.

Allenby entered the holy city on December 11, dismounting and walking through the Jaffa Gate. His "Christmas present to the British nation," a nation that had expected a war over by Christmas 1914, was captured on film and eagerly exhibited across the country. Beaverbrook's strategy was working.

Beaverbrook was rewarded in March 1918 with the chairmanship of the newly created Ministry of Information, which consolidated all propaganda efforts. That sounds something like success, but the stream of lies wore away public trust, particularly among those who fought. Many soldiers were aghast to see battles that haunted them the rest of their lives portrayed as jollies in which they'd been bumped a little.

In 1920 Gibbs published *The Realities of War*, in which he confessed his qualms about British leadership in the war. The American edition of the book was named *Now It Can Be Told*, but it's not a mea culpa. "What I have written here does not cancel, nor alter, nor deny anything in my daily narratives of events on the western front as they are now published in book form," he writes in the introduction. "They stand, I may claim sincerely and humbly, as a truthful, accurate, and tragic record of the battles in France and Belgium during the years of war, broadly pictured out as far as I could see and know."[14]

Now It Can Be Told is beautifully written, and it fills in his earlier work with details that would have never made it past the censors. The waxen faces of the dead, steam rising from the entrails of downed horses, scraps of red French Army trousers still waving from prickly shrubs and barbed wire in old battlefields, these vivid images are all there, as is brutal criticism of the British Army leadership, a point of view that was gaining ground by the 1920s. A general callously sentences a British soldier to die between bites of an egg; other brass gambol around general headquarters looking for tennis partners, oblivious to the privations of the men knee-deep in mud a few miles north of them.

But Gibbs never questions why Britain fought this war in the first place nor whether his writing had any part in encouraging men to keep signing up for a chance to jump into the meat grinder. The dissociative quality of Gibbs's postwar writing makes one wonder if he experienced what we now know as post-traumatic stress disorder. Considering his years on the front, it would have been remarkable if he did not.

Gibbs was knighted the same year he published *The Realities of War*. He died in 1962. The Ministry of Information was disbanded in November 1918, and all its records were destroyed.

"The only alternative to what we wrote would have been a passionate denunciation of all this ghastly slaughter and violent attacks on British generalship," Gibbs wrote in 1920. "Even now I do not think that would have been justified. As Bernard Shaw told me, 'While the war lasts one must put one's own soul under censorship.'"[15]

11

WE DID MISS THE BOYS

On July 8 Paddy Crossan stepped off the field of battle and into the realm of legend when he walked into Henencourt Wood.

He told his incredulous colleagues he'd laid buried by the shell that landed between him and the men from the Eleventh Suffolks outside Quadrangle trench. He woke up covered with dirt next to their bodies. He was unable to see or hear properly but somehow made it back to the front, crawling for several days amid the corpses of no-man's-land before finding the British lines and an aid station. He made it to camp a day before a draft of men from other units began to restock the Sixteenth Royal Scots.[1]

Even back home when he had one foot on the ball, the Handsomest Man in the World always kept a toe or two in the land of myth. It was no small achievement that he did the same at the Somme, where a week earlier enfilade fire had finally ripped the language of gallantry in two.

No more would the brave charge the foe on steeds, the sweet wine of youth pouring from their fallen comrades as they dashed on to glory.[2] No, now they jumped the bags and walked to their deaths, their entrails in their hands as they lay screaming for hours in no-man's-land, where snipers might pick off any stretcher-bearer foolish enough to try to help them.

But how could ordinary language suffice for a week in which Paddy died, and was buried, and rose again? Burials by shell explosion weren't uncommon in World War I. On December 2, 1916, the *Edinburgh Evening News* reported on the award of a Distinguished Conduct Medal to Pvt. Mark Archibald of Gorgie, who was "buried by a shell explosion, but a second shell loosened the earth and enabled him to extricate himself. Although greatly shaken, he refused to rest and at once set about to work and successfully dug out several of his comrades who had also been buried."

Nor was it unusual for soldiers to stay out in no-man's-land for days. After the morning of July 1, Pvt. John Gaughan of the Tyneside Irish spent five days lying next to two dead men in a shell hole, performing first aid on himself with their field dressings.[3] Several of the wounded McCrae's lads, Jack Alexander writes, spent days after the attack living off the rations and water of dead men in the parched expanses no-man's-land before being discovered.

That was where Lionel Coles's body was found. You can visit his grave today at Gordon Dump, a peaceful cemetery down a long grassy path from the road that runs between Contalmaison and La Boisselle. Harry Wattie, Duncan Currie, and Ernie Ellis are commemorated three miles away on the Thiepval Memorial for men with no known graves.

Another legend ended two weeks later with a phone call to the Thirty-Fourth Division headquarters at 8:00 PM. Maj. Gen. Edward Charles Ingouville-Williams, who had commanded the division since it formed in Ripon, had been killed an hour earlier while reconnoitering near Mametz Wood. Ingouville-Williams always chafed at being stuck at headquarters and, as his visit to Scots Redoubt showed, always traveled as close as he was allowed to the danger his men faced. (Enlisted men were replaceable, the thinking went; generals, less so.) Ingouville-Williams was returning to his car with his aide-de-camp, 2nd Lt. Thomas Grainger Stewart of McCrae's, when a shell fell on him at the top of a bank. He was buried the next day at Warloy-Baillon Communal Cemetery.

"So died the first commander and the maker of the Thirty-Fourth Division—an absolutely fearless man; a stern disciplinarian, but with a tender heart," John Shakespear wrote in the divisional history. Ingouville-Williams "worked his men hard, but he loved them, and looked after their well-being and comfort. Only two days before his death he wrote, 'Never shall I cease singing the praises of my old 34th Division, and I shall never have the same grand men to deal with.' All ranks felt they had lost a great leader and a kind friend."[4] Eight officers and 160 enlisted men from McCrae's took part in the ceremony, serving as his last honor guard.

Sadly, there were few men from the Edinburgh days to join them. "We had a match the other evening, but, oh, Mr. M'C., we did miss the boys," Annan Ness wrote in a letter to John McCartney published in part by the Glasgow *Daily Record* on July 27. "Talk about football—it made the tears come to our eyes." Ness signed off as much possible of the cheer Western Front soldiers usually tried to manage in their letters home: "But have a good heart, guv'nor, we shall soon be in Berlin. My best regards to the directors and yourself."

The bad news was beginning to reach Edinburgh. "Mr. M'Cartney is in receipt of letters which make it only too clear that a good many well-known players in this noted contingent have been put out of action," the *Record* wrote two weeks earlier, "but until official notification is received names not be mentioned further than to say that Briggs, Crossan, Hazeldean, and M'Guire have all sent intimation that they were wounded in the great attack." McGuire was in the hospital in Glasgow with an arm wound, the *Record* went on. Hazeldean was in England with a bullet wound in his left thigh. Alfie Briggs was in the worst state of the correspondents, at a hospital in Epsom with awful wounds to his head, arm, and foot. And Crossan, well, "Crossan appears to have been so little damaged that he has already left hospital and rejoined his battalion."

That battalion's leader got a new second-in-command two days before Paddy's resurrection: Maj. Arthur Stephenson of the Ninth King's Own Yorkshire Light Infantry. It also received more officers and enlisted men: 42 on July 9; 64 from the Sixteenth Highland Light Infantry the next day; 254 from the Fifth and Sixth Scottish Rifles, 44 from other Royal Scots Territorial units the day after that.

At 6:15 PM on July 25 Maj. Gen. Sir Cecil Lothian Nicholson arrived at Thirty-Fourth Division headquarters to take over for Ingouville-Williams. Lt. Gen. Sir William Pulteney had inspected the division's 111th and 112th Infantry brigades earlier that afternoon. "Putty" had overseen the III Corp's disastrous day on the Somme, so flush with confidence beforehand he'd disregarded warnings from his gunners that they might not have cut all the enemy's wire defenses. Nicholson came from the Sixteenth Brigade and had been wounded at Neuve-Chapelle the year before. He visited the headquarters of the same brigades Pulteney had inspected the next day, and may have gotten to the others had a phone call not come in from III Corps on the twenty-seventh. The Thirty-Fourth Division was going back into the line.

It would do so without its artillery, which had moved to the former German lines in Sausage Valley to support the ongoing Somme offensive. "Our mess dug-outs have been well creosoted, but there are still a good many dead Boches [German soldiers] to be removed from blocked-up entrances, etc.," a battery commander wrote in the unit's diary. Removing those bodies was "very smelly work," he noted.[5]

At his château, Haig received a letter from Wully Robertson on July 29. "The powers-that-be are beginning to get a little uneasy in regard to the situation," Robertson wrote from London. Unlike readers of British papers, they'd seen the ghastly casualty figures from the offensive's first days and wondered "whether a loss of say 300,000 men will lead to really great results, because, if not, we ought to be content with something less than we are doing now." Ever the optimist, Haig replied that the Germans would soon run out of reinforcements, and that "steady offensive pressure will result eventually in his complete overthrow."[6]

July 30 was a hot, cloudless day, and the roads were dusty as Thirty-Fourth Division marched toward Bazentin-le-Petit, where a two-thousand-foot-long trench north of a heart-shaped wood carpeted with bodies wrecked by shellfire and decaying in the unyielding sun was proving difficult for the British to clear. "Intermediate Trench" lay two miles northeast of Contalmaison, which (what was left of it, at least) had finally fallen on July 10. German troops occupied the western end of the trench, and the British were in the east. Between their "respective spheres of influence," as Shakespear's divisional history put it, were two barricades.

McCrae's tried to evict the trench's original tenants as August 1 turned to August 2, hitting them with grenade attacks to no immediate effect. The next night brought better results: 120 yards of additional trench captured after a grim bombing raid led by Capt. James Hendry.

But those yards came at a high price. Hendry was severely wounded, as were twenty-five enlisted men of D Company. Five other ranks were killed. Retaliatory shellfire wounded Jimmy Boyd.

Sir George was about 2,300 feet behind them at Bazentin-le-Petit's cemetery, where he'd established a headquarters in less-than-ideal conditions. Brigade headquarters on the northwest of the wood "wasn't a salubrious place" either, Shakespear wrote. It was a former German dressing station that had been "repaired with sand-bags, into which had been shoveled various parts of human anatomy, German I hope. As the weather was very hot, the smell was strong." The Grimsby Chums' headquarters staff were sleeping in a deep, dark German dugout that they found so stuffy they decided to clean it, whereupon they realized they'd been sleeping on top of three dead Germans. "Life at Bazentin was unpleasant," Shakespear wrote.[7]

More unpleasantness was to come. A and B Companies were ordered to assault the German side of the trench on the night of the third alongside two companies from the Eleventh Suffolks on the right and an attack by troops from two other divisions. They were yanked at the last minute, but the Sixteenth Royal Scots and the Suffolks were ordered to go ahead without them. The Sixteenth Royal Scots and the Suffolks were to follow a twelve-minute barrage into the trench, capture the line, and establish a machine gun position. Except for the marginal importance of the trench, and the Germans occupying High Wood a half mile away with machine guns in perfect enfilade position—Nineteenth Division troops had tried the same assault a few days earlier and come under heavy enfilade fire—it was a reasonable plan.

Everything that could go wrong did. To get to their jumping-off positions before zero hour, A and B companies had to move through a crowded ditch while their replacements moved up. The Eleventh Suffolks got lost; only a small force was in position when the whistles blew at 1:10 AM, and it met with such intense artillery fire that it had to pull back. Capt. Napier Armit sent a runner to Sir George to tell him of the fiasco. When Sir George's report reached division headquarters, Nicholson was furious and ordered the Royal Scots to attack again immediately. They did so at 4:51. It was suicide. Armit and Lt. J. G. Mackenzie were killed, along with sixty other men.

Jimmy Boyd was missing and presumed dead. The stretcher-bearers taking him to an aid station had vanished as well.[8]

Nicholson blamed Sir George for the bungled attack, writing in a report that praised his "personal gallantry" and "unfailing cheerfulness" and concluded, "I do not consider that he is qualified to command a battalion in the field."[9]

This was a very serious charge, and in the time-honored tradition of British Army sackings, Nicholson recommended that someone he felt unqualified to lead a battalion be given a different battalion instead.

The Thirty-Fourth Division left what Shakespear called "the hell pot of the Somme" on August 15, after half a dozen other attempts on Intermediate Trench yielded inconsequential results.[10] In a report he added to Shakespear's book, Nicholson blamed enfilade fire from machine guns and artillery, and the fact that all its attacks were "carried out as isolated operations, and never as part of an attack on a wide front."[11] McCrae was apparently no longer at fault.

The division returned to its old stomping grounds of Armentières, where on August 19 Sir George went to the hospital for ptomaine poisoning, which Alexander writes was actually typhoid fever. It was the beginning of the end of McCrae's time on the front.

Haig's assault on the Somme was still straining to reach the objectives he'd set for its first day, and on September 15 he deployed a new weapon, the Mk I "tank," a bizarre rhomboid vehicle that Churchill preferred to call a "land battleship." He sent forty-nine, twenty-five of which actually made it across no-man's-land, capturing the villages of Martinpuich, Flers, and Courcelette. The Guards Division shared the machines' advance. Raymond Asquith, son of the prime minister, was shot in the chest and died, but not before lighting a cigarette. Another future prime minister, Harold Macmillan, was serving with the guards and was injured that day as well.

The kaiser had replaced Gen. Erich von Falkenhayn with Field Marshal Paul von Hindenburg as chief of the general staff in late August. The day Haig's tanks lumbered across two thousand yards of Picardy, Hindenburg ordered the German armies to "hold fast all positions" on all five fronts it was fighting as well as the involuntary deportment of seven hundred thousand Belgians to work on the German war effort. The next day Hindenburg ordered army units on the Somme to begin work on a fortified line behind the current ones that would stop any further advances.

Sir George returned to his battalion on September 19, and the division "settled down to 'peace time' war" near Armentières, which was "much as we left it," Shakespear wrote. "The *patisserie* with its pretty waitresses still flourished. The fair Lucienne still welcomed her guests with smiles, and danced while they dined, and played draughts with the favoured ones when they had finished." Major Herbert Warden of McCrae's reopened the divisional training school, which Shakespear said had been "closed for the holidays, i.e., the Somme episode."[12]

In addition to fair Lucienne's smiles, Armentières offered a laundry where the enlisted men could bathe once a week, a remarkable luxury. Spare socks and gum boots were kept in stock, and the division constructed rest houses in the basements of ruined houses. A worn-out soldier could get out of wet clothes, warm up by the fire, and drink soup and cocoa for a little while. There were also regular buses to the officers' club the 2nd Anzacs Corps—Australian and New Zealand troops—in Bailleul, where the brass could attend lectures. In these lines, Shakespear wrote, everyone "could live in a fug which is absolutely indescribable, and that is what everyone wants at the front."[13]

Even the trenches were relatively blissful compared to the Somme with German shells and *Minenwerfer*, or "Minnies," sailing through the air at times, answered by British Stokes mortars and artillery. There were also raids, "stirring little fights" to Shakespear that nonetheless added up to a "considerable number" of casualties.

Stephenson wrote a report on September 18 about one raid that had taken place on the night before. Lt. Robert Martin led the raid, which took place on a dark, cloudy night. At 11:58 PM, Martin and his men laid out along the Courau, a small stream with two-foot-deep water that ran through no-man's-land. They waited for an artillery barrage that was supposed to last for two minutes, but went for five, with one gun continuing for twenty minutes. Their approach announced, Martin and his men were greeted by machine-gun fire and Very lights in front of the trench, where they found gleaming new wire installed five or six strands deep. Rifle fire from loopholes in the trench joined the "emma gees," so Martin ordered a withdrawal. A signaler who went out to help guide the party home was wounded, and the British had to send out a party to fetch him after realizing the Germans had dispatched a patrol to try to do the same. Everyone was back in the trenches by 4:10 AM. "In conclusion, while much regretting that the raid failed in its object, I feel confident that it would have been quite impossible to have got a party of any useful size into the enemy trench in view of the extreme difficulty of penetrating the wire under the fire of the Machine guns and rifles," Stephenson wrote.[14]

On October 9, a shell struck a parapet of a British trench, injuring Paddy Crossan. "Shrapnel did the damage to P. Crossan, the Heart of Midlothian back," the *Daily Record* wrote on November 3. "It knocked two holes in one of his feet." Paddy bid adieu to his McCrae's pals as he was sent to hospital—there was little chance he'd be returned to his unit after he went to the hospital. There, Jack Alexander writes, Paddy's foot was scheduled to be amputated when a German surgeon volunteered to try to save it. He did, and Paddy got a trip home to recover.

Back on the Somme, rain and mud became problems nearly as big as machine guns and artillery. But Haig pressed on—his day-one objectives were nearly within reach. On November 18 the fields turned to pudding, and Haig finally closed the operation. That putrefied patch of Picardy claimed the lives of 95,675 British soldiers, as well as 50,729 French and 164,055 Germans. Rather than a turning point, it was a preview of the mud and blood that would define 1917.

Sir George ordered a raid on enemy trenches on November 23. Capt. George Cowan led two officers and forty-two other ranks across no-man's-land, only to find that the wire wasn't well cut. The Germans fired red, white, and green lights in the air as they decided to quit. Sir George wrote that he was "highly satisfied" with their conduct.

Sir George was unwell. Alexander writes that he was visibly exhausted "and almost entirely gray." That report was among his last acts as commander of his eponymous battalion. On November 25, the battalion diary notes, he was "ordered to proceed to ENGLAND and report to the War Office." The event, momentous for the men of McCrae's, doesn't even get a mention in the divisional history. Arthur Stephenson assumed its command.

The Entente powers made the changes they could. On December 3 Joffre lost his position to Gen. Robert Nivelle, a hero of Verdun. In London, Asquith fell, too, his government replaced by a coalition led by David Lloyd George, a media-savvy Welshman. "Poor old Squiff," Haig wrote in his diary. He hated Lloyd George. The king wasn't a fan, either, and promoted Haig to field marshal to tick off the prime minister.

The never-ending winter rain flooded the trenches in the Thirty-Fourth Division's lines. You had to take care when stepping on a trench board that you didn't shoot forward and land facedown in stinking muddy water. Some of the men got really into ratting, keeping score of how many they bagged. And the divisional theater company, the Chequers, presented the men a pantomime for Christmas: *Aladdin*, starring "two real French actresses, whose looks were a good deal better than their acting," Shakespear wrote.[15] The performances were always packed.

Haig inspected the Thirty-Fourth Division on December 22, the men having put up a huge screen to block the view of German gunners along the Armentières–Estaires road to protect him. The Sixteenth couldn't meet him, alas—they were in the lines.

At times, that feudal language favored by British officers mixed well with bureaucratese. The Thirty-Fourth Division's year-end accounting of lives lost and maimed is called a "statement of wastage," and for 1916 it listed the following: 1,522 men killed, 3,140 missing and almost certainly dead, 9,740 wounded, and 1,578 sick.

Of the Hearts lads who'd joined, only Annan Ness was still with McCrae's that Christmas, in the war that was supposed to have been wrapped up two years before that date.

After his visit to Armentières, Haig sent the division a telegram thanking them for their service. A few months later, he paid another visit to the Somme battlefield and jotted down a few thoughts in his diary. For a man uniformly described as "inarticulate," the 239 words he accords to the tens of thousands who died are almost florid:

> No one can visit the Somme Battlefield without being impressed with the magnitude of the effort made by the British Army. For five long months this battle continued. Not one battle, but a series of great battles, were methodically waged by numerous Divisions in succession, so that credit for pluck and resolution has been earned by men from every part of the Empire. And credit must be paid, not only to the private soldier in the ranks, but also to those splendid young officers who commanded platoons, companies and battalions. Although new to this terrible "game of war" they were able, time and again, to form up their commands in the darkness of night, and in spite of shell holes, wire and other obstacles, lead them forward in the grey of the morning to the attack of these tremendous positions. To many it meant certain death, and all must have known that before they started. Surely it was the knowledge of the great stake at issue, the existence of England as a free nation, that nerved

them for such heroic deeds. I have not the time to put down all the thoughts which rush into my mind when I think of all those fine fellows, who have either given their lives for their country, or have been maimed in its service.

Haig could have ended there. But he was apparently unable to resist taking a shot at Lloyd George and his other enemies in Whitehall. "Later on," he wrote, "I hope we may have a Prime Minister and a Government who will do them justice."

12

THE MOPPERS-UP

The newspaper notice promised "well-known Scottish football players" and struggled a bit to deliver under those terms; members of junior clubs like Shettleston and Strathclyde would take the field in Belfast the following evening alongside players whose team names were familiar, even if their surnames weren't. But one name scheduled to appear on behalf of "Scottish Command Depot," which was to play Distillery Selected for a benefit match on Saturday, May 19, 1917, was in fact fairly famous: Private Crossan of Heart of Midlothian.

Six months after nearly losing his foot, Paddy was back on the field.

His wound first took him to England's Black Country, where a trio of auxiliary hospitals around the town of Stourbridge provided a range of services, including convalescence in the ivy-covered mansion Studley Court.

Football was still a tonic for Paddy, even if the game at Belfast's Grosvenor Park wasn't particularly hard fought: the military side got the first goal before Distillery equalized, then headed in a winning goal.

In August, Paddy popped up on the small field again, this time at Hearts' season opener against St. Mirren alongside George Sinclair and Alfie Briggs. All three men were greeted rapturously by six thousand fans who came out in heavy rain to see the greats return.

The game got a little weird. St. Mirren's Harry Higginbotham had "a word or two with Crossan," according to a *Daily Record* account.

When a fan took Paddy's side in the dispute, Higginbotham, "apparently anxious to chastise him," according to the *Sunday Post*, scaled the fence and dove into the stands.[1] To the St. Mirren player's dismay, the freelance critic scrambled away. On Higginbotham's return, the *Record* wrote, referee G. G. Mackenzie informed the St. Mirren player his "services would be required no more that afternoon."

Down by a man, St. Mirren lost by a goal scored by Sinclair. Briggs "is a wonder," the *Record* gushed. Crossan was "the pick of the backs."[2] Even if they were home for a brief stop, it was good to see them wearing maroon again.

The warmth faded a little the next week at Hampden Park in Glasgow, where Paddy hurt his right leg in a game against Queen's Park and had to leave after the first half. The amateur team was up 1–0 at that point but went on to sink three more goals after Hearts forward Bert Denyer took over Paddy's position. The team returned to Edinburgh with naught but a tantalizing glimpse of what might have been.

The war years had been tough on the team, and especially hard on McCarthy, whose choices were to try to build a team and hope its members didn't all get drafted (Parliament passed the Military Service Act in January 1916, imposing conscription), or make do with men engaged in the war effort plus soldiers passing through town or stationed nearby. This dynamic, as always seems to be the case in Scotland, favored the Glasgow teams, whose shipbuilders and munitions workers were exempt from the draft, and thus able to keep Rangers and Celtic stocked up. A football fan in Glasgow was likely to have his "favourite Saturday afternoon dish served up hot and strong," wrote William Reid, an *Edinburgh Evening News* journalist writing under the pen name Diogenes. In Edinburgh the foreseeable future held only weak sauce: "One great trouble is that none of the present-day players can play the game." Reid's column appeared on August 4, 1917. It was the third anniversary of Britain's declaration of war.

McCartney had developed a pair of hobbies that kept his mind a bit off the grim state of Hearts: sending footballs to British troops abroad and publishing articles about the "entire cosmopolitan crew of kill-joys and motley parasites" who focused so much ire on football players before Hearts' enlistment.[3] Sending the balls made a real difference in the lives of soldiers overseas. Writing about it also appeared to provide an outlet for feelings that had evidently not quite cooled, as seen in this passage quoted in the *Daily Record* of June 8, 1917:

> How these parasites finding a landing on the bodies of responsible people is one of the seven wonders. They are neither fitted for fighting nor willing to fight, but their rudimentary, fragmentary, and hearsay knowledge of things has the unfortunate tendency to further distort their limited powers of observation. . . . [When Hearts enlisted] bishops on the ecclesiastical screen were showing 'the portals of Hell open wide,' lords of creation were supplicating for Zeppelin raids on football grounds, and sleek skins were bellowing for other fellows' hides. How magnanimous! Truly, football players and supporters must have marvelled at the attentions of Snobocracy.

Since the British retreat at Mons, soldiers had been writing Heart of Midlothian asking the club to send footballs. "Applications began to pour in to such an extent that it was quite impossible for the Heart of Midlothian Football Club to comply," McCartney remembered later. With Reid's help, McCartney established a fund to send footballs to the front and to British soldiers held in German prisoner-of-war camps, eventually putting 1,700 balls into service.

Even getting them to Germany wasn't an issue until the end of 1916, McCartney later recalled, until a government agency called the Central Prisoners of War Committee got onto his case. The body "swooped down upon us and commanded that no more footballs were to be sent to German prison camps by means of any other agency than their own good selves." Worse, the bureaucrats demanded McCartney's fund purchase the balls from shops in London, for the outrageous price of twelve shillings, six pence. The balls would arrive saying they were from the Red Cross Society.

JOHN McCARTNEY

Played for:	*Manager and Secretary:*
CARTVALE F.C.	BARNSLEY F.C.
GLASGOW THISTLE F.C.	ST. MIRREN F.C.
GLASGOW RANGERS F.C.	HEART OF MIDLOTHIAN F.C.
COWLAIRS F.C.	PORTSMOUTH F.C.
NEWTON HEATH F.C. (Manchester United)	LUTON TOWN F.C.
LUTON TOWN F.C.	
BARNSLEY F.C.	

Author page for John McCartney's *The Sport in War,* one of two pamphlets he wrote about his team's enlistment and his work sending balls to troops.

The "self-elected busy-bodies had to have their line of red tape in operation," McCartney fumed. "They must do something to justify their existence." In *The "Hearts" and the Great War*, a pamphlet he published in 1918 about the effort, he also swiped at critics who "suggest that too much has been made of this element of sport in relation to the fighting man." Those people "belong to the exclusive set of elderly sixties and youthful seventies who frolic and gambol in the aristocratic parlour at ping pong, or become breezy over an exciting tidley-wink contest. They pull crackers for exercise, and wear paper hats as a preventive to ice rinks forming on their domes."

McCartney had serious points to make in addition to all the score settling: "Youthful exuberance fired with zeal, energy, and exercise can alone win the war," he wrote. "The athlete you simply cannot subdue."[4]

His pamphlets offered testimony from the recipients of footballs, including Foch, the King of Belgium, and Joffre. More affecting were the quotes from soldiers who received them.

"You can rest assured that the football will be enjoyed as we have just finished twenty-six days in the trenches, and although it has been a bit costly, they (the Huns) can make no impression on the good old 2nd Royal Scots," wrote privates Sharp and McCardle from France. (McCardle later died in France, McCartney noted.) "Most thankful for the magnificent ball you sent, and we greatly appreciate your kindness," wrote M. Tirol, a French prisoner of war in Germany. "It will help us pass the time quickly, and keep us in good form for the time of our return home." And Corporal Briggs of the Sixteenth Royal Scots wrote in as well to say thanks, "Had our first match with it, and playing in army boots, we were like a lot of 'Clydesdales.' Football is the game to keep us fit, and raises enthusiasm that may prove bad for the Germans."

There were also letters from men who'd been touched by the Hearts' lads. "Tell Geordie Sinclair this letter is from the Piper who shook hands with him when he rode past the Royal Scots on the day after Mons," wrote Corporal G. Groves of the Second Royal Scots. A Scottish prisoner of war in Minden, Germany, named Sergeant Hill wrote to say thanks for a ball and that he was sorry to hear about Harry Wattie's death. "We played together as children," Groves said.

Edinburgh businesses and citizens donated to the drive, but McCartney credits a wounded Canadian soldier named Pvt. R. C. F. Hyslop with the biggest contribution: £182 8s. 5d. Hyslop, working "from the confines of his little wheel-chair," McCartney writes, was "a familiar figure sitting at the door of his home with his 'Footballs for Soldiers' collection box beside him." He raised more than Edinburgh's Tramway Company, which sold penny tickets for the cause and raised £132.

The club had its own trouble raising money. Ticket sales plummeted as the product McCartney could put on the field grew shaggier. Elias Fürst was able to keep the wolves at bay by negotiating with creditors about the club's obligations from building its new stand. He also played a role in the continuing operations of Chelsea Football Club in London. That organization still owed Hearts £750 for the transfer of Lawrence Abrams. Hearts obtained a court order in August 1916 to force repayment, but declined to enforce it after Chelsea appealed, saying it would have to fold if it paid that debt. Fürst and Hearts decided to let it slide.

Most football clubs were experiencing difficulties. The league forced Aberdeen, Raith Rovers, and Dundee to withdraw from the 1917–1918 season. It was difficult, expensive, and time consuming for clubs around Edinburgh and Glasgow to reach Aberdeen in particular, and spotty train service during wartime made it almost impossible. Players' families also felt the pinch of their new salaries. An infantry private made seven shillings, seven pence per week, much less than the four pounds per week most Hearts players were making before the war. McCartney quietly arranged grocery deliveries for families who were having trouble making ends meet.

———————

On February 4 German forces began moving back to the newly constructed defensive positions Hindenburg had ordered. The new positions were made from reinforced concrete, with wire obstacles designed to make it easier than ever for machine gunners to sweep attacking troops. Wherever possible, the Germans placed their positions on reverse slopes. The geographic advantage Germany had on the Somme was now doctrine.

The new line was straighter and twenty-five miles shorter, freeing up army reserves. Germany was fighting on many fronts and faced another opening if Romania entered the war. The Verdun offensive, which ended the previous fall, was costly to the attackers, too. Its old line probably couldn't withstand another mammoth assault by the British and French once the weather improved. Between the old lines and what the British called the "Hindenburg line," German troops devastated the French countryside, destroying houses, poisoning wells, ripping up roads, and slaughtering livestock, leaving the troops that followed only a smoking bull's-eye to live in.

In addition to the defensive realignment, Hindenburg and Gen. Erich Ludendorff, the pair of commanders who replaced Falkenhayn in August 1916, convinced the kaiser to take the bold step of declaring unrestricted submarine warfare in hopes of knocking Britain out of the war. In the event that this new policy brought the United States into the war, Germany made diplomatic overtures to Mexico, promising to help it retake Texas, Arizona, and New Mexico. At the same time, the Mexican ambassador to the United States asked for $50,000 to help influence congressmen. The British intercepted coded telegrams for both schemes.

Haig's position was still not secure, and he managed to make things worse by granting an interview to French journalists on February 1. He spoke to them of the primary importance of the Western Front and said he expected in the new year to see "the decision of the war on the field of battle." Lloyd George was interested in challenging Germany on other fronts, especially Italy. Haig's habitual optimism could be, and was, read as insubordination back in London.

At the end of the month, Lloyd George began to put the screws to Haig. At a conference in Calais about the new year's efforts, the prime minister moved to put Haig firmly under the command of Nivelle. The new French top commander was promising an offensive that would dramatically shorten the war. Haig was appalled—"madness" was how he characterized the plan in his diary—and threatened to resign. Wully Robertson and Imperial War Cabinet secretary Maurice Hankey were able to forge a compromise that required Haig to "conform his plans of operations" with Nivelle's for this operation only. As a coup, it left a lot to be desired: Haig remained in place, his resentment and sense of injury growing.

The British were to open the offensive with a diversionary attack at Arras. Five days earlier, the Thirty-Fourth Division tried out a new weapon, the Livens projector. It was a kind of mortar that delivered canisters full of poison gas, or burning oil, at its targets. It was inaccurate, but useful enough that the British kept it in their arsenal into World War II. The projector's inventor, Royal Engineers officer William Howard Livens, also came up with the Livens large gallery flame projector, a fifty-six-foot-long monster used at Mametz and Carnoy during the Battle of the Somme. (The director Peter Jackson later used the machine as inspiration for his portrayal of the dragon Smaug in *The Hobbit*, which was written by a signals officer stationed on the Somme, John Ronald Reuel Tolkien of the Eleventh Battalion, Lancashire Fusiliers.)

On April 6, 1917, the United States declared war on Germany. The suppositions behind Nivelle's offensive kept changing, but his plan didn't.

The Sixteenth Royal Scots had moved to Arras at the end of March. The planning for this attack showed the British staff were evolving and adjusting after the disappointments of the previous year. A system was forming. In it, a new artillery tactic called the "creeping barrage" would lay a "curtain" of fire in front of advancing infantry. Narrow parts of no-man's-land would have trench mortar fire rather than artillery. The infantry's goals were clear: three lines, each assigned a color, to be taken on a realistic timetable.

April 8 was Easter Sunday, and Haig, as was his custom, attended a Church of Scotland service at his headquarters. The Reverend George

Duncan preached the importance of the "unconquerable mind," a phrase Haig enjoyed so much he mentioned it in his diary.

The next morning was misty and gray. McCrae's were in position by 5:05 AM and went over the top at 5:30. The contrast between this attack and the first day of the Somme in the battalion's war diary is remarkable:

> 5:34 AM: Barrage lifted to 2nd Line. Front line taken & being mopped up.
> 5:37 AM: Barrage lifted to 3rd Line. 2nd Line taken & being mopped up.
> 5:40 AM: Barrage went forward by lifts of 50 yards to 4th Line. 3rd Line taken and being mopped up.

Other members of the division didn't have such a smooth time. A hidden machine gun vexed two battalions of the Tyneside Irish. "I therefore made up my mind to put a stop to its activities," Lance Corporal Thomas Bryan later told his regimental journal.[5] Creeping from one shell hole to another, he surprised the gun crew team, shooting them from afar. (Two witnesses said they saw him finish the job with his bayonet.)

Nicholson ordered McCrae's to dig in on the "Green" line, sending out patrols to try to find the Germans. They couldn't find many. The Sixteenth Royal Scots captured six Germans in a gun pit, along with a siege gun that made a fine souvenir.

The first day of the Battle of Arras was a triumph for the British Expeditionary Force, for its commander General Edmund Allenby, and for his boss, Field Marshal Sir Douglas Haig. The new tactics had worked splendidly, and the Canadian Corps led by Lt. Gen. Sir Julian Byng captured most of the Vimy Ridge in the Arras offensive's northern sector.

What no one counted on was the weather. Overnight on the ninth, heavy rain changed to snow, accompanied by gale-force winds. By April 11 Shakespear wrote, "The rain and snow made digging almost impossible." Men began to get sick. The winter-in-spring caused big-picture problems, and aerial observation became impossible. Allenby was unaware that German reinforcements were arriving as he ordered further gains.

The results were predictable. Casualty figures began to rise along the line. By April 14, 3,598 Canadians had died holding Vimy Ridge. Seven thousand were wounded. The Thirty-Fourth Division alone had 2,767 casualties during the six-day offensive—341 killed, 2,074 wounded, 315 missing, 37 sick. They lost 137 officers and 2,630 other ranks to misfortune. "Rather different to the appalling totals of the first few days of the previous July," Shakespear wrote, "but still heavy enough to make one think furiously, when one remembers that in all reports the barrage is described as feeble, and the machine gun fire as weak."[6]

On April 15, three divisional commanders—Maj. Gen. Sir Percival S. Wilkinson, Gen. Sir Henry de Beauvoir De Lisle, and Maj. Gen. Sir Philip Robertson—held a very unusual meeting to condemn Allenby's mounting casualties. They communicated their "no confidence" vote to Haig, who suspended operations the same day.

Nivelle's offensive began the next day. It, too, quickly became a disaster.

That didn't mean the Royal Scots would be excused from contributing to the gathering calamity. The battalion's operational strength was 12 officers and 277 other ranks—about the size one of its companies a year earlier—when the men assembled on the Lille Road after coming out of the lines on April 14. After being bused to Averdoingt, McCrae's began a reorganization. Lt. Cuthbert Lodge and three other officers moved to A Company, which had lost every last one of its officers at Arras. The same day saw the arrival of 105 drafts—"indifferently trained men, many of whom had not yet been under fire," Shakespear called them.[7] More rebuilding should have followed, but five days later they were on the march again. The French had put pressure on Haig to continue pushing out from Arras to help save Nivelle's flagging offensive.

April 23 was a beautiful spring morning as the battalions of the Thirty-Fourth Division, reduced to an average strength of 520 men apiece, marched through Blangy Park along the banks of the river Scarpe. That night, the 101st Brigade would take over seven hundred yards of some of the nastiest trenches they'd seen so far, on the outskirts of a commune called Roeux.

The trenches were part of a German second-line system from which the Ninth Division had expelled the German 65th Infantry Regiment and 65th Reserve Infantry Regiment during the opening of the Arras battle. They'd moved to the other side of Roeux but had established some thorny machine-gun and sniper positions in houses, Roeux's château, and in the town's chemical works. Just getting into the trenches would have been difficult for experienced troops.

The trenches had *C* names—Cap, Care, Cusp, Ceylon. To their right was a small wooded area just in front of the spot the trench curved down to the river Scarpe. To their left was a railway. Clambering through a cutting on the way to the position, Rowse was surprised to see German doctors still on duty operating in a dressing station cut into the bank. They were treating men from both sides.

It was an evil little spot. The soldiers had to deepen the trenches to make them attack-ready, and the Germans kept sending up Very lights so they could train guns on the working parties. On the twenty-seventh they learned they'd attack the next day. The Fifteenth Royal Scots would attack on the right, going toward what was left of the town, and all the buildings within it. Behind them would be two companies of the Sixteenth Royal Scots, as "moppers-up." The Grimsby Chums would attack in the center, toward a cemetery and a crossroads. They'd have one mopping-up company from McCrae's behind them. And the Eleventh Suffolks would go around the left side of the château toward the chemical works. They got a company of the Sixteenth to mop up as well. Zero hour was set at 4:25 AM. On their way into position, big containers of cold lamb chops came out, and the men in the trenches passed them to one another silently. That cold hunk of meat on the bone would be the day's high point. April 28 "began badly, continued badly, and ended worse," Shakespear wrote later.[8]

An excellent hand-drawn map in the Grimsby Chums' war diary shows exactly how a machine gun from the château was able to spray fire all over their flank. Ahead of them was another machine gun in a house. The fire was so heavy some had to retreat to their lines. Others dove into shell holes.

On the right, a party of the Fifteenth Royal Scots had preceded the rest, trying to clear out the small woods to their right. It was a dreadful task in a dark area filled with barbed wire and machine guns. The ruined village itself offered little resistance from the Germans, but they soon learned why: the British artillery was shelling it.

The Suffolks fared little better, facing machine-gun fire from a trench that had escaped the artillery's attention. When those who could got back in the trench, they had about three hundred men left, plus sixty from the Sixteenth Royal Scots.

At 5:30 AM the Germans launched a counterattack from the right. Some moved through the woods, up the right of the line, and then began attacking the British lines from the rear. "Our fellows were firing from both sides of the trench," Rowse remembered. There was a gap between the woods and the trench, and the battalion's snipers picked off as many men who were running through it as they could. Maj. Walter Vignoles, who'd been shot through four fingers at the Somme, set up a Lewis gun and squelched the rest of the counterattack.

Back near the village, Lt. Leonard Robson and Capt. Gavin Pagan of the Fifteenth Royal Scots were with about two hundred men, including the moppers-up, trying to find a place to dig in and defend themselves against the counterattack. But the ground was too wet from the recent snow and rain; all they could make were indentations in mud. By 8:30 AM Robson was down to about thirty men, cut off from the lines and with no way to tell anyone how much trouble they were in. He'd been shot in the leg and a bullet had hit his haversack, injuring his back. He decided to improvise. He crawled down to the river and tried to swim to the British line. "Presently I found myself being helped to my feet—minus equipment—by two of my men under enemy supervision," he later told Shakespear.[9]

In the evening the Chums sent out a stretcher party for the wounded. Among their own soldiers they found some members of the Fifty-First Division who'd been lying out wounded for five days. In his report, Stephenson was scathing about the artillery, which "opened very raggedly" and "was absolutely inadequate" at taking out machine guns in houses and the woods. The Sixteenth went in with 18 officers and 416 other ranks; it left with 8 officers and 205 enlisted men. Early the next morning two battalions of the Tyneside Scottish made another run at the chemical works, to ambivalent results.

There weren't enough troops to try another attack. The next day was quiet as those who lived through the first day's action held the lines until they could be relieved. When they went out on the evening of the thirtieth "nobody had any law or order, their packs were slung on somehow and rifles were almost dragged along," Rowse remembered. Of his company, about sixty men were left. Then the Scottish units' pipers started playing. "It's unbelievable the effect that had on the lads," he said, choking up. "The packs came on, their rifles came up, they started to march, and we marched the rest of the way behind the pipe band of the Royal Scots. That was most impressive."[10]

Roeux finally fell on May 10. It took the British nine attempts to clear out the Germans. During the assault, 1,475 men of the Thirty-Fourth Division died or went missing, and 1,169 more were wounded.

The Nivelle offensive actually gained Entente forces a little ground, just not as much as promised. Nivelle paid for the oversold plan with his job. In May, France replaced him with Philippe Pétain. Haig got along great with Pétain. Lloyd George wasn't in danger of losing his position, but his enthusiastic backing of Nivelle meant he had less standing in London when Haig began campaigning for approval for the assault he thought would finish the Germans once and for all. He wanted to take another crack at the Flemish region around Ypres, especially near a village called Passchendaele.

In the meantime he had some mopping up of his own to do. Allenby had come to him on May 1 worried about the high casualties on the restarted Arras battle. Haig continued the assault. Allenby returned on

May 7 to warn him that the troops left weren't trained. Haig had him sacked.

The move rebounded on Haig in a way that only makes sense in a career spent stepping on rakes: Lloyd George and Churchill had Allenby sent to Palestine to run their feel-good campaign of taking Jerusalem by Christmas. Among his troops was a recently joined member of the Territorial Army's 1/4th Royal Scots: Pvt. Patrick James Crossan. His wage book bore the inscription "Gone to Egypt."

13

CLOGGED WITH MUD
AND USELESS

G avrilo Princip died in an Austrian prison hospital on April 28, 1918. He was twenty-two and had tuberculosis. Few newspapers carried more than a sentence or two on the man whose actions set the worst war yet seen on earth into motion. He died as little more than a footnote.[1]

"No one can describe it," D. W. Griffith said when contemplating World War I. It was as unfilmable as it was indescribable. Words fail all the time, but they failed this war in new and important ways. *Battle*, for instance, comes from a Latin word meaning "to beat," which an optimist might read as "to win." But on the Western Front the word reverted to its origins in Roman cookery: "to pound repeatedly." This is why, by drawing a tight frame around events, poetry and painting can be some of the best ways to understand this war. Words and images that evoke show more than photographs or words that simply describe. When the poet Isaac Rosenberg describes a man, stuck underground, envying the freedom of a rat, it teaches more about trench warfare than a dozen oral histories.

How would you know if you won this war unless you knew what you were fighting for? Princip lit a fire with his Browning, but Europe's wood was cleft and dry. Even a quick survey of the causes of World

War I sounds like a parody. Germany needed to honor its alliance with Austria-Hungary, which wanted to preserve its dominion over the Slavs, who wanted autonomy and with whom Russia wanted to make common cause against Germany, which wanted a stronger border against Russia as well as a bigger navy and more places to board ships, so it could better compete with Britain, which viewed Germany's navy as a threat to its economy and colonies and had an agreement with France—which wanted Alsace and Lorraine back from Germany—and Russia to protect Belgium, whose ports were uncomfortably close to Britain's, and Serbia (remember Serbia?) wanted a port as well, and also everyone was beginning to need oil, which meant dealing with the Turks, whose empire controlled much of the Middle East and with whom the Germans were trying to make common cause. Is it even worth mentioning that Kaiser Wilhelm II was Tsar Nicholas's cousin, King Edward VII's nephew, and technically a high-ranking officer in Britain's Royal Navy? Millions of people vanished from the earth for *this*?

Woodrow Wilson was at least able to make a case for the prosecution of the war. "The world must be made safe for democracy," he told the US Congress on April 2, 1917. Never mind that more than half the US population was forbidden by law to vote at the time—America finally gave the war a decent marketing slogan.

What the United States couldn't yet supply was an army, at least one that could fight on the industrial scale demanded by the gears of technology and futility grinding against each other on the Western Front. Wilson dispatched John J. "Black Jack" Pershing, perhaps best known at the time for pursuing (and failing to capture) Pancho Villa, to turn what was basically a frontier force into a world-class army. The generals of France and Britain thought this meant the United States would send fresh recruits for them to deploy. They expected Pershing would leap at the chance to learn from them, to work for them.

Pershing viewed things a little differently. His job was to straighten out the mess in Europe once and for all. He had no patience for incremental progress in epic battles like the Somme, which Haig described in a December 1916 dispatch as the "Opening of the Wearing-Out Battle."

Haig's defenders argue that the much-derided breakthroughs he was passionate about are better viewed as sensible contingency plans for success in a war he recognized could only be fought through attrition. That belief always seemed to become more pronounced following disappointments.

The Allied powers now began to think of the war as ending in 1919, or even 1920. "Is it not obvious that we ought not to squander the remaining armies of France and Britain in precipitate offensives before the American power begins to be felt on the battlefield?" Winston Churchill asked in Parliament on May 10, 1917.

Haig had a different argument. Flanders might be where the Germans might finally break. And he actually made a pretty good case for the battle that has come to be known as Passchendaele. Like the war itself, it was almost impossible to abandon or justify the Ypres salient. It dated back to October 1914, when British and French troops carved a roughly V-shaped line around a lovely Flemish market town and proceeded, with German help, to turn it into arguably the worst place on earth. Gas and flamethrowers both made their debut at Ypres. Artillery fire destroyed the drainage systems of the flat land between the lines, turning the loamy soil into mud so deep people and horses could, and frequently did, drown in it. The elbow-shaped salient was open to German fire from three sides.

But the Belgian coast was only a few miles away from the high ground the Germans occupied across from the city. If the British could advance past that to the coast, they'd remove not only the rail junction of Roulers but a vital submarine base that was threatening the whole war. Haig had planned an offensive in Flanders in 1916, but Verdun and the Somme prevented him from following through. Here at last was a chance to *win.*

On June 7 the British detonated nineteen mines under Messines ridge, killing some ten thousand German soldiers and making prisoners of seven thousand more. The Germans withdrew to the east four days later under heavy artillery bombardment and infantry attack. The explosions were meant to be a prelude to a larger attack, but the War

Cabinet asked Haig to come to London first to sell an ever-skeptical cabinet on his plans.

"Don't argue that you can finish the war this year, or that the German is already beaten," Wully Robertson wrote Haig on June 13. "Argue that your plan is the best plan—as it is—that no other would even be *safe* let alone decisive, and then leave them to reject your advice and mine. They dare not do that."

Six days later, Haig went to London and told the cabinet the war could be won in 1917 and that the Germans were as good as beaten. "I stated that Germany was within six months of total exhaustion of her available manpower, *if the fighting continues at its present intensity,*" he wrote in his diary that night, after having tea with his children, who "looked very thin and pinched."

On June 27 Haig visited French, who apologized for snooping around France on Lloyd George's behalf. "I shook him by the hand and congratulated him on speaking out like a man," Haig wrote in his diary. "I invited him to France and we parted the best of friends. I was with him for about half an hour."

After its miserable spring, the Thirty-Fourth Division finally got some well-deserved time away from battle in June, taking over a quiet sector near Péronne. On their retreat to the Hindenburg Line the Germans left that beautiful town on the river Somme and its surrounding region a smoldering husk. "Wrecking farmhouses, cutting down ornamental shrubs, smashing farm implements (all laid out in a row for the purpose), sawing through spokes of farm carts, fouling ponds and water supplies," was how one officer described the wreckage.

The devastation was so thorough the division's soldiers found the liberated French who were left were eager to sell appurtenances of rest and rebuilding at bargain prices: "The peevish destruction of purely civilian property has had a great effect in stiffening up the French, and has saved us from paying fancy prices for brick rubble, timber, strawberries, currant tart, and gooseberry fool," Shakespear wrote.[2]

On July 20 the War Policy Committee issued a report that cleared the way for Haig to begin his summer offensive. Planning began immediately. On the morning of July 31 artillery fire woke Haig up. "The whole ground was shaking with the terrific bombardment," he wrote in his diary. The battle had begun. The morning's offensive went well. And then it began to rain.

The "Blighty wound" held a special place in the fantasies of British troops. It was an injury serious enough that you'd have to go home to recuperate but at the same time wouldn't leave you permanently damaged. "When Tommy receives a 'soft one' (a slight wound)," Lorenzo Smith wrote in his *Lingo of No Man's Land*, "he not infrequently shouts 'Hooray, I'm off for Blighty.'"

There were no Blighty wounds at Passchendaele. Often the only way across the deadly mud was narrow duckboard tracks. If you were too hurt to walk or if you fell off the track you were liable to drown in the mud, a slow, agonizing death from which even a determined rescuer couldn't always save you. The rain only let up for three days the entire month of August. The shell holes filled with slime, debris, and bodies. General Hubert Gough floundered, ordering the Battle of Langemarck for August 16. The pattern was modest success followed by crushing counterattack. Gough couldn't pick the lock.

In late August Haig replaced Gough with Gen. Herbert Plumer, who'd led the somewhat successful prelude to Passchendaele. When the skies finally dried in September, the fighting began anew.

On October 9 the Sixteenth Royal Scots had moved back north and went to work repairing the Langemarck–Poelcappelle road. It was not a glamorous detail. "The work was done under heavy shell fire and under very bad weather conditions as it rained continuously," the battalion's diary reads. The work went on day after brutal day. Ten men died, thirty-four were wounded, and sixteen were missing. By the thirteenth the battalion's strength was down to 22 officers and 607 other ranks.

The battalion moved to Saragossa Farm to prepare for an assault. German planes made rest impossible, dropping bombs "in the neighbourhood," the diary recorded. At 3:00 PM on October 18 they actually hit D Company's camp, killing eight and wounding eighteen, including 2nd Lt. Thomas Grainger Stewart, Ingouville-Williams's former aide-de-camp. On the twentieth, the war diary records, Stephenson was "slightly gassed" while visiting the front lines. That evening the battalion was shelled while approaching the front lines and had fifty casualties.

Germany had introduced a new, somehow more awful form of chemical warfare. Mustard gas smelled strongly of horseradish, lingered after being dispersed, and attacked your body, making masks less effective. It soaked your clothes, burned your skin, and would blind you if you rubbed your eyes. In June 2010 a clam boat pulled up some World War I–era mustard gas shells that had apparently been disposed off the coast of Long Island. One broke, causing burns to a crew member. "What is stunning to everyone is it is still so potent after all this time," a doctor treating the injured man said.[3]

As bad as things were behind the lines, fighting in the Ypres salient was worse. It took two hours to walk to the front. Shakespear wrote, "The walk was over country which was a mass of shell craters, salvage, guns, and men. The ground surface being impossible, all walking had to be done on duckboard tracks, which went to within about one thousand to one thousand five hundred yards of the front line, and were prolonged nightly."[4]

The battalion's diary is difficult reading. The front line was just "a line of shell hole positions." An officer of the Fifteenth Royal Scots said the "conditions were past speaking about, mud and filth up to the neck." The assault was set for the morning of October 22 but on what it's not exactly clear—the map shows some huts and a crossroads. The afternoon before the attack German airplanes flew low over the position and strafed the men, who were moving in twos and threes down the duckboard path. "There were several instances of individual men being pursued," a report reads.

A party trying to lay tape for the attacking parties came under such heavy fire the project had to be abandoned. The Sixteenth's four companies were supposed to assault in two waves at 5:30 AM, but shellfire was so harsh they could only muster one. A gap opened up between McCrae's and the Fifteenth Royal Scots on their right, leaving their flank "in the air." The battalion's rifles "were clogged with mud and useless." A second lieutenant and twenty men got cut off and "nothing further was heard of them." When the battalion was relieved the following night, its strength was seven officers and twenty-seven other ranks.

A subsequent report points out that Cpl. H. Fox stayed out all night administering to the wounded. Bandages and dressings got lost on the way to the position, so Fox searched the dead under shellfire for replacements.

Passchendaele ground on until November 10, when Haig finally gave up on getting to Roulers. Sixty-two thousand British soldiers died, and 164,000 were wounded. German losses were even heavier.

Allenby swept through the Holy Land, pursuing the Turks through heavy rain and taking Jerusalem on December 11. He entered the city on foot, drawing a deliberate contrast to the kaiser, who rode in on horseback in 1898. That night, his soldiers marched past the Garden of Gethsemane and camped on the Mount of Olives.

"I have landed in the Holy Land, and it is a lovely place," Paddy Crossan wrote John McCartney. "I would rather be fighting against Turks than Germans. The Turk is a clean fighter and they have just had an awful smashing. We have just captured Jerusalem—in fact all Palestine has been lost to the Turks. I am beside Neil Moreland (another Hearts player)."[5] The two tried to find the Wailing Wall but were turned away by a festival celebrating the Turks' departure, Crossan wrote, so they set out into the countryside to try to find the Pillar of Salt, but that expedition, too, was fruitless.

Paddy's Christmas card for 1917 included a little poetry:

> The bonnie blooming heather and the
> hilltops clad wi' snaw,
> Our hearts are aye in Scotland tho'
> we're faur, faur, awa'.[6]

14

THE RENDEZVOUS
OF ALL SPORTSMEN

"**B**attalion disbanded."
The Sixteenth Royal Scots told the story of their end with extreme economy on May 16, 1918. They were in Louches, a commune little more than twenty miles away from the Boulogne port where so many British units had begun their tours in France. Three officers and 328 other ranks were sent off to reinforce other units; fifty men and a handful of officers stayed behind to help train American troops. There was an unusual honor for Regimental Sgt. Maj. Annan Ness on the battalion's last day; he received a commission in the field. The rock of McCrae's, the man who helped train all his teammates back in Edinburgh, would finish the war as a lieutenant.

The Thirty-Fourth Division's battalions were training newly arrived American troops when the ax fell. Each US brigade would be affiliated with an "English brigade," Shakespear wrote. Or, ahem, a Scottish one: the Sixteenth's training cadre stuck with the 111th Infantry Regiment, a Pennsylvania unit founded by Ben Franklin, until the middle of June, when they departed south and the 309th Regiment showed from Brooklyn. Their last assignment was the Mississippi Rifles—Jefferson Davis's old outfit. On August 16, the last pieces of McCrae's were sent to the Ninth Royal Scots.

The Sixteenth Royal Scots had dwindled over the early months of 1918 but still had a knack for being in important action. They were at Croisilles when the Germans ignited their first massive offensive on the Western Front in March, crossing back over the Somme battlefields on March 24 before the air went out and the food crisis in Berlin began to starve onrushing troops. They were at Erquinghem when "Operation Georgette," the last major offensive in April, pushed British troops so far that Haig issued an order pledging that "with our backs to the wall and believing in the justice of our cause each one of us must fight on to the end." Jack Alexander writes that Ness guarded a bridge over the Lys and a wounded soldier with nothing but his rifle while others made their retreat.

The Sixteenth held their own in heavy fighting, even as the British fell back. Shakespear describes the French citizens' rush from Nieppe, just north of Erquinghem, as the Germans pushed into town: "Grandmother in armchair on wheelbarrow, pushed by grandson; mother, with sack of cooking gear, leading cow; small girl with calf; old man pushing a bicycle, used as a sort of pack animal, carrying two beds, small boy bearing family clock. All dressed in best Sunday black. Devoted but perspiring swain carrying off a hefty young lady sitting side saddle on the top bar of the cycle he is riding."[1]

On April 29, Georgette ended. The Germans were running out of food and, with large numbers of American soldiers arriving every day, running out of time. That spring, starved for men, Britain recalled to France troops who'd conducted campaigns elsewhere. "Back to France once more," Paddy Crossan wrote John McCartney. "Have been in Italy and Palestine." Crossan mentioned he'd seen Sandy Grosert from Hibs heading to the front lines. He had other concerns: "Would rather face the whole Prussian Guard than those big ugly brutes—trench rats."[2]

On April 22, former Hearts goalkeeper John Allan was the last member of the team to die in France before the war ended. He was with the Ninth Royal Scots and was killed at Roeux, where the Sixteenth Royal Scots had pressed their doomed assault the year before. His body was never found.

That summer American troops helped the French turn away a German advance toward Paris. Haig began to press back on the western end of the line, and the war finally turned mobile, even at times offering the cavalry a renewed place in the British weapons system. The offensive now known as the "Hundred Days" broke the Hindenburg Line and, working as a coalition, brought the German Army to the brink of collapse before armistice halted further fighting. The decision to stop fighting before the Germans were soundly defeated allowed a poisonous notion to go home to Germany with the troops—that they'd been "stabbed in the back" by politicians. It was an idea that helped the political rise a few years later of a returning soldier named Adolf Hitler.

THE END AT LAST the *Evening News* proclaimed on Monday, November 11, 1918. At 11:00 that morning, an armistice signed by German and Allied representatives in a railway car in Compiègne, France, took effect. The war ceased its active ravages 1,559 days after it began.

Princes Street became "exceedingly animated" as the clock struck eleven, the *Evening News* reported. University students led impromptu processions through the streets, and soldiers on leave marched at the front of many. The city hoisted flags at its chambers and instructed all the church bells to play a joyful peal. The lord provost lifted the order to darken windows at night "so that there may be at least this change from the dark and dismal war street lights." The board of trade temporarily lifted early closing hours for restaurants and clubs.

The next morning, Edinburgh and all of Britain faced problems much bigger than hangovers. The casualty counts told only part of the story. More than 886,000 British people died in military service during those years, an average of 568 every day. More than two million were wounded.

Some wounds weren't always apparent. The sustained horrors of the war continued to visit soldiers' minds as they slowly demobilized and returned home. In 1915 the military psychologist Charles Myers popularized the term *shell shock* as a way of describing the trauma, and it was just inaccurate enough to be useful. Eighty thousand soldiers were officially traumatized, but the real figure was likely much, much higher.

A spectrum cast into law a decade later placed the mentally ill on a spectrum from "moral defectives" to "idiots." People at the severe end tended to end up in hospitals where, if they were lucky, electric shock treatment was a secondary therapy. One of the best facilities was in Edinburgh. Craiglockhart, where William H. R. Rivers treated the poets Siegfried Sassoon and Wilfred Owen during the war. Men from the upper classes often had artistic outlets to express their trauma and account for much of our understanding of the condition, while the working classes were largely expected to "get on with it." Women who'd spent years fearing the arrival of the postman were lucky to be diagnosed with "hysteria." Children who'd lost a parent or grown used to the idea that death could manifest in the skies from zeppelins or Gotha bombers were not accounted for by any official statistics.[3]

It was especially wrenching for many that their loved ones' bodies were never found. In many families from Edinburgh's and Glasgow's working classes before and after the war, communion with a body was an essential part of finding peace with a loved one's passage. A body would remain in the home for three days for viewing, with men often standing vigil overnight.[4] The missing bodies of so many soldiers robbed many families of any feeling of closure.

Men averse to expressing their emotions are sometimes found in Scotland, and their returns home were especially frustrating. Many were haunted by the inability of those at home to comprehend their experiences; few of them were able or wanted to communicate what they'd seen. The Ministry of Pensions treated all applicants with extreme suspicion, especially when it came to claims of mental illness. Families of those men who managed to win financial support had the cost of the patient's care deducted first. Quack remedies—tonics, pills, patent medicines—abounded for those who sought treatment at home instead.

There was always alcohol, consumed in pubs where other patrons were likely to leave you plenty of space to self-medicate. For those who needed to scream, there was still professional football.

Hearts hammered Falkirk 5–0 at Tynecastle the week after the armistice. They'd finished the previous season in tenth place on the league table despite prodigious scoring from a new signing named Andy Wilson, who joined the Hearts after a shattered arm sent him home from the war. Players who returned from the war expecting their old salaries were disappointed to learn their teams wouldn't, or more likely couldn't, pay them more than a pound per week. Profitable clubs could pay up to three pounds per week after January 1, 1919, by making a special application to the league.[5]

On January 11, 1919, both Hearts and Hibernians took the field at Tynecastle with some familiar names among their starters. Peter Nellies and George Sinclair were on the pitch, as they had been for many matches over the previous years. Sandy Grosert was starting for Hibs. But the twelve thousand at Tynecastle that Saturday were especially delighted to see Paddy Crossan wearing maroon and playing right back once again. Andy Wilson scored three goals before the first half; Grosert managed to answer with one in the second.

Paddy's return to Edinburgh was accompanied by an appropriately legendary anecdote. As the historian Jack Alexander tells the story, Crossan had been gassed in France in August and was recovering in Edinburgh when his old mate in McCrae's John Veitch visited:

> Crossan's bed was by a window, looking out over Arthur's Seat. When Veitch asked him what he intended to do when he recovered, Pat replied, "First I'm going to run up yon wee hill, then I'm going back to play for Hearts."[6]

The week after Paddy returned, Willie Wilson came home to Hearts as well, playing on the left wing against Third Lanark at Cathkin Park. Wilson's shoulder, which he'd injured during a slippery game against Raith Rovers in November 1912, kept getting knocked out of shape by rifle recoil, and he bounced on and off active duty throughout the war, finally doing a hitch with McCrae's, or what was left of it, in the winter of 1917–1918. Willie Wilson and George Miller set up a goal by Andy Wilson in the first fifteen minutes, but the home team tied, then found two more goals in the second half. Paddy got injured toward the end, probably from Cathkin's "treacherous footing," the *Scotsman* noted.[7] Nevertheless, he stayed in the lineup until the end of March, and played most games through the end of the season.

Hearts finished seventh on the league table, an improvement over the previous season, at least. Attendance was up, and the club was finally able to begin paying off its new stand. But friction was growing amid the board as McCartney tried to rebuild the team. Despite the attentions of Jimmy Duckworth, the soldier-players were unlikely to return to their 1914 form. They needed to be restocked, and McCartney proposed to do so the same way he'd built the prewar squad. Fürst was suffering from heart problems and unable to give his friend the support he needed. McCartney resigned in mid-October. As the Dundee *Courier* related the story on October 18, "For some little time it has been an open secret that things were not going smoothly and that two minds were at work in regard to the selection of the team." Hearts' directors, the account reads, "accepted the resignation with regret, and both locally and generally the severance of a fairly long and intimate association will be regretted."

With so much apparent ill feeling swirling around the manager's departure, the appointment of his replacement was a bit of a surprise: Hearts chose McCartney's son, William. Amid the unrest, Hearts were inconsistent, and the on-field product quickly became a write-off, though rising attendances and ticket prices put the club back on solid financial ground. One minor miracle occurred on December 27 when Paddy Crossan scored two goals, both from penalty kicks.

That May, Hearts replaced sixty-eight-year-old Jimmy Duckworth as trainer. "Old Duck" trained runners before he applied those skills to football, and reveled in making his charges sprint. He died of heart disease three months later in Newton Mearns, a suburb of Glasgow. "He

could not bear with slackers, and his cure for inertia was the spikes,"
read a typical obituary in the *Arbroath Herald*. Describing a visit to
Tynecastle in heavy rain, the author asked Duckworth how the boys were
getting on. The trainer opened a door to show a small group drilling in
the rain. "That's how they are gettin' on," Duckworth told his visitor
with a smile. "But wait till I get them on the track in the mornin'."[8]

Hearts finished third the following season, their best since the war
began. It was a fluke. The following year saw a disastrous start, when
Hearts lost their first nine games.

Amid the nail biting, the club's war memorial was unveiled on
April 10 at Haymarket. A tall pylon with clocks by James Ritchie &
Son embedded in its yellow stone edifice, Harry Gamley's design chis-
eled the names of various engagements into the sides: Vimy, Ypres,
Gaza, Somme. A plaque on the front reads ERECTED BY THE HEART OF
MIDLOTHIAN FOOTBALL CLUB TO THE MEMORY OF THEIR PLAYERS AND
MEMBERS WHO FELL IN THE GREAT WAR 1914–1919. Above the inscrip-
tion is a heart surrounded by a wreath.

Thirty-five thousand people turned out for the opening ceremony,
where Secretary for Scotland Robert Munro would speak and the memorial would be handed over to the corporation of Edinburgh. Among
the dignitaries present were Sir James Leishman, Elias Fürst, and Sir
George McCrae.

Sir George had thrown himself back into policy since returning
home, taking up the cause of housing reform at the Local Government
Board, which merged with the Scottish Insurance Commission in 1922
to become the Scottish Board of Health.

The event called for a saga, not a speech, Munro said, but he tried
anyway. The members of Hearts hadn't hesitated to answer the call to
war, and some of them "fell in the Battle of the Somme in the morning of their days with the dew of youth still upon their brows." There
were many wreaths laid at the bottom of the memorial that day, including tributes from the league, Hearts players, and other clubs including
Celtic, Leith Athletic, and Portsmouth, where John McCartney was now
manager. A pipe dirge brought the ceremony to a close, followed by the

British bugle call "Last Post" and the national anthem. Edinburgh's lord provost promised the memorial would be "preserved with all reverence and honour in all coming time."[9]

A week later, Hearts' players undertook a preservation effort of their own, hoping to win the last game of their season and avoid relegation to a lower league. The contest took place at—where else?—Aberdeen, where the weather was atrocious, and so was the football. The *Aberdeen Daily Journal* said the play that day could not "have been mistaken for the efforts of teams other than those at the bottom of the table."[10] But Willie Wilson kept the offense alive throughout the game, setting up a goal by Frank Stringfellow within the last fifteen minutes. The home-town crowd, twelve thousand strong, applauded the visitors.

Despite having been gassed, twice wounded, and becoming a bit heftier as time went by, Paddy Crossan remained in the Hearts first team for nearly three years after the memorial was dedicated. You can attribute his perseverance in part to the malaise that affected almost every team in Britain after the war—experienced footballers were likely to have served overseas during the war, and many had been wounded. And yet Paddy was a fan favorite, for sure. A possibly apocryphal headline is part of his legend: PADDY CROSSAN KICKS FOOTBALL FROM TYNECASTLE TO NEWCASTLE. The conceit being, of course, that a goods train was passing the stadium when, like Paul Bunyan, he heaved a ball out of the stadium and into a goods train bound for England.[11]

Crossan's larger-than-life off-field persona can obscure the fact that he was a very good player. The team won or drew 68 percent of the games he was on the field, a tribute to his defending. By February 1925 Paddy was in his early thirties and slowing down. On the seventh of that month, Hearts traveled to Rugby Park to play Kilmarnock at home. It was Paddy's 310th game in maroon. Hearts' defense crumbled within minutes of the opening whistle, and Kilmarnock scored twice, the second goal trickling in past goalkeeper William White after Crossan and left back Jock Wilson got tangled up. Jock White eventually scored for the Edinburgh side, but the papers blamed Paddy, not the forwards, for the loss. "Inside ten minutes Crossan had let his side down," the

Scotsman opined on February 9, making a point of mentioning the "weakness of the Hearts' defence." A Sunday *Post* recap on February 8 noted how easily Kilmarnock's R. M. Rock had beat Crossan, which "must have given Hearts' Directors seriously to think."

Crossan sat in March and left the team in April. He "does not care playing second fiddle" to Tom Reid, the *Falkirk Herald* wrote. He moved across town to Leith Athletic for the first part of the 1925–1926 season. There he faced Hearts on August 20, in a match where he "did not seem to be in the best of condition, but played quite a good game," one sportswriter observed.[12]

That autumn, Paddy found something he liked almost as much as playing football. He opened a bar on Rose Street and named it after himself. A new career as a gentleman publican beckoned. With respectability came a marriage long in the planning. On January 21, 1926, Mary Alice Wattie and Patrick James Crossan bound their families together at St. Mary's on York Place in Edinburgh. On September 17, 1927, the bloodlines became one when Patrick John Crossan was born.

Paddy's Bar billed itself as "the Rendezvous of All Sportsmen," but its location coincided with Rose Street's rise as the heart of literary Edinburgh. Poets and artists were among Paddy's best customers in the handsome establishment, where the bar staff wore white coats and the taps gleamed. Mary Alice wore a hat when she served the public; Paddy tended to work the room, greeting well-wishers and fans among the regulars. This became a business issue over time; Paddy's most loyal fans would often end up leaving with a carton of cigarettes and bottle of Paddy's Special Whisky on the house.

In April 1926 Hearts traveled to Selkirk for what was billed as a "missionary" game. There Hearts would play a local side with their old center half, Bob Mercer, back in the lineup. Mercer began his football career in Selkirk, so the match at Ettrick Park was a double homecoming. But a few minutes in, Mercer fell to the ground with a shout, and was carried off the field unconscious. A doctor arrived too late. Mercer died playing for Hearts.

Paddy Crossan and Mary Alice Wattie at St. Mary's in Edinburgh on their wedding day, January 21, 1926.
Courtesy of the Crossan family

Mercer volunteered for McCrae's back in 1914 but an injured knee kept him from joining his teammates. In October 1916 he volunteered for the Royal Garrison Artillery, and he arrived in France in January 1918. That spring, he was gassed on the Somme. He never fully recovered. Mercer continued to play for Hearts until 1921, when his breathing problems became too much for the team. He played briefly for Dunfermline, and returned to Hearts as a coach in 1925. He was thirty-six when he died.

Other members of the 1914 team began other careers. Annan Ness trained as a dental surgeon. Jimmy Hazeldean became a bottle blower. Willie Wilson was a tinsmith. Alfie Briggs found work as a boilermaker. And George Sinclair, too, entered the pub business, opening Sinclair's Bar on Montrose Terrace, which later became a favorite watering spot for Hibs players (including, for a brief period at the end of the 1970s, the legendary British footballer George Best).

Some stayed with football a bit longer. Jimmy Frew played for Leeds United and Bradford City before opening a sporting goods shop in Leeds. Neil Moreland kicked around Scotland's lower leagues, playing for Broxburn United, Albion Rovers, and Dykehead. And Bob Preston left Tynecastle in 1922 for two English teams, Torquay United and Plymouth Argyle.

Meanwhile, Paddy was cultivating more legends off the field. There are rumors that one of Al Capone's henchmen used to frequent Paddy's Bar on whisky-acquisition trips during Prohibition. One of the best stories involves a customer who brought a Shetland pony into the pub after Paddy's son, also nicknamed Paddy, had been born. Crossan, after a few whiskies, agreed that no boy should be without such an animal, and purchased it. That evening, he brought it home to the third-floor tenement house the family shared on Pitt Street, to Mary Alice's dismay. The beast's eventual fate is, sadly, lost to history.

Another era ended on December 27, 1928, when Sir George McCrae passed away in his home in North Berwick. He was sixty-eight and suffered from heart disease. His obituary in the *Scotsman* begins with a rare apology for being the bearers of such awful news: "We regret to announce the death of Sir George McCrae."

The list of his accomplishments required two columns: the Local Government Board, Edinburgh's finances, acquisition of tramways and electric lighting, rebuilding the North Bridge, Parliament, his famous battalion, and then, after he returned home, a surprising return to politics that saw him lose a parliamentary election in 1922 to a Socialist candidate, win in another district the next year, and then lose again in 1924, after which he worked ever more on the issue of housing. The obituary was followed by a recap of his time in France with the Sixteenth Royal Scots, and a timetable of the events of July 1, 1916.

Sir George's funeral on Saturday, January 5, took place at Lady Glenorchy's Church in Edinburgh, before a gun carriage carried him to Grange Cemetery. The streets were packed, and on Drummond Street police had to keep back the mourners. He received full military honors, and members of the battalion were part of his cortege. Sir George's casket was covered with a Union Jack and his sword.

Back on Rose Street, Paddy continued the work of becoming a civic asset anew. In 1932 he gave an interview to the *Evening News* on the subject of football today. Crossan was still a Hearts fan and a "regular frequenter of Tynecastle," and he observed the game closely, noting its differences rather than judging them inferior. For example, Paddy offered, the threat of relegation to lower leagues had forced teams to play more aggressively than before: "The old scientific Scottish game has departed; the 'pattern-weaving industry' is bankrupt; artistry is at a discount, and cut-and-thrust methods have taken their place," the author of the piece wrote, channeling the veteran's words.

Such energetic play couldn't help but shorten careers, Crossan said, "the pace and energy demanded are so great that the average player cannot be expected to maintain the pressure over a period of years as his predecessors did."[13]

Paddy had a few downs amid the ups. In August 1929 an Edinburgh constable noticed a car parked in a tramway island at the intersection of Lothian Road and Princes Street, near the grand Caledonian Hotel.

The policeman approached the car, where he detected the scent of alcohol, and a driver, Paddy Crossan, whose eyes were "watery and hazy" and whose "speech was thick."[14] Crossan was invited to the West End Police Station where a doctor pronounced him under the influence of alcohol. Paddy's personal doctor visited the station and pronounced him just fine. His two passengers gave evidence in court that Paddy was sober. He said he was driving them home. Despite all the character evidence—the judge in the case, Paddy's grandson Peter notes, was one of the passengers—the charge was found proved, and Paddy was ordered to pay two pounds.

Mostly it was good, this businessman's life. Paddy filled out, enjoying the less strenuous regime of his new career. In 1932 he presented prizes at the East Calder Burns Club's singing and reciting competition, including a special gold badge to a young girl named Mary Hastie. It was real pillar of the community stuff, and he excelled at it.

The turn of 1933 brought more hard news. John McCartney died on January 18 at home on Moat Street. Heart disease and diabetes did the great man in; the *Evening News* revealed he'd had a leg amputated and ever since, "his sphere of activity, previously great, became rather circumscribed." McCartney had great stories about his playing career, and "sundry hard 'scraps'" when his old club Cowlairs played Hibernian, the obituary read, but it was his management of what it called "the people's game" that made his life's work so remarkable. "To what failings of temperament he had one could not be otherwise than kind when he remembers the open-hearted nature of the man, his kindly disposition, his rare geniality," the send-off read. "A hater of humbugs of all sorts, Mr M'Cartney was disliked by all humbugs, but he will long retain a very kindly place in many hearts in Edinburgh as in the other spheres of his labours."[15]

McCartney's funeral was another civic occasion, the cortege from his house to North Merchiston Cemetery observed by hundreds of people lining Slateford Road. His final resting place was but a thousand feet from Tynecastle. His son William was among the pallbearers, and representatives from football teams all over Scotland attended. A photograph of the occasion shows people crowding in and around the cemetery walls, some perched on shoulders, for one last look at Hearts' legendary manager.

And 1933 wasn't yet done with its deprivations. Paddy's lungs were still laboring to recover from the poison gas he'd inhaled in France. That spring, he entered Southfield Sanitorium in Edinburgh to recover from pulmonary tuberculosis. On April 28 Paddy Crossan died.

Paddy's death certificate said he was thirty-nine. According to the date on his birth certificate, he was 41. It doesn't really matter—time was too picayune a metric for the Handsomest Man in the World anyway. His passing occasioned banner headlines in Edinburgh, as well as a lovely obituary in the *Midlothian Advertiser* back home in oil shale country. "He was always a personality on the field, and there was no resisting the gay abandon of his play," it read. "How the crowd loved his mammoth kicking, his daring interventions, and his flying tackles! He was breeziness itself, and many a time his dauntless courage inspired a jaded Hearts team to renewed efforts."[16]

A funeral mass was said at St. Mary's Cathedral on May 2, before Paddy was laid to rest in Mount Vernon Cemetery, where hundreds of mourners paid their respects. The *Scotsman* noted a "large number of wreaths, including one in the shape of a heart from the club with which he had been associated practically throughout his football career."[17]

That Saturday the players of Hearts and Hamilton Academical wore black armbands to honor Paddy Crossan during an Alliance Shield game. Hearts crushed Accies 5–0.

Paddy's death hurt Mary Alice Wattie profoundly. Young Paddy was only five when his father died, and as soon as Mary Alice could, she sent him away to boarding school in Fort Augustus, near Inverness. Her sister Louise, who everyone called Louie, moved in, and Mary Alice set about running the bar.

Another war came and went, but not before the clock committed more and more robberies. Elias Fürst in June 1942. Annan Ness in

December of the same year. The "Big Chief," Harry Julian, McCrae's tallest man and a worldwide force in Scouting, in 1943.

A silent 1955 film tour of Edinburgh shows the bar staff of Paddy's Bar, still sharp in their white coats, rushing to serve a business packed with customers. Men with hats and long coats take up most of the standing space by the shiny bar, but there are lots of women in the seated area. Paddy's Bar became a favorite of some rather famous artists. Hugh MacDiarmid appeared there regularly, as did Sydney Goodsir Smith. John Ogdon dropped in whenever he was in town.

But for all that booming business, Mary Alice inherited a good number of regulars with monumental unpaid tabs, some of whom tried to finesse the situation with checks that didn't clear. By the early 1960s the bar was teetering financially. Mary Alice's health declined. Her son, Paddy, now in his thirties, felt he had no choice but to try to get the bar back on track. He and his wife, Jean, began the long process of sorting out the finances, enduring boors who would harangue them with stories about the great Paddy Crossan, and gently informing others they'd have to pay in cash going forward.

Mary Alice died on November 18, 1965, of breast cancer. She was seventy-eight. Paddy and Jean sold the bar and most of the memorabilia within it in 1968. While they planned to stay out of the hospitality business, they opened another bar, the Tilted Wig, two years later and ran it successfully until 1992, when they retired. The Wig became an Edinburgh landmark, with a small beer garden, real ales, and a faithful clientele, many of whom worked in the law. Paddy died in 2012, and was remembered as "one of Edinburgh's last 'old school' pub landlords." Peter, who worked in the bar when he was younger, says his dad lived a lot of his life in Paddy's shadow, to the point that he downplayed his father's profession while trying to get Peter a place at Edinburgh Academy, where he assumed rugby and cricket would be the sort of sports the staff followed. During an interview, the headmaster asked him, "Are you any relation to the famous Paddy Crossan?" As Paddy tried to gather himself, the headmaster added, "I'm a great Hearts fan, and your father was a great man."

Paddy and many of the other Hearts lads would be remembered throughout Edinburgh for decades, but what of the other men who served in the battalion? An association was formed in 1919, and annual reunion dinners brought the survivors together. They petitioned the city for a memorial adequate to their sacrifice, but Alexander writes that their appeals were ignored by a community ill informed about the war and trying to move on.

Eight months after the Haymarket memorial to Hearts' war dead made its debut before tens of thousands outdoors in a busy intersection, a dedication ceremony for a memorial to the Sixteenth Royal Scots took place in stately but comparatively low-key circumstances. On December 17, 1922, a tablet was unveiled in St. Giles' Cathedral, down the Royal Mile from Edinburgh Castle. The church was full, the *Scotsman* reported, as Sir George handed over the battalion's colors to the cathedral, which promised to preserve them forever.

The tablet is beautiful, sculpted in rose limestone by Pilkington Jackson and designed by Sir Robert Lorimer. You can find it in the Albany Aisle, a chapel in St. Giles's northwest corner that also has a memorial to John Knox. On it the archangel St. Michael stands defiantly over a vanquished dragon, flaming sword in right hand, a shield in the other. An inscription over gilded stone below reads:

> To the Glory of God
> In Honoured Memory Of
> Eight Hundred Officers
> Non-Commissioned Officers
> And Men
> Of the 16th (S) Battalion
> The Royal Scots (2nd Edin R)
> Who Fell in the War
> 1914–1919

General Pulteney sent a message praising the battalion for its "magnificent work" at the Somme, and Douglas Haig sent a "special tribute to a Scottish regiment which, on the 1st July 1916, suffered such heavy loss and served its country so well." Haig continued, "I hope that the day will never come when Scotsmen will fail to answer to the call of duty, or fear to follow, if need be, in the footsteps of the brave kinsmen who have gone before us."

A *Scotsman* correspondent added "an impression" to the paper's account:

> There were the C. O., looking not greatly changed; the Padre, looking a little grayer; and all around were familiar and many more unfamiliar faces, for there were more "Sixteenths" than one, and total strangers found themselves linked, as it were, by familiar blue "tabs" in one common allegiance. Names "familiar in the mouth as household words" were by them freshly remembered, for not a man but had come to honour a friend— some comrade of those blithe, far-away days in Heriot's, of sunny days "in rest" behind the line, of the terrible baptismal day at La Boisselle, of the muddy agony of Passchendaele, or of those languorous later days on the right beside the French. There were others who had to honour more than friends. The colour looked strangely new as it was borne slowly forward beneath the overhanging lines of dusty, ragged, and shell-torn colours overhead; but none, one felt, represented sterner fields or celebrated more honourable service or prouder sacrifice.[18]

The service concluded with a lament on the pipes, the last post, reveille, and the national anthem. Outside St. Giles's west door is the Heart of Midlothian mosaic embedded in the street, the site of the Old Tolbooth and the Walter Scott novel from which the football team took their name in 1874. Scots today spit on the Heart as they pass it because the Old Tolbooth held a debtors prison and sites for public executions.

But while that tradition remains well known, the story of Sir George McCrae and his volunteers got told more quietly over the years as its survivors succumbed to time, the British public reevaluated the Great War (to the great cost of Haig's reputation), and an even bigger world war elbowed out the complex memory of the horrible one that preceded it.

Bob Preston died in 1945; he'd retired to Northern Ireland and opened a pub, as well as managed Distillery, the club that hosted Paddy Crossan for that one-off match in May 1917. Alfie Briggs died in 1950, followed five years later by Willie Wilson, and four years after that by George Sinclair. Jamie Low died in 1960. He'd retired from playing football and ran his family's fishing-net business. Jimmy Frew died in 1967 in Leeds. Jimmy Hazeldean died in 1980.

For years, someone kept tying a fresh Heart of Midlothian scarf around Patrick Crossan's grave at Mount Vernon Cemetery. The graveyard is south of Edinburgh in the hillside suburb of Liberton. Tynecastle is about seven miles to the northwest, as the crow flies, and the magnificent mountain Arthur's Seat is in view directly to the north. Paddy Crossan looks out on "yon wee hill" for eternity.

EPILOGUE
The Last Post

An American visiting Picardy is traveling in other people's memories. The gently rolling fields full of soft wheat and rioting poppies are interrupted by tiny redbrick villages of a dozen or so buildings and names that tore holes in British and German families a hundred years before. Puisieux. Beaumont-Hamel. Bucquoy. Foncquevillers.

Much of the area where the hundredth anniversary of the Battle of the Somme would be remembered on July 1, 2016, was in a perimeter closed to traffic, and very early that morning I was driving from Arras toward the Albert airport on a route that was making my phone's GPS scream in protest. The villages and the land weren't all that memorable on their own, but they were surrounded by places where grandparents and great-grandparents had fought and died under circumstances that are almost inconceivable. I saw German tourists alighting from buses at some of the sites on previous days, but most of the commemorative spots I saw were there for people from Britain or Commonwealth countries. Gommecourt. Hawthorn Ridge. Lochnagar.

In the airport complex I waited in a line with about fifteen other cars as it began to get light. A French policeman yelled at a fellow ahead of me who used the lull to repeatedly exit his small car to change items of clothing. Sandals off. Sweater on. He smiled and waved, and snaked

The Scots and French flags fly together at Contalmaison church, near the farthest point that British troops reached on July 1, 1916. The village finally fell on July 10. A cairn memorializes the Fifteenth and Sixteenth Royal Scots. Heart of Midlothian fans leave mementos at the base of the cairn year-round.
Andrew Beaujon

the spot I was going to park in when we finally got to the muddy field where we'd leave our cars. After going through security and showing my passport, I walked down a corrugated plastic track to a bus headed to Contalmaison. Some people were in kilts, some wore suits, many wore middle-class British outdoor gear—puffy vests and chambray shirts over jeans. A few were in military attire. I sat next to a gentleman wearing a Raith Rovers jersey under a tweed jacket, and as we rode we talked about the Brexit referendum the week before, and places each of us had visited in the other's country.

Our bus stopped just south of Contalmaison's church, on the road that leads up from Fricourt. Hearts supporters in maroon jerseys, some looking a bit wrung out from their time in the hotel bar in Arras the night before when their team played FC Infonet, wandered around chatting softly. I nodded to a few of the people I'd met there and got in line for a miniature cup of coffee at some card tables in a tent across the street from a monument to the Fifteenth and Sixteenth Royal Scots.

It's in the shape of a cairn, a pile of stones that people have used for thousands of years to mark places of significance: shrines, battlefields, landmarks. The Sixteenth Royal Scots discussed building a pair of cairns to mark their history, one in Edinburgh, one here. They had to settle for a tablet in St. Giles' instead.

After pipers and the Royal Scots Regimental Association brought in the colors, we heard a short welcome from Maj. Gary Tait, the chairman of McCrae's Battalion Trust. Then a prayer and a speech by a slight fellow in a white shirt, khakis, and a black tie. Jack Alexander is the reason the cairn is there. Jack Alexander is the reason we all were there.

Alexander spoke in Scots English and rough French, welcoming us to what he took pains to emphasize was the hundredth anniversary of the *eighth* day of the Battle of the Somme. It began with a weeklong bombardment, he told the crowd from a lectern draped with the French and Scottish flags. Remember the bombardment. Alexander spoke of the "duty of remembrance," the labor involved in never forgetting.

He understands that work deeply. Alexander began collecting information on McCrae's battalion for a book in 1990 and saw it published thirteen years later. The McCrae's Battalion Trust organized fundraising for the cairn but hardly stopped there after it was finished in 2004. It is responsible for organizing a gravestone for piper Willie Duguid, the renaming of the square by the Usher Hall as McCrae's Place, as well as these annual pilgrimages. Memory isn't easy. Memory is hard work.

July 1, 1916, was a day of hard ironies that bewilder memory. Haig's belief in God's help and the ability of his own shells to cut barbed wire. The plan for a breakthrough victory that turned out to be a blueprint for incremental gains. The beautiful weather that enveloped a day of slaughter. Literary critics say irony inevitably becomes myth, a fact anyone who wants to learn how to remember the Somme will appreciate. The action was too vast to describe, and excruciatingly difficult to reconstruct. Battle alters memory, and those fuzzy memories alter how we think of war.

No-man's-land. In the trenches. Shell shock. The linguistic contributions of World War I have long since slipped their dreadful moorings. I'm from a country that fought at the very end of the war, and while our soldiers experienced depravity and abominations just like everyone else's, theirs aren't as tightly woven into the United States' collective psyche as the experiences of soldiers are in Britain's, France's, Germany's, or Russia's. For us, World War I is less an act of remembering than an interesting subject of study. For many of us, that war is something that happened to someone else.

At Contalmaison we heard the last post played on a bugle that belonged to a member of the Sixteenth Royal Scots and that hadn't been played since July 1, 1916. We observed a moment of silence, where all you could hear was halyards making bells of flagpoles, a rooster crowing somewhere else in town, and birds singing. It was cool and dry, another beautiful morning. Pipes skirled, then played "Flooers o' the Forest." The bugle sounded again, playing reveille.

The representatives of various organizations laid wreaths at the cairn, upon which Sir George's rifle leaned. Scots Redoubt is a few hundred yards behind the memorial. It was time to lay wreaths of paper poppies. *On behalf of the people of Fife, Provost Jim Leishman, MBE. On behalf of Hibernian Football Club, Tom Wright. On behalf of Raith Rovers Football Club, Marshall Bowman.* There was Hearts legend John Robertson, laying a wreath on behalf of the club. There was the mayor of Contalmaison, walking beside an Edinburgh councilmember. There were two young men from West Calder High School. The church's bells struck ten.

Then came family members, called one by one. *In memory of Lieutenant Colonel Sir George McCrae, Callum Robertson. In memory of the family of Lance Corporal Jimmy Boyd, Sandy Potter.* The French women who'd passed out the lyrics for "God Save the Queen" and "La Marseillaise" were sitting on the steps of the church, smoking. *In memory of the family of Archibald West, Rory and Kenny West. In memory of the family of Paddy Crossan, Peter Crossan.*

We sang the anthems, then heard Craig Herbertson and Ed Westerdale sing "Dumbarton's Drums," the regimental quick march of the Royal Scots, but also a folk song with a different tune. (It all makes sense if you're Scottish.) It was beautiful, and we applauded.

Accounts of trench warfare always mention the larks. It's a reasonable question how anyone could hear a bird singing during a bombardment, but soldiers about to go over the top at the Somme swear they heard the whistling call amid the crashes and explosions.

Maybe that was because of what the literary historian Paul Fussell called "the necessity of fiction in any memorable testimony about fact." Maybe if your only view was of muddy walls, the sky held abiding interest and your ears grew keener. Maybe the larks were a symbol of the earth's renewal, or pins in the memories that passed down through language, through pop culture, through an Edinburgh University student's obsession with a battalion everyone else had forgotten, through the crushing and inexplicable pain of wives, parents, siblings, partners, children, and friends. How did they die? Why did they have to die? What did they die *for*?

I have heard the larks at Contalmaison, and let me tell you: larks may not be louder than trench warfare, but there are worse sounds on which to hang a memory. They are very loud, and their song stays with you forever.

ACKNOWLEDGMENTS

I spent most of my time working on this book from the wrong side of the ocean, and I'm so thankful to the people who made that distance less of an issue than it could have been.

Thank you to Andrew Macdonald and Peter Hart for granting me permission to quote from their work.

Special acknowledgement must be made to the librarians and archivists I consulted: Dr. Anne Cameron of the Archives and Special Collections, University of Strathclyde; Fraser Simm, archivist of the George Heriot's Trust; Victoria Garrington, curator of the Curatorial and Engagement Team, Edinburgh Museums and Galleries; Jennie Cartwright of Lincs Inspire Libraries in Grimsby, England; Douglas Wright of Edinburgh Central Library; and Alison Metcalfe of the National Library of Scotland. An extra-special thanks to Sybil Cavanagh, formerly of the West Lothian Local History Library, who found so much information about Addiewell and the Crossan family. Sybil, I honestly can't thank you enough.

Three football historians helped me: Gus Martin, author of terrific books about West Lothian Football; David Speed of Heart of Midlothian Football Club, who gave me an impromptu lesson in geography when we were both standing around in Contalmaison; and Matthew McDowell of the University of Edinburgh. Matt especially put up with a ridiculous number of questions and emails.

Kevin Williams of Swansea University educated me on British media and propaganda in the course of a long interview. Claire Haymes helped me with German translations.

While in France, I met so many wonderful people, including Sandy Potter and Craig Potter. Sandy has written a play about the McCrae's men called *The Scarf,* which you can and should watch on YouTube. Craig and I kicked around Arras and just kind of hung out. We also spent some time walking to my Airbnb to pick up my laptop so everyone could watch the Hearts game on the hotel TV. We were accompanied on this quest by Kenny West, descendant of Sgt. Archibald West and owner of the excellent bar Scotch Hop in Edinburgh, which serves homemade pies and delicious house-brewed beer. Do not miss it if you're in town. I'd also like to thank Mme. Patricia Leroy, the mayor of de Contalmaison, and John Dalgleish of the McCrae's Battalion Trust, who helped me out with media credentials.

I was fortunate to meet many descendants of the McCrae's soldiers and others, and I especially want to thank Peter, Edward, and Simon Crossan. Peter gave me a thorough interview and shared with me some gems from the family collection. Peter, you're a gent. Joanna Wright took time to tell me about her great-grandfather, David Anderson, who if even half the legends about him are true was one of the biggest badasses who ever lived.

Jack Alexander very graciously met with me when I was starting this project. His book, *McCrae's Battalion,* is the best thing ever written about these men. More than anyone, he has kept the story of McCrae's from receding into history. He's not just a hero to Hearts fans; he's truly a hero of Scotland. You should buy his book *right now.*

While you've got your wallet handy, please consider donating to the McCrae's Battalion Trust, which is a remarkable organization. That cairn outside the church in Contalmaison? Their work. The gravestone for piper Willie Duguid? Yep. The trust and Jack have guided or had a hand in every important commemoration of McCrae's, from the replacement of the Haymarket memorial to the renaming of the plaza around the Usher Hall. They lead an annual pilgrimage to Contalmaison and the battlefields of northern France and Belgium. Consider joining them; I promise you it will be the trip of a lifetime.

I was able to finish this book on time thanks to my friends Tim and Karen Graf, who loaned me their cabin in beautiful Basye, Virginia, during my last two weeks of writing when my wife, Ewa, suggested she'd kind of rather I worked somewhere else. My parents, Dick and Janet Couch, and my mother-in-law, Ewa Golabek, provided food, child-care, and space to work in Sault Ste. Marie, Canaan, and Edinburgh. The entire Hamilton-Golabek-Maguire-Persson-Beaujon-Couch-Riley-Ackermann-Baughman clan kept me going; I love you all.

I want to give a special thanks to Roy Peter Clark at the Poynter Institute, who not only introduced me to my agent, Jane Dystel, but whose books on writing recharged me every day.

Jane Dystel sustained me, guided me, and encouraged me through this whole process. Miriam Goderich and Amy Bishop at Dystel & Goderich Literary Management provided invaluable help as well. Jerome Pohlen brought this book to Chicago Review Press and was a trusty guide and editor. Lindsey Schauer gave the book an excellent edit, and Miki Caputo gave it a copyedit that I deeply appreciate.

My bosses at *Washingtonian* were generous with leave and made it easier on me to work on this project than I deserved. My editor, Michael Schaffer, was always around to kick around ideas, read drafts, and to urge me on. Our owner, Cathy Merrill Williams, has nurtured a workplace where creativity flourishes. I am so grateful to work with them and all my cherished colleagues at the best damn magazine in Washington.

My friends know who they are and that I love them. Thanks to John Rickman and Emily Rickman for putting off our band Talk It for a year while I did this thing instead. We will now commence once more to rock, my friends.

Finally, I must thank my children, Cameron and Euan, who put up with their dad being exhausted all the time for a whole year of getting up at 5:00 AM on weekdays, and being a ghost through most week-ends. There's no way I can adequately thank my wife, Ewa Beaujon, who helped fact-check this book, and offered patience—so, so much of that—support, and love. Who would have known when she first told me about the memorial at Haymarket, while we sat around her mother's kitchen table in Bruntsfield, that it would come to this? As the quaich she gave me after we married at the Sacred Heart on Lauriston Street reads, *seas between us braid hae roar'd*. And yet we always make land together.

NOTES

Chapter 1: A Company of Sportsmen

1. Alex Wood, "The MP's Secret: Respect Your Ancestors—But Don't Always Believe Them," *The Scottish Genealogist* 58, no. 1 (March 2011): 42–45.
2. *Scotsman*, November 25, 1914.
3. Jack Alexander, *McCrae's Battalion: The Story of the 16th Royal Scots* (Edinburgh: Mainstream, 2004), 48.
4. *Bath Chronicle and Weekly Gazette*, July 2, 1908.
5. Martin Gilbert, *The First World War: A Complete History* (New York: RosettaBooks, 2014), loc. 2411, Kindle.
6. *Punch, or the London Charivari*, October 21, 1914.
7. *Edinburgh Evening News*, November 26, 1914.
8. *Edinburgh Evening News*, November 26, 1914.
9. Alexander, *McCrae's Battalion*, 61.
10. Dundee *Courier*, August 17, 1914.
11. Glasgow *Daily Record*, November 28, 1914.
12. *Courier*, November 28, 1914.
13. *Daily Record*, November 27, 1914.
14. Alexander, *McCrae's Battalion*, 80–81.
15. *Edinburgh Evening News*, December 7, 1914.

Chapter 2: The Scientific Game

1. www.addiewellheritage.org.uk/page_id__62_path__0p4p45p35p19p31p38p20p .aspx.

2. "Addiewell in 1910: A Miniature Hell of Slums," *Forward* 4, no. 46, www .addiewellheritage.org.uk/page_id__110.aspx.

3. *Falkirk Herald and Linlithgow Journal*, November 22, 1877.

4. *Falkirk Herald and Linlithgow Journal*, November 22, 1877.

5. *Edinburgh Evening News*, October 15, 1888.

6. *Edinburgh Evening News*, October 15, 1888.

7. *Edinburgh Evening News*, October 15, 1888.

8. Gus Martin, *West Lothian's Scottish Cup History* (Dechmont, UK: self-published, 2015), 10.

9. *Daily Record*, October 26, 1914.

10. Matthew McDowell, interview with author, May 11, 2016.

11. Alexander, *McCrae's Battalion*, 66–67.

12. William Reid, *The Story of 'The Hearts': A Fifty Years' Retrospect 1874–1924*, (Edinburgh: Heart of Midlothian Football Club, 1924), 61.

13. *Scotsman*, March 10, 1913.

14. *Courier*, March 31, 1913.

15. John McCartney, *The "Hearts" and the Great War* (Edinburgh: self-pub., 1918), 20.

16. *Scotsman*, November 3, 1913.

17. *Courier*, November 24, 1913.

18. *Daily Record*, January 19, 1914.

19. *Courier*, February 27, 1914.

Chapter 3: The Sport in War

1. *Edinburgh Evening News*, December 2, 1914.

2. *Edinburgh Evening News*, December 2, 1914.

3. *Edinburgh Evening News*, December 2, 1914.

4. *Scotsman*, December 1, 1914.

5. *Edinburgh Evening News*, December 2, 1914.

6. *Edinburgh Evening News*, December 2, 1914.

7. *Scotsman*, December 3, 1914

8. *Edinburgh Evening News*, December 3, 1914.

9. *Scotsman*, December 5, 1914.

10. *Edinburgh Evening News*, December 5, 1914.

11. *Edinburgh Evening News*, December 5, 1914.

12. *Scotsman*, December 16, 1914.

13. Until 1971 the British pound was divided into 20 shillings, or 240 pence. Helen Clark and Elizabeth Carnegie's book *She Was Aye Workin'* gives the example of a typical tenement-dwelling Scots family in 1913: the husband brought home thirty-two shillings each week. After housekeeping expenses (15 shillings, 11 pence), rent (6 shillings), coal, clothing, etc., they'd finish the week nine pence ahead.

14. *Edinburgh Evening News*, December 5, 1914.

15. *Edinburgh Evening News*, December 5, 1914.

16. *Edinburgh Evening News*, December 26, 1914.

17. *Edinburgh Evening News*, December 12, 1914.

18. *Scotsman*, December 16, 1914.

19. *Edinburgh Evening News*, December 14, 1914.

20. *Edinburgh Evening News*, December 14, 1914.

21. Fraser Simm, "Our Grassmarket Buildings: A Brief History," *Quadrangle: George Heriot's School Development Newsletter* (September 2006): 3.

22. *Edinburgh Evening News*, February 8, 1915.

23. *Scotsman*, December 30, 1914.

24. *Daily Record*, December 21, 1914.

25. *Scotsman*, December 25, 1914.

Chapter 4: In Sunshine and in Shadow

1. All of Haig's diary entries are from *The Private Papers of Douglas Haig, 1914–1919*, ed. Robert Blake London: Eyre & Spottiswoode, 1952).

2. Richard Holmes, *The Little Field Marshal: A Life of Sir John French* (London: Wiedenfeld & Nicolson, 1981), 48.

3. Charles à Court Repington, *Vestigia: Reminiscences of Love and War* (Boston: Houghton Mifflin, 1919), 74.

4. *Private Papers of Douglas Haig*, 20.

5. *Private Papers of Douglas Haig*, 35.

Chapter 5: Rare Sport, My Masters

1. *Edinburgh Evening News*, February 13, 1915.

2. *Edinburgh Evening News*, February 15, 1915.

3. *Edinburgh Evening News*, January 28, 1915.

4. *Daily Record*, March 1, 1915.

5. *Daily Record, March 1, 1915.*

6. *Edinburgh Evening News*, March 22, 1915.

7. *Sunday Post*, April 4, 1915.

8. *Daily Record*, April 5, 1915.

9. *Courier*, April 5, 1915.

10. *Daily Record*, April 12, 1915.

11. *Daily Record*, April 12, 1915.

12. *Manchester Evening News*, April 15, 1915.

13. *Scotsman*, April 16, 1915.

14. *Daily Record*, April 19.

15. Erik Larson, *Dead Wake: The Last Crossing of the* Lusitania (New York: Broadway Books, 2015), loc. 3519, Kindle.

16. *Scotsman*, May 10, 1915.

17. *Scotsman*, May 17, 1915.

18. *Edinburgh Evening News*, May 21, 1915.

19. *Scotsman*, May 22, 1915.

20. *Edinburgh Evening News*, May 24, 1915.

21. *Scotsman*, June 1, 1915.

22. *Scotsman*, June 9, 1915.

23. *Edinburgh Evening News*, June 18, 1915.

Chapter 6: Get the Devils on the Run

1. *Private Papers of Douglas Haig*, 98.

2. *Private Papers of Douglas Haig*, 121.

Chapter 7: In Search of Adventure

1. *Edinburgh Evening News*, December 6, 1915.

2. *Edinburgh Evening News*, August 2, 1915.

3. *Edinburgh Evening News*, July 24, 1915.

4. *Edinburgh Evening News*, July 31, 1915.

5. Rowse, W. F., oral history, catalog no. 24870, Imperial War Museum.

6. *Edinburgh Evening News*, July 31, 1915.

7. McCartney, John, *The Sport in War* (Edinburgh, self-published, 1930), 21.

8. Malcolm Ernest Hancock, oral history, catalog no. 7396, Imperial War Museum.

9. J. W. Sandilands and Norman MacLeod, *The History of the 7th Battalion Queen's Own Cameron Highlanders* (Stirling, UK: Eneas MacKay, 1922), 32.

10. John Sheen, *Tyneside Irish: 24th, 25th, 26th & 27th (Service) Battalions of Northumberland Fusiliers* (Barnsley, UK: Pen and Sword, 2010), loc. 1149, Kindle.
11. *Edinburgh Evening News*, October 23, 1915.
12. *Liverpool Echo*, October 25, 1915.
13. *Edinburgh Evening News*, October 28, 1915.
14. *Edinburgh Evening News*, November 3, 1915.
15. *Edinburgh Evening News*, December 6, 1915.
16. *South Staffordshire Chronicle*, March 20, 1915.
17. *Edinburgh Evening News*, March 10, 1916.
18. Bill Smith, "Monday 6th December 1915," *Captain Tunstill's Men: A Day-by Day Account of One Company in the Great War* (blog), December 5, 2015, http://tunstillsmen.blogspot.com.au/2015/12/monday-6th-december-1915.html.
19. *Edinburgh Evening News*, March 10, 1916.
20. Sidney Albert Amatt, oral history, catalog no. 9168, Imperial War Museum.
21. *Edinburgh Evening News*, March 10, 1916.
22. *Edinburgh Evening News*, March 10, 1916.
23. *Edinburgh Evening News*, March 10, 1916.
24. *Scotsman*, December 28, 1928.
25. John Shakespear, *The Thirty-Fourth Division, 1915–1919* (Luton, UK: Andrews, 2012), 20.

Chapter 8: I Think We Can Do Better than This

1. Keating's diary belongs to the Royal Welsh Fusiliers; the Wrexham County Borough Museum and Archives is compiling a transcription. I transcribed this passage from images of Keating's diary in a 2015 BBC story, "1915 WW1 Diary Gives Account of Second Christmas Truce" by Nick Bourne.
2. Philip Gibbs, *Now It Can Be Told*, (New York: Harper & Brothers, 1920), 18.
3. Jack Sheldon writes in *The German Army on the Somme 1914–1916*, "In order to deliver the daily ration of 350 grams of uncooked meat per man, one of the Bavarian corps estimated that it slaughtered and butchered an average of forty beef cattle and fifty to ninety pigs per day, with peaks on occasions of sixty cattle and one hundred and sixty pigs."
4. Thirty-Fourth Division, general staff war diary, June 1916.
5. Shakespear, *Thirty-Fourth Division*, 28.
6. Jack Sheldon, *The German Army on the Somme 1914–1916* (Barnsley, UK: Pen and Sword, 2005), loc. 2616, Kindle.
7. Gibbs, *Now It Can Be Told*, 215.

8. Sheldon, *German Army*, loc. 2738.

9. Sheldon, *German Army*, loc. 2896.

10. Sheldon, *German Army*, loc. 2930.

Chapter 9: Over the Top

1. Thirty-Fourth Division, general staff war diary, June 1916.

2. Andrew Macdonald, *First Day of the Somme* (Auckland: HarperCollins, 2016), 217.

3. Alexander, *McCrae's Battalion*, 155.

4. Cecil Lewis, *Sagittarius Rising* (London: Frontline Books, 2009), loc. 1080, Kindle.

5. Lewis, *Sagittarius Rising*, loc. 1197.

6. Alexander, *McCrae's Battalion*, 156.

7. Hart, *Voices from the Front: An Oral History of the Great War* (New York: Oxford University Press, 2016), loc. 2778, Kindle.

8. Lewis, *Sagittarius Rising*, loc. 1217.

9. Sheldon, *German Army*, loc. 2886.

10. Graham Stewart and John Sheen, *Tyneside Scottish: 20th, 21st, 22nd & 23rd (Service) Battalions of the Northumberland Fusiliers* (Barnsley, UK: Pen and Sword, 1999), loc. 2628, Kindle.

11. Stewart and Sheen, *Tyneside Scottish*, loc. 2628.

12. Stewart and Sheen, *Tyneside Scottish*, loc. 2638.

13. *Scotsman*, September 2, 1916.

14. David's great-granddaughter Joanna Wright loves this particular story, but as a cop herself she's unsure of its accuracy. Where did the surrendered soldiers go?

15. *Scotsman*, September 2, 1916.

16. Tenth Battalion, Lincolnshire Regiment, war diary, July 1916.

17. *Edinburgh Evening News*, August 4, 1916.

18. Sheldon, *German Army*, loc. 3488.

19. Alexander, *McCrae's Battalion*, 159.

20. Ray Westlake, *Tracing British Battalions on the Somme* (Barnsley, UK: Pen and Sword, 1994), loc. 1509, Kindle.

21. Shakespear, *Thirty-Fourth Division*, 42.

22. Michael Kernan, "Day of Slaughter on the Somme," *Washington Post*, June 27, 1976.

23. Alexander, *McCrae's Battalion*, 161.

24. Alexander, *McCrae's Battalion*, 162.

25. Peter Hart, *The Somme* (London: Phoenix, 2012), loc. 2985, Kindle.

26. Hart, *Somme*, loc. 2985.

27. Hart, *Somme*, loc. 2993.

28. Sheldon, *German Army*, loc. 3507.

29. Alexander, *McCrae's Battalion*, 164.

30. Hart, *Somme*, loc. 3045.

31. Shakespear, *Thirty-Fourth Division*, 46.

32. Shakespear, *Thirty-Fourth Division*, 47.

33. Alexander, *McCrae's Battalion*, 172.

34. Shakespear, *Thirty-Fourth Division*, 48.

35. Alexander, *McCrae's Battalion*, 178.

36. Shakespear, *Thirty-Fourth Division*, 49.

Chapter 10: The City of Beautiful Nonsense

1. *Edinburgh Evening News*, July 3, 1916, quoting Gibbs.

2. *New York Times*, April 9, 1915.

3. Granville Roland Fortescue, *At the Front with Three Armies, My Adventures in the Great War* (London: Andrew Melrose, 1915), 50.

4. Phillip Knightley, *The First Casualty* (Baltimore: Johns Hopkins University Press, 2004), 99.

5. Gary S. Messinger, *British Propaganda and the State in the First World War* (Manchester: Manchester University Press, 1992), 30.

6. Knightley, *First Casualty*, 101.

7. Gibbs, *Now It Can Be Told*, 29.

8. Stephen Badsey, *The British Army in Battle and Its Image, 1914–18* (London: Continuum, 2009), 196.

9. There's an excellent account of this incident in Knightley, *First Casualty*, 106–8.

10. Messinger, *British Propaganda*, 42.

11. Anthony Slide, ed., *D. W. Griffith: Interviews* (Jackson: University Press of Mississippi, 2012), 94.

12. *Financial Times*, April 30, 2014.

13. Badsey, *British Army in Battle*, 181.

14. Gibbs, *Now It Can Be Told*, vii.

15. Gibbs, *Now It Can Be Told*, 30.

Chapter 11: We Did Miss the Boys

1. Alexander, *McCrae's Battalion*, 181. Peter Crossan, Paddy's grandson, told me he'd heard this story as well.

2. In *The Great War and Modern Memory* (Oxford: Oxford University Press, 1975) Paul Fussell identifies this diction as the "essentially feudal language" of upper-class men raised on "the boys' books of George Alfred Henry; the male-romances of Rider Haggard; the poems of Robert Bridges; and especially the Arthurian poems of Tennyson and the pseudo-medieval romances of William Morris" (21). It persists in some histories of the war like John Shakespear's *The Thirty-Fourth Division*, in which cheery troops endured rough handling from "the Boche" but nonetheless "took up their positions readily, quite keen at the thought of another battle" (199).

3. Sheen, *Tyneside Irish*, loc. 2126.

4. Shakespear, *Thirty-Fourth Division*, 65.

5. Shakespear, 67.

6. Gilbert, *First World War* Kindle, loc. 6126.

7. Shakespear, *Thirty-Fourth Division*, 67.

8. Alexander, *McCrae's Battalion*, 195.

9. Alexander, 193.

10. Shakespear, *Thirty-Fourth Division*, 72.

11. Shakespear, 73.

12. Shakespear, 76.

13. Shakespear, 78.

14. Sixteenth Royal Scots, war diary, September 1916.

15. Shakespear, *Thirty-Fourth Division*, 85.

Chapter 12: The Moppers-Up

1. The Sunday *Post*, August 19, 1917.

2. *Daily Record*, August 20, 1917.

3. *Daily Record*, June 8, 1917. (Also: McCartney, *"Hearts" and the Great War*, 8.)

4. McCartney, *"Hearts" and the Great War*, 35.

5. Sheen, *Tyneside Irish*, loc. 3126.

6. Shakespear, *Thirty-Fourth Division*, 109.

7. Shakespear, *Thirty-Fourth Division*, 111.

8. Shakespear, *Thirty-Fourth Division*, 114.

9. Shakespear, *Thirty-Fourth Division*, 120.

10. Rowse, oral history.

Chapter 13: Clogged with Mud and Useless

1. Princip died in Theresienstadt, which was then a part of Austria-Hungary.
2. Shakespear, *Thirty-Fourth Division*, 134.
3. *Boston Globe*, June 8, 2010.
4. Shakespear, *Thirty-Fourth Division*, 156.
5. McCartney, *Sport in War*, 19.
6. McCartney, 29.

Chapter 14: The Rendezvous of All Sportsmen

1. Shakespear, *Thirty-Fourth Division*, 224.
2. McCartney, *The Sport in War*, 25.
3. Suzie Grogan's excellent *Shell Shocked Britain: The First World War's Legacy for Britain's Mental Health* discusses these points in detail.
4. Helen Clark and Elizabeth Carnegie, *She Was Aye Workin': Memories of Tenement Women in Edinburgh and Glasgow* (Oxford: White Cockade, 2003), 180.
5. Tom Purdie, *Hearts at War, 1914–1919* (Gloucestershire: Amberley, 2014), loc. 2085, Kindle.
6. Alexander, *McCrae's Battalion*, 256.
7. *Scotsman*, January 20, 1919.
8. *Arbroath Herald and Advertiser*, August 27, 1919.
9. *Scotsman*, April 10, 1922.
10. *Aberdeen Daily Journal*, May 1, 1922.
11. Peter Crossan told me about this headline, which I was unable to find but would very much like to believe exists.
12. *Scotsman*, August 20, 1925.
13. *Edinburgh Evening News*, April 30, 1932.
14. *Scotsman*, August 16, 1929.
15. *Edinburgh Evening News*, January 19, 1933.
16. *Midlothian Advertiser*, May 5, 1933.
17. *Scotsman*, May 3, 1933.
18. *Scotsman*, December 18, 1922.

BIBLIOGRAPHY

War Diaries

All are from the UK National Archives.
10th Battalion, Lincolnshire Regiment
11th Battalion, Suffolk Regiment
16th Battalion, Royal Scots
15th Battalion, Royal Scots
34th Division, General Staff Diary
III Corps Summary of Operations

Author transcribed the diaries and, where possible, checked them against transcriptions in Martin Mace and John Grehan's *Slaughter on the Somme 1 July 1916: The Complete War Diaries of the British Army's Worst Day*.

Books, Other Publications, Sources, and Further Reading

Alexander, Jack. *McCrae's Battalion: The Story of the 16th Royal Scots*. Edinburgh: Mainstream, 2004.

Badsey, Stephen. *The British Army in Battle and Its Image, 1914–18*. London: Continuum, 2009.

Brown, Lawrence. *The British Soldier*. Bayeux, France: Casemate, 2016.

Byledbal, Anthony, David Rakowski, Peter Barton, Simon Jones, Jeremy Banning, Iain McHenry, Jonathan Porter, and Richard Porter. "La Boisselle

Study Group Archaeological Report: 2012." La Boisselle Project, 2013. www.laboisselleproject.com/wp-content/uploads/2013/07/La-Boisselle-Study-Group-Archaeological-Report-2012-English-version-low-res.pdf.

Carlin, Dan. "*Blueprint for Armageddon IV.*" August 17, 2014. Episode 53. *Hardcore History.* Podcast. www.dancarlin.com/hardcore-history-53-blueprint-for-armageddon-iv/.

Clark, Helen, and Elizabeth Carnegie. *She Was Aye Workin': Memories of Tenement Women in Edinburgh and Glasgow.* Oxford: White Cockade, 2003.

Crossan, Peter. Interview with author. August 3, 2016.

Fenby, Jonathan. *France: A Modern History from the Revolution to the War with Terror.* New York: St. Martin's, 2015.

Fortescue, Granville Roland. *At the Front with Three Armies, My Adventures in the Great War.* London: Andrew Melrose, 1915.

Fussell, Paul. *The Great War and Modern Memory.* Oxford: Oxford University Press, 1975.

Gibbs, Philip. *Now It Can Be Told.* New York: Harper & Brothers, 1920.

Gilbert, Martin. *The First World War: A Complete History.* New York: RosettaBooks, 2014. Kindle.

Grogan, Suzie. *Shell Shocked Britain: The First World War's Legacy for Britain's Mental Health.* Barnsley, UK: Pen and Sword, 2014.

Haig, Douglas. *The Private Papers of Douglas Haig, 1914–1919.* Edited by Robert Blake. London: Eyre & Spottiswoode, 1952.

Hart, Peter. *Voices from the Front: An Oral History of the Great War.* Oxford: Oxford University Press, 2016. Kindle.

———. *The Somme.* London: Phoenix, 2012. Kindle.

Holmes, Richard. *The Little Field Marshal: A Life of Sir John French.* London: Wiedenfeld & Nicolson, 1981.

Kershaw, Robert. *24 Hrs at the Somme: 1 July 1916.* London: W. H. Allen, 2016.

Knightley, Phillip. *The First Casualty: The War Correspondent as Hero and Myth-Maker from the Crimea to Iraq.* Baltimore: Johns Hopkins University Press, 2004.

Knox, W. W. *Industrial Nation: Work, Culture and Society in Scotland, 1800–Present.* Edinburgh: Edinburgh University Press, 1999.

Larson, Erik. *Dead Wake: The Last Crossing of the* Lusitania. New York: Broadway Books, 2015. Kindle.

Lewis, Cecil. *Sagittarius Rising*. London: Frontline Books, 2009. Kindle.

Liveing, Edward G. D., and Philip Gibbs, *Walking into Hell: The Somme Through British and German Eyes*. Stratford-upon-Avon: Coda Books, 2014. Kindle.

Macdonald, Andrew. *First Day of the Somme*. Auckland: HarperCollins, 2016.

Mace, Martin, and John Grehan. *Slaughter on the Somme 1 July 1916: The Complete War Diaries of the British Army's Worst Day*. Barnsley, UK: Pen and Sword, 2013.

Martin, Gus. *The Broxburn Football Story*. Dechmont, UK: Brian Currie Printers, 2002.

———. Interview with author. May 16, 2016.

———. *West Lothian's Scottish Cup History*. Dechmont, UK: self-published, 2015.

McCartney, John. *The "Hearts" and the Great War*. Edinburgh: self-published, 1918.

———. *The Sport in War*. Edinburg: self-published, 1930.

McDowell, Matthew. Interview with author. May 11, 2016.

Messinger, Gary S. *British Propaganda and the State in the First World War*. Manchester: Manchester University Press, 1992.

Pennell, Catriona. *A Kingdom United: Popular Responses to the Outbreak of the First World War in Britain and Ireland*. Oxford: Oxford University Press, 2012.

Purdie, Tom. *Hearts at War, 1914–1919*. Gloucestershire: Amberley, 2014. Kindle.

Reid, William. *The Story of 'The Hearts': A Fifty Years' Retrospect 1874-1924*. Edinburgh: Heart of Midlothian Football Club, 1924.

Repington, Charles à Court. *Vestigia: Reminiscences of Love and War*. Boston: Houghton Mifflin. 1919.

Rowse, W. F. Interview by Dr. Keith Chambers. November 18, 1975. Transcribed by author. Catalog no. 24870, Imperial War Museum.

Sacco, Joe. *The Great War: July 1, 1916: The First Day of the Battle of the Somme; An Illustrated Panorama*. New York: W. W. Norton, 2013.

Sandilands, J. W., and Norman MacLeod. *The History of the 7th Battalion Queen's Own Cameron Highlanders*. Stirling, UK: Eneas MacKay, 1922.

Shakespear, John, *The Thirty-Fourth Division, 1915–1919*. Luton, UK: Andrews, 2012. Digital edition.

Sheen, John. *Tyneside Irish: 24th, 25th, 26th & 27th (Service) Battalions of Northumberland Fusiliers*. Barnsley, UK: Pen and Sword, 2010. Kindle.

Sheffield, Gary. *The Chief: Douglas Haig and the British Army*. London: Aurum Press, 2011. Kindle.

———. *Forgotten Victory: The First World War; Myths and Realities*. London: Endeavour Press, 2014. Kindle.

Sheldon, Jack. *The German Army on the Somme 1914–1916*. Barnsley, UK: Pen and Sword, 2005. Kindle.

Simms, Fraser. "Our Grassmarket Buildings: A Brief History." *Quadrangle: George Heriot's School Development Newsletter* (September 2006).

Simpson, C. R. *The History of the Lincolnshire Regiment 1914–1918*. London: Medici Society, 1931.

Slide, Anthony, ed. *D. W. Griffith: Interviews*. Jackson: University Press of Mississippi, 2012.

Smith, Lorenzo N. *Lingo of No Man's Land; or, War Time Lexicon*. Boston: W. K. Hawthorne, 2012. Kindle.

Stewart, Graham, and John Sheen. *Tyneside Scottish: 20th, 21st, 22nd & 23rd (Service) Battalions of the Northumberland Fusiliers*. Barnsley, UK: Pen and Sword, 1999. Kindle.

Tardi, Jacques. *It Was the War of the Trenches*. Seattle: Fantagraphics, 2010.

Westlake, Ray. *Tracing British Battalions on the Somme*. Barnsley, UK: Pen and Sword, 1994. Kindle.

Williams, Kevin. Interview with author. October 21, 2016.

Wood, Alex, "The MP's Secret: Respect Your Ancestors—But Don't Always Believe Them." *The Scottish Genealogist* 58, no. 1 (March 2011): 42–45.

Wright, Joanna. Interview with author. February 27, 2017.

During the course of my research I also consulted hundreds of articles from British newspapers, which I accessed through the invaluable British Newspaper Archive. I cross-checked game information against the astonishing database held by the London Hearts Supporters Club, which lists every player and every goal in every match the club has played in its history. They watch matches at the Famous Three Kings pub next to the West Kensington tube station, and I hope to join them someday.

INDEX

Italic page numbers refer to photos.